1

Table of Contents

INTRODUCTION

Congratulations on preparing to take the first step to becoming an officer in the United States Air Force! The AFOQT is an important exam for many reasons, but mostly because it lets the Air Force know where your strengths and weaknesses lie, and how they can best utilize your abilities. It gives them a glimpse of your raw abilities in a few subjects, but will also test your ability to stay calm under pressure. Some sections, such as Math and Science, will test your raw knowledge and intellect, not to mention how hard you prepared (or not) for the exam. Other sections are deceptively simple, in that the task is something you might think a 6 year old could do. The catch though is that you have an absurdly short amount of time on these sections and the task is usually designed to seem easier than it really is. Their goal in this case is to see how you respond when the odds are stacked against you and you know that you won't be able to finish. Do you panic and make mistakes, or push through diligently and do your best? This study guide will prepare you for both aspects of this challenging exam. The AFOQT is a competitive test, so you need to aim high…no pun intended.

Sections on the AFOQT

There are 12 sections on the AFOQT and will follow this order:

1) Verbal Analogies – 25 questions, 8 minutes
2) Arithmetic Reasoning – 25 questions, 29 minutes .
3) Word Knowledge – 25 questions, 5 minutes
4) Math Knowledge – 25 questions, 22 minutes
5) Instrument Comprehension – 20 questions, 6 minutes
6) Block Counting – 20 questions, 3 minutes
   (10 minute break)
7) Table Reading – 40 questions, 7 minutes
8) Aviation Information – 20 questions, 8 minutes
9) General Science – 20 questions, 10 minutes
10) Rotated blocks – 15 questions, 13 minutes
11) Hidden Figures – 15 questions, 8 minutes
12) Self-Description Inventory – 220 questions, 40 minutes

As you can see, there are a few sections with minimal time limits, giving you only 10-15 seconds per question in some cases. The only section we will NOT cover in this study guide is the "Self-Description Inventory". This is not a section you can "study" for and there are no tricks here. It is simply a personality questionnaire, so be sure to be totally honest and straightforward in your answers. Don't give answers for what you think 'they want to hear'.

Scoring on the AFOQT

You will be given scores in five areas:

- Pilot
- Navigator
- Academic Aptitude
- Verbal
- Quantitative

Each score is made up of different combinations of the 12 sections of the AFOQT and each has a different minimum score. In all 5 cases, the scores are percentiles, which range from 1 to 99. An average score would fall in the upper 40's, but it is recommended that for those who want to be a pilot, that a score of 70 or higher is necessary across the board in all 5 scores to be considered with a mix of 85-95 scores being a strong score. The sections comprising each score and the minimum required score to be considered is listed below for your reference:

- **Pilot**
  - Minimum Score to be pilot: 25
  - Minimum Combined Pilot & Navigator score: 50
    - (Note: Must have a minimum of 10 Navigator Score)
  - Score Comprised of sections:
    - Arithmetic Reasoning
    - Math Knowledge
    - Instrument Comprehension
    - Table Reading
    - Aviation Information

- **Navigator**
  - Minimum Score to be Navigator: 25
  - Minimum Combined Pilot & Navigator score: 50
    - (Note: Must have a minimum of 10 Pilot Score)
  - Score Comprised of sections:
    - Verbal Analogies
    - Arithmetic Reasoning
    - Math Knowledge
    - Block Counting
    - Table Reading
    - General Science

- **Academic Aptitude**
  - No minimum; composite of Math and Verbal sections
  - Score Comprised of Sections:
    - Verbal Analogies
    - Arithmetic Reasoning
    - Word Knowledge
    - Math Knowledge

- **Verbal**
  - Minimum Score for all candidates: 15
  - Score Comprised of Sections:
    - Verbal Analogies
    - Word Knowledge

- **Quantitative**
  - Minimum Score for all candidates: 10
  - Score Comprised of Sections:
    - Arithmetic Reasoning
    - Math Knowledge

Test Day Procedures

On test day, be prepared for a 3.5 hour test day, including administrative information and instructions. You will have one 10 minute break halfway through the exam. You do not want to waste time reading instructions, you should be totally familiar with those before sitting down. Pencils and paper will be provided, you may NOT use a calculator. No food or drink is allowed during the test.

It is important to note that there is no wrong answer penalty on the AFOQT. Again....

THERE IS NO PENALTY FOR WRONG ANSWERS!

This means, under no circumstance, on any section of the entire test, should you EVER leave a question blank even if it is a wild guess.

Additional Important Information about the AFOQT

One of the most important factors to take into consideration is that you may only take the AFOQT twice. Never, ever think of the first exam as a "practice round". You need to study diligently and do your absolute best the very first time you take it.

If you decide to take the exam a second time, keep in mind you must wait 180 days (6 months) and your second score will become your official score, even if you do worse! Your most recent score is the only one anyone will see. In some extremely rare circumstances, you might secure a waiver to take the AFOQT a third time, but that is highly unlikely for most candidates.

Finally, it is important to consider that the USAF looks at the whole package you send them. For example, if the average score for candidates who earn a pilot position is 90, just because you might only have a 85 does not mean it is impossible to win a spot. Conversely, just because you have a 99 does not automatically guarantee anything. They will look at your entire application package, including your GPA and the other 4 scores you receive.

One more time, just to be sure: DO NOT EVER LEAVE A QUESTION BLANK!!!! You will better understand as you work through the different sections just how short the time limits are and that you cannot allow yourself to be caught off guard with only 5 seconds left and you don't have time to fill in any answers before the buzzer. You must maintain situational awareness of the clock, which is best done by practicing under timed conditions.

Chapter 1: Verbal Analogies

A number of relationship objectives are contained on the Verbal Analogies section. With these types of analogies, you must determine the relationship between the words and complete the analogy with the correct choice. There are 25 questions with a time limit of 8 minutes, giving you roughly 20 seconds per question. The key here is to become familiar with analogies and get some practice, and most people will find that 20 seconds is ample. We will first review some of the type of analogies you might run into, then do a practice test. The concept of analogies is pretty straight forward, but don't brush it off because it is the subtleties that lose points.

Similarity/Contrast

Most often, similarities and contrasts involve synonyms (words that mean the same thing) or antonyms (words that have opposite meanings). An analogy that involves synonyms is primarily a definition of terms – determining one word that could be replaced with another word. In such a relationship, you must ascertain what a word means and how it is connected to the others in the analogy. An analogy that involves contrasts shows the relationship between a word and its opposite.

Example:

zenith : summit :: vale (a. nadir   b. yang   c. arboreal   d. gorge)

Answer: Choice (D) is correct. Zenith and summit are both words that refer to the highest point of something, like a mountaintop. Therefore, look for the pair of words that are synonyms. Vale and gorge both refer to low points – synonyms – so choice D is best.

Whole-Part/Part-Whole

This type of analogy denotes the relationship between a whole thing (house, for example) and a part of the whole (room).

autocracy : individual :: meritocracy : (a. unwise   b. talented   c. multitude   d. indigent)

Answer: Choice (B) is correct. An autocracy is a system in which one individual is rewarded with power. Therefore, look for the answer choice in which the second word is the most important part of the first word. In a meritocracy, distribution of power is based on people's ability and talent.

Membership

A membership analogy is very similar to the whole-part analogy. It shows the relationship between a whole group and a member of the group.

Example:

xenophile : foreign :: (a. hippophile b. bibliophile   c. anglophile d. oenophile) : wine

Answer: Choice (D) is correct. A xenophile is a person who is interested in foreign cultures, and an oenophile is a person who is interested in wine.

Object/Characteristic

In this type of analogy, you must establish the relationship between a person or object and its characteristic.

Example:

carnivore : lion :: piscivore : (a. tiger   b. penguin   c. reptile   d. beetle)

Answer: Choice (B) is correct. A lion is a carnivore, which means it is a meat-eater. Therefore, the relationship between the two words is categorical – lions are a type of carnivore. Choice (B) is correct, because penguins are piscivores, or fish-eating.

Cause/Effect

This type of analogy involves analyzing the relationship between a word and the outcome or result it causes. Occasionally, the analogy may be written with the effect first, and you must determine the cause.

Example:

sycophant : flatters :: raconteur : (a. critiques   b. repels   c. regales   d. leads)

Answer: Choice (C) is correct. In the initial part of the analogy, a sycophant is a person who flatters others. So, in the answer choices, look for the pair in which the second word describes the effect of the first term's behavior. A raconteur is a storyteller – one who regales others with tales.

Agent/Object

This analogy type is one that shows the relationship between a person and a tool or object that he/she uses. You might also see similar analogies that involve a non-living thing – an object – and how it is used.

Example:

codicil : supplement :: condiment : (a. assault   b. pronounce   c. revere   d. flavor)

Answer: Choice (D) is correct. A codicil is an appendix to a will; its function is to supplement or explain further. Therefore, look for the answer choice in which the second term describes the function of the first term. The purpose of condiments is to flavor food. Therefore, choice (D) is correct.

Order

In order analogies, the words are related by sequence or in a reciprocal (or opposite) circumstance.

Example:

Alpha ; omega :: Delaware : (a. Oregon   b. Florida   c. Maine   d. Hawaii)

Choice (D) is correct. Alpha is the first letter of the Greek alphabet and omega is the last letter. Delaware was the first state admitted to the union, and Hawaii was the last state admitted.

Verbal Analogies Practice Test Questions

1.   carat : weight :: fathom :
   - a. capacity
   - b. perspective
   - c. mass
   - d. depth

2.   mollify : enrage :: quell :
   - a. exonerate
   - b. bifurcate
   - c. incite
   - d. denounce

3.   Electron :_____ :: satellite : planet
   - a. proton
   - b. nucleus
   - c. atom
   - d. neutron

4.   Habitat : location :: _____ : role
   - a. capacity
   - b. competition
   - c. niche
   - d. predation

5.   26 : even :: _____ : prime
   - a. 8
   - b. 11
   - c. 15
   - d. 20

6.   Cytology : cells :: _____ : fungi
   - a. mycology
   - b. ornithology
   - c. oncology
   - d. phrenology

7. Darwin : evolution :: Mendel :
   a. blood groups
   b. popular culture
   c. relative dating
   d. genetics

8. Sacramento : California :: _____ : Florida
   a. Orlando
   b. Tallahassee
   c. Miami
   d. Jacksonville

9. appease : placate :: obviate :
   a. disregard
   b. clarify
   c. decide
   d. preclude

10. Cortez : Mexico :: Cartier :
    a. North America
    b. Canada
    c. East Indies
    d. Florida

11. chicken : brood :: cats :
    a. clowder
    b. herd
    c. swarm
    d. army

12. _____ : Missouri :: Granite : New Hampshire
    a. Tar Heel
    b. Sunshine
    c. Show Me
    d. Buckeye

13. latitude : longitude :: parallels :
    a. lines
    b. equator
    c. degrees
    d. meridians

14. *Gulliver's Travels* : Jonathan Swift :: *Frankenstein* : _____
        a. John Keats
        b. George Eliot
        c. Mary Shelley
        d. Alexander Pope

15. newton : force :: _____ : power
        a. joule
        b. tesla
        c. watt
        d. hertz

16. 0° latitude : equator :: 23.5° south latitude : _____
        a. prime meridian
        b. tropic of Capricorn
        c. middle latitude
        d. tropic of Cancer

17. clarinet : _____ :: cello : string
        a. brass
        b. woodwind
        c. percussion
        d. horn

18. hatching : parallel lines :: stippling : _____
        a. squares
        b. dots
        c. perpendicular lines
        d. curves

19. capacity : liter :: mass : _____
        a. meter
        b. kilometer
        c. gram
        d. pound

20. inaugurate: President :: coronate : _____
        a. pope
        b. cardinal
        c. bishop
        d. monarch

21.   positive : negative :: _____ : flat
        a. sharp
        b. tone
        c. bass
        d. treble

22.   Poseidon : sea :: _____ : war
        a. Hades
        b. Ares
        c. Apollo
        d. Pan

23.   Hindi : India :: _____ : Brazil
        a. Spanish
        b. English
        c. Portuguese
        d. French

24.   Michelangelo : painter :: Frank Lloyd Wright : _____
        a. writer
        b. sculptor
        c. playwright
        d. architect

25.   Judaism : temple :: Islam : _____
        a. church
        b. synagogue
        c. mosque
        d. mecca

Verbal Analogies Practice Test Answer Key

1. D
2. C
3. B
4. C
5. B
6. A
7. D
8. B
9. D
10. B
11. A
12. C
13. D
14. C
15. C
16. B
17. B
18. B
19. C
20. D
21. A
22. B
23. C
24. D
25. C

Chapter 2: Arithmetic Reasoning

The Arithmetic reasoning tests your ability to use fundamental math concepts to solve word problems. During the test, you will have 29 minutes to answer 25 problems. The most important step in solving any word problem is to read the entire problem before beginning to solve. You shouldn't skip over words or assume you know what the question is from the first sentence. The following are the general steps used to solve word problems:

General Steps for Word Problem Solving:
Step 1: Read the entire problem and determine what the problem is asking for.
Step 2: List all of the given data.
Step 3: Sketch diagrams with the given data.
Step 4: Determine formula(s) needed.
Step 5: Set up equation(s).
Step 6: Solve.
Step 7: Check your answer. Make sure that your answer makes sense. (Is the amount too large or small; are the answers in the correct unit of measure; etc.)
Note: Not all steps are needed for every problem.

In the Math Knowledge, you will be given a list of the most commonly-made mistakes on the mathematics knowledge test – they will apply here as well. Even if an answer you calculated is a given answer choice, that doesn't make it the correct answer. Remember that not all of the information given in a problem is needed to solve it.

> For example:
>> Kathy had $12.45, John had $10.30, and Liz had $6.90. How much money did the girls have combined?

> The amount John has is not needed to solve the problem, since the problem is only asking for the combined amounts of Kathy and Liz.

Mistakes most commonly occur when answers for only a part of the problem are given as answer choices. It's very easy to get caught up in thinking, "That's the number I have here! It looks right, so I'll go with that." Trust yourself, and always check your answers. The best way to prepare for the arithmetic section is to practice! At first, don't concern yourself with how long it takes to solve problems; focus on understanding how to solve them, and then time yourself.

This section will go over some of the most common types of word problems found on the Arithmetic Reasoning Section, but keep in mind that any math concept can be turned into a word problem.

Key Words

Word problems generally contain key words that can help you determine what math processes may be required in order to solve them. Here are some commonly-used key words:

- **Addition:** Added, combined, increased by, in all, total, perimeter, sum, and more than.
- **Subtraction:** How much more, less than, fewer than, exceeds, difference, and decreased.
- **Multiplication:** Of, times, area, and product.
- **Division:** Distribute, share, average, per, out of, percent, and quotient.
- **Equals:** Is, was, are, amounts to, and were.

BASIC WORD PROBLEMS

A word problem in algebra is the equivalent of a story problem in math, only word problems are solved by separating information from the problems into two equal groups (one for each side of an equation). Examine this problem:

Sara has 15 apples and 12 oranges. How many pieces of fruit does she have?

We know that the sum of 15 and 12 is equal to the total amount of fruit. An unknown number or value is represented by a letter. The total number of pieces of fruit is unknown, so we will represent that amount with x. When the value that a particular variable will represent is determined, it is defined by writing a statement like this:

Let x = Total Amount of Fruit.

Once again, the sum of 15 apples and 12 oranges is equal to the total amount of fruit. This can be used to translate the problem into an equation:

$15 + 12 = x$

$x = 27$

Sara has 27 pieces of fruit.

Of course, you could probably have solved this problem more quickly without having set up an algebraic equation. But knowing how to use an equation for this kind of problem builds your awareness of which concepts are useful; some of them are even critical to solving much harder problems.

Examples:

1. A salesman bought a case of 48 backpacks for $576. He sold 17 of them for $18 at the swap meet, and the rest were sold to a department store for $25 each. What was the salesman's profit?

> Calculate the total of the 17 backpacks, which you know the cost to be $18:
> $17 * \$18 = \$306$.
> Calculate how many backpacks were sold at $25: $48 - 17 = 31$.

Calculate the total amount of profit for the backpacks sold at $25: 31 * $25 = $775.
Add the two dollar amounts for backpacks sold: $306 + $775 = $1081.
Subtract the salesman's initial cost: $1081 - $576 = $505.
The answer to the question asked about his profit is: $505.

2. Thirty students in Mr. Joyce's room are working on projects over the duration of two days. The first day, he gave them 3/5 of an hour to work. On the second day, he gave them half as much time as the first day. How much time did the students have altogether?

1st day = 3/5 of an hour.
2nd day = 1/2 (3/5) = 3/10 of an hour.
Total = 3/5 + 3/10 = 6/10 + 3/10 = 9/10 of an hour.
An hour has 60 minutes, so set up a ratio:
9/10 = x/60.
x = 54.
So the students had 54 minutes altogether to work on the projects.
Another way to do this problem is to calculate first the amount of time allotted on the first day: 3/5 * 60 minutes = 36 minutes.
Then take half of that to get the time allotted on the second day:
36 minutes * 1/2 = 18 minutes.
Add the two together for your total time! 36 + 18 = 54.

CONSECUTIVE NUMBER PROBLEMS

Examples:

1. Two consecutive numbers have a sum of 91. What are the numbers?

To begin solving this problem, define the variable. You do not know what the first consecutive number is, so you can call it x.

The First Consecutive Number = x.

Since the numbers are consecutive, meaning one number comes right after the other, the second number must be one more than the first. So, $x + 1$ equals the second number.

The Second Consecutive Number = $x + 1$.

The problem states that the sum of the two numbers is 91. This can be shown in the equation like the following: $x + (x + 1) = 91$. That equation can be solved as follows:

Initial Equation: $x + (x + 1) = 91$.
Combine Like Terms: $2x + 1 = 91$.
After subtracting 1 from each side: $2x = 90$.
After dividing each side by 2, $x = 45$.
Careful! In a situation like this, it's almost a sure thing that one of the answer choices will be "45" on the test. This is a trap! You aren't done with your problem yet. Remember, x only equals the value of the first consecutive number – you want the sum of *both*.
Since x equals 45, and the Second Consecutive Number equals $x + 1$, you can simply add 1 to 45 to find that Second Consecutive Number. It should be shown like the work below:

Let x = The First Consecutive Number = 45.
Let $x + 1$ = The Second Consecutive Number = 46.
$x + (x + 1) = 91$.

Don't forget to check your work!
$2x + 1 = 91$.
$2x = 90$.
$x = 45$.

Sometimes you will encounter a problem which has more than two consecutive numbers, such as:

2. When added, four consecutive numbers have a sum of 18. What is the largest number?
   You can solve this much like the previous problem. The difference is that you will have to define four numbers (instead of two).

   Note: Each consecutive number is found by adding 1 to the previous number.
   The First Consecutive Number = x.
   The Second Consecutive Number = $x + 1$.
   The Third Consecutive Number = $x + 2$.
   The Fourth Consecutive Number = $x + 3$.
   Your equation will look like this: $x + (x + 1) + (x + 2) + (x + 3) = 18$.
   $4x + 6 = 18$.
   $4x = 12$.
   $x = 3$.
   Remember the problem asked for largest number, x represents the smallest; so you aren't done!
   $x + 3 = 3.\ 3 + 3 = 6$.

24

EVEN or ODD CONSECUTIVE NUMBERS

The only difference between ordinary consecutive numbers and even or odd consecutive numbers is the space between each number. Each consecutive number would add 2 instead of 1. The trick here is to remember that your first consecutive number will determine whether or not the following consecutive numbers will be even or odd. If the problem calls for even consecutive numbers, then your first number must be even; if odd, then the first number must be odd.

Many problems lend themselves to being solved with systems of linear equations.

1. The admission fee at a small fair is $1.50 for children and $4.00 for adults. On a certain day, 2,200 people enter the fair, and $5,050 is collected. How many children and how many adults attended?

    Using a system of equations allows the use of two different variables for the two different unknowns.

    Number of adults: a.
    Number of children: c.
    Total number: $a + c = 2200$.
    Total income: $4a + 1.5c = 5050$.

    Now solve the system for the number of adults and the number of children. Solve the first equation for one of the variables, and then substitute the result into the other equation.

    Because $a + c = 2200$, we know that:

$$a = 2200 - c$$
$$4(2200 - c) + 1.5c = 5050$$
$$8800 - 4c + 1.5c = 5050$$
$$8800 - 2.5c = 5050$$
$$-2.5c = -3750$$
$$c = 1500$$

    Now go back to that first equation: $a = 2200 - (1500) = 700$. There were 1500 children and 700 adults.

2. A landscaping company placed two orders with a nursery. The first order was for 13 bushes and 4 trees, and totaled $487. The second order was for 6 bushes and 2 trees, and totaled $232. The bills do not list the per-item price. What were the costs of one bush and of one tree?

25

First pick variables ("*b*" for the price of bushes and "*t*" for the price of trees) and set up a system of equations:

First order: $13b + 4t = 487$.

Second order: $6b + 2t = 232$.

Multiply the second row by 2, so when they are subtracted, one variable is eliminated.

To subtract, multiple the second row by negative 1. Then you have: $13b + 4t = 487$.
$-12b - 4t = -464$

This says that $b = 23$. Back-solving, you will find that $t = 47$. Bushes cost \$23 each; trees cost \$47 each.

PERCENTAGE WORD PROBLEMS
Basic Equations:
Percent Change:
> Amount of Change ÷ Original Amount * 100

Percent Increase:
> (New Amount – Original Amount) ÷ Original Amount * 100

Percent Decrease:
> (Original Amount – New Amount) ÷ Original Amount * 100

Amount Increase (Or Amount Decrease):
> Original Price * Percent Markup (Or, for Amount Decrease, Markdown)

Original Price:
> New Price ÷ (Whole - Percent Markdown)

Original Price:
> New Price ÷ (Whole + Percent Markup)

Many percentage problems consist of markup and markdown. For these, you calculate how much the quantity changed, and then you calculate the percent change relative to the original value.

Examples:
1. A computer software retailer used a markup rate of 40%. Find the selling price of a computer game that cost the retailer \$25.

The markup is 40% of the $25 cost, so the equation to find markup is: $(0.40) * (25) = 10$.

The selling price is the cost plus markup: $25 + 10 = 35$. The item sold for $35.

2. A golf shop pays its wholesaler $40 for a certain club, and then sells it to a golfer for $75. What is the markup rate?

First calculate the markup: $75 - 40 = 35$.

Then find the markup rate: $35 is (some percent) of $40, or: $35 = (x) * (40)$.

...so the markup over the original price is: $35 \div 40 = x$. $x = 0.875$.

Since the problem asks for a percentage, you need to remember to convert the decimal value.

The markup rate is 87.5%.

3. A shoe store uses a 40% markup on cost. Find the cost of a pair of shoes that sells for $63.

This problem is somewhat backwards. You are given the selling price, which is "cost + markup", and the markup rate. You are not given the actual cost or markup.

Let x be the cost. The markup, being 40% of the cost, is $0.40x$. The selling price of $63 is the sum of the cost and markup, so:

$63 = x + 0.40x$.
$63 = 1x + 0.40x$.
$63 = 1.40x$.
$63 \div 1.40 = x$.
$x = 45$. The shoes cost the store $45.

4. An item originally priced at $55 is marked 25% off. What is the sale price?

First, find the markdown. The markdown is 25% of the original price of $55, so: $x = (0.25) * (55)$. $x = 13.75$.

By subtracting this markdown from the original price, you can find the sale price: $55 - 13.75 = 41.25$. The sale price is $41.25.

5. An item that regularly sells for $425 is marked down to $318.75. What is the discount rate?

First, find the amount of the markdown: 425 – 318.75 = 106.25. Then calculate "the markdown of the original price", or the markdown rate: $106.25 is (some percent) of $425, so:

106.25 = (x) * (425).

...and the markdown over the original price is: $x = 106.25 ÷ 425$. $x = 0.25$.

Since the "x" stands for a percentage, remember to convert this decimal to percentage form. The markdown rate is 25%.

6. A bike is marked down 15%; the sale price is $127.46. What was the original price?

This problem is backwards. You are given the sale price ($127.46) and the markdown rate (15%), but neither the markdown amount nor the original price.

Let "x" stand for the original price. Then the markdown, being 15% of this price, will be $0.15x$. The sale price is the original price, minus the markdown, so: $x – 0.15x = 127.46$.

$1x – 0.15x = 127.46$.

$0.85x = 127.46$.
$x = 127.46 ÷ 0.85$.

$x = 149.95$. The original price was $149.95.

Note: In this last problem, we ended up – in the third line of calculations – with an equation that said "eighty-five percent of the original price is $127.46". You can save yourself some time if you think of discounts in this way: if the price is 15% off, then you're only actually paying 85%. Similarly, if the price is 25% off, then you're paying 75%, etc.

Note: While the values below do not refer to money, the procedures used to solve these problems are otherwise identical to the markup - markdown examples.

7. Growing up, you lived in a tiny country village. When you left for college, the population was 840. You recently heard that the population has grown by 5%. What is the present population?

First, find the actual amount of the increase. Since the increase is five percent of the original population, then the increase is: (0.05) * (840) = 42.

The new population is the old population plus the increase, or: 840 + 42 = 882.

The population is now 882.

8. You put in an 18 X 51 foot garden along the whole back end of your backyard. It has reduced the backyard lawn area by 24%. What is the area of the remaining lawn area?

The area of the garden is: (18) * (51) = 918. This represents 24% of the total yard area, or 24% of the original lawn area. This means that 918 square feet is 24% of the original, so: 918 = 0.24x.

918 ÷ 0.24 = x.

3825 = x.

The total back yard area is 3825 square feet, and we know from the problem that the width is 51 feet. Therefore, to find the length: 3825 ÷ 51 = 75. The length then is 75 feet. Since 18 feet are taken up by the garden, then the lawn area is: 75 − 18 = 57 feet deep. The area of the lawn now measures 51' X 57'.

WORK WORD PROBLEMS

"Work" problems involve situations such as: two people working together to paint a house. You are usually told how long each person takes to paint a similarly-sized house, and then you are asked how long it will take the two of them to paint the house when they work together.

There is a "trick" to doing work problems: you have to think of the problem in terms of how much each person/machine/whatever does in a given unit of time.

Example:

Suppose one painter can paint the entire house in twelve hours, and the second painter takes eight hours. How long would it take the two painters together to paint the house?

If the first painter can do the entire job in twelve hours, and the second painter can do it in eight hours, then (here is the trick!) the first painter can do 1/12 of the job per hour, and the second guy can do 1/8 per hour. How much then can they do per hour if they work together?

To find out how much they can do together per hour, add together what they can do individually per hour: $1/12 + 1/8 = 5/24$. They can do 5/24 of the job per hour. Now let "t" stand for how long they take to do the job together. Then they can do $1/t$ per hour, so $5/24 = 1/t$. When for $t = 24/5$, $t = 4.8$ hours. That is:

Hours to complete job:

      First painter: 12.

      Second painter: 8.

      Together: t.

Work completed per hour:

      First painter: 1/12.

      Second painter: 1/8.

      Together: $1/t$.

Adding their labor:

      $1/12 + 1/8 = 1/t$.

      $5/24 = 1/t$.

      $24/5 = t$.

      $t = 4\ 4/5$ hours.

As you can see in the previous example, "work" problems commonly create rational equations. But the equations themselves are usually pretty simple.

More Examples:

1. One pipe can fill a pool 1.25 times faster than a second pipe. When both pipes are opened, they fill the pool in five hours. How long would it take to fill the pool if only the slower pipe is used?

    Convert to rates.

      Hours to complete job:

        Fast pipe: f.

        Slow pipe: $1.25f$.

        Together: 5.

      Work completed per hour:

        Fast pipe: $1/f$.

        Slow pipe: $1/1.25f$.

        Together: 1/5.

Adding their labor:
$$1/f + 1/1.25f = 1/5.$$

Solve for f:
$$5 + 5/1.25 = f.$$
$$5 + 4 = f.$$
$$f = 9.$$

Then $1.25f = 11.25$, so the slower pipe takes 11.25 hours.

If you're not sure how I derived the rate for the slow pipe, think about it this way: if someone goes twice as fast as you, then you take twice as long as he does; if he goes three times as fast, then you take three times as long. In this case, one pipe goes 1.25 times as fast, so the other takes 1.25 times as long.

This next one is a bit different:

Ben takes 2 hours to wash 500 dishes, and Frank takes 3 hours to wash 450 dishes. How long will they take, working together, to wash 1000 dishes?

For this exercise, you are given *how many* can be done in one time unit, rather than *how much* of a job can be completed. But the thinking process is otherwise the same. Ben can do 250 dishes per hour, and Frank can do 150 dishes per hour. Working together, they can do 250 + 150 = 400 dishes an hour. That is:

Ben: 500 dishes / 2 hours = 250 dishes / hour.

Frank: 450 dishes / 3 hours = 150 dishes / hour.

Together: (250 + 150) dishes / hour = 400 dishes / hour.

Next find the number of hours that it takes to wash 1000 dishes. Set things up so units cancel and you're left with "hours":

(1000 dishes) * (1 hour / 400 dishes).

(1000 / 400) hours.

2.5 hours.

It will take two and a half hours for the two of them to wash 1000 dishes.

2. If six men can do a job in fourteen days, how many would it take to do the job in twenty-one days?

Convert this to man-hours, or, in this case, man-days. If it takes six guys fourteen days, then:

(6 men) * (14 days) = 84 man-days.

That is, the entire job requires 84 man-days. This exercise asks you to expand the time allowed from fourteen days to twenty-one days. Obviously, if they're giving you more time, then you'll need fewer guys. But how many guys, exactly? (x men) * (21 days) = 84 man-days.

...or, in algebra: $21x = 84$. $x = 4$. So, only four guys are needed to do the job in twenty-one days.

You may have noticed that each of these problems used some form of the "how much can be done per time unit" construction, but aside from that each problem was done differently. That's how "work" problems are; but, as you saw above, if you label things neatly and do your work orderly, you should find your way to the solution.

DISTANCE WORD PROBLEMS

"Distance" word problems, often also called "uniform rate" problems, involve something travelling at a fixed and steady ("uniform") pace ("rate" or "speed"), or else moving at some average speed. Whenever you read a problem that involves "how fast", "how far, or "for how long," you should think of the distance equation, $d = rt$, where d stands for distance, r stands for the (constant or average) rate of speed, and t stands for time. It is easier to solve these types of problems using a grid and filling in the information given in the problem.
Warning: Make sure that the units for time and distance agree with the units for the rate. For instance, if they give you a rate of feet per second, then your time must be in seconds and your distance must be in feet. Sometimes they try to trick you by using two different units, and you have to catch this and convert to the correct units.

1. An executive drove from his home at an average speed of 30 mph to an airport where a helicopter was waiting. The executive boarded the helicopter and flew to the corporate offices at an average speed of 60 mph. The entire distance was 150 miles; the entire trip took three hours. Find the distance from the airport to the corporate offices.

	d	r	t
driving	d	30	t
flying	$150 - d$	60	$3 - t$
total	150	---	3

The first row gives me the equation $d = 30t$.
Since the first part of his trip accounted for d miles of the total 150-mile distance and t hours of the total 3-hour time, you are left with $150 - d$ miles and $3 - t$ hours for the second part. The second row gives the equation: $150 - d. d = 60(3 - t)$.
This now becomes a system of equations problem.
Add the two "distance" expressions and setting their sum equal to the given total distance:
$150 - d = 60(3 - t). d = 30t. 150 = 30t + 60(3 - t)$.
Solve for t: $150 = 30t + 180 - 60t. 150 = 180 - 30t. -30 = -30t. 1 = t$.

32

It is important to note that you are not finished when you have solved for the first variable. This is where it is important to pay attention to what the problem asked for. It does not ask for time, but the time is needed to solve the problem.

So now insert the value for t into the first equation: $d = 30$.

Subtract from total distance: $150 - 30 = 120$.

The distance to the corporate offices is 120 miles.

2. Two cyclists start at the same time from opposite ends of a course that is 45 miles long. One cyclist is riding at 14 mph and the second cyclist is riding at 16 mph. How long after they begin will they meet?

	d	r	t
slow guy	d	14	t
fast guy	$45 - d$	16	t
total	45	---	---

Why is t the same for both cyclists? Because you are measuring from the time they both started to the time they meet somewhere in the middle.

Why "d" and "$45 - d$" for the distances? Because I assigned the slower cyclist as having covered d miles, which left $45 - d$ miles for the faster cyclist to cover: the two cyclists *together* covered the whole 45 miles.

Using "$d = rt$," you get $d = 14t$ from the first row, and $45 - d = 16t$ from the second row. Since these distances add up to 45, add the distance expressions and set equal to the given total:
$45 = 14t + 16t$.

Solve for t, place it back into the equation, to solve for what the question asked. $45 = 30t$.

$t = 45 \div 30 = 1\frac{1}{2}$. They will meet 1 ½ hours after they begin.

SIMPLE INTEREST

Formula for simple interest: $I = PRT$.

I represents the interest earned.

P represents the principal which is the number of dollars invested.

T represents the time the money is invested; generally stated in years or fractions of a year.

R represents the rate at which the principal (p) is earned.

Formula for Amount: $A = P + I$.

A represents what your investment is worth if you consider the total amount of the original investment (*P*) and the interest earned (*I*).

Example: If I deposit $500 in an account with an annual rate of 5%, how much will I have after 2 years?
    1st year: $500 + (500 * .05) = $525.
    2nd year: $525 + (525 * .05) = $ 551.25.

RATIO PROBLEMS

To solve a ratio, simply find the equivalent fraction. To distribute a whole across a ratio:
1. Total all parts.
2. Divide the whole by the total number of parts.
3. Multiply quotient by corresponding part of ratio.

Example: There are 81 voters in a room, all either Democrat or Republican. The ratio of Democrats to Republicans is 5:4. How many republicans are there?
1. 5 + 4 = 9.

2. 81 ÷ 9 = 9.

3. 9 * 4 = 36. 36 Republicans.

PROPORTIONS

Direct proportions: Corresponding ratio parts change in the same direction (increase/decrease).
Indirect proportions: Corresponding ratio parts change in opposite directions; as one part increases the other decreases.
Example (Indirect Proportion): A train traveling 120 miles takes 3 hours to get to its destination. How long will it take if the train travels 180 miles?
    120 miles : 180 miles
        is to
  x hours : 3 hours
  Write as a fraction and cross multiply: 3 *180 = 120*x*.
  540 = 120*x*. *x* = 4.5 hours. It will take the train 4.5 hours to reach its destination.

Arithmetic Reasoning Practice Test Questions

1. Employees of a discount appliance store receive an additional 20% off of the lowest price on an item. If an employee purchases a dishwasher during a 15% off sale, how much will he pay if the dishwasher originally cost $450?
    a) $280.90.
    b) $287.
    c) $292.50.
    d) $306.
    e) $333.89.

2. The city council has decided to add a 0.3% tax on motel and hotel rooms. If a traveler spends the night in a motel room that costs $55 before taxes, how much will the city receive in taxes from him?
    a) 10 cents.
    b) 11 cents.
    c) 15 cents.
    d) 17 cents.
    e) 21 cents.

3. Grace has 16 jellybeans in her pocket. She has 8 red ones, 4 green ones, and 4 blue ones. What is the minimum number of jellybeans she must take out of her pocket to ensure that she has one of each color?
    a) 4.
    b) 8.
    c) 12.
    d) 13.
    e) 16.

4. You need to purchase a textbook for nursing school. The book costs $80.00, and the sales tax is 8.25%. You have $100. How much change will you receive back?
    a) $5.20.
    b) $7.35.
    c) $13.40.
    d) $19.95.
    e) $21.25.

5. Your supervisor instructs you to purchase 240 pens and 6 staplers for the nurse's station. Pens are purchased in sets of 6 for $2.35 per pack. Staplers are sold in sets of 2 for $12.95. How much will purchasing these products cost?
    a) $132.85.
    b) $145.75.
    c) $162.90.
    d) $225.25.
    e) $226.75.

6. **Two cyclists start biking from a trailhead at different speeds and times. The second cyclist travels at 10 miles per hour and starts 3 hours after the first cyclist, who is traveling at 6 miles per hour. Once the second cyclist starts biking, how much time will pass before he catches up with the first cyclist?**
    a) 2 hours.
    b) 4 ½ hours.
    c) 5 ¾ hours.
    d) 6 hours.
    e) 7 ½ hours.

7. **Jim can fill a pool with water by the bucket-full in 30 minutes. Sue can do the same job in 45 minutes. Tony can do the same job in 1 ½ hours. How quickly can all three fill the pool together?**
    a) 12 minutes.
    b) 15 minutes.
    c) 21 minutes.
    d) 23 minutes.
    e) 28 minutes.

8. **A study reported that, in a random sampling of 100 women over the age of 35, 8 of the women had been married 2 or more times. Based on the study results, how many women over the age of 35 in a group of 5,000 would likely have been married 2 or more times?**
    a) 55.
    b) 150.
    c) 200.
    d) 400.
    e) 600.

9. **John is traveling to a meeting that is 28 miles away. He needs to be there in 30 minutes. How fast does he need to go in order to make it to the meeting on time?**
    a) 25 mph.
    b) 37 mph.
    c) 41 mph.
    d) 49 mph.
    e) 56 mph.

10. **If Steven can mix 20 drinks in 5 minutes, Sue can mix 20 drinks in 10 minutes, and Jack can mix 20 drinks in 15 minutes, then how much time will it take all 3 of them working together to mix the 20 drinks?**
    a) 2 minutes and 44 seconds.
    b) 2 minutes and 58 seconds.
    c) 3 minutes and 10 seconds.
    d) 3 minutes and 26 seconds.
    e) 4 minutes and 15 seconds.

11. Jim's belt broke, and his pants are falling down. He has 5 pieces of string. He needs to choose the piece that will be able to go around his 36-inch waist. The piece must be at least 4 inches longer than his waist so that he can tie a knot in it, but it cannot be more that 6 inches longer so that the ends will not show from under his shirt. Which of the following pieces of string will work the best?
    a) 3 feet.
    b) 3 ¾ feet.
    c) 3 5/8 feet.
    d) 3 1/3 feet.
    e) 2 ½ feet.

12. In the final week of January, a car dealership sold 12 cars. A new sales promotion came out the first week of February, and the dealership sold 19 cars that week. What was the percent increase in sales from the last week of January compared to the first week of February?
    a) 58%.
    b) 119%.
    c) 158%.
    d) 175%.
    e) 200%.

13. If two planes leave the same airport at 1:00 PM, how many miles apart will they be at 3:00 PM if one travels directly north at 150 mph and the other travels directly west at 200 mph?
    a) 50 miles.
    b) 100 miles.
    c) 500 miles.
    d) 700 miles.
    e) 1,000 miles.

14. During a 5-day festival, the number of visitors tripled each day. If the festival opened on a Thursday with 345 visitors, what was the attendance on that Sunday?
    a) 345.
    b) 1,035.
    c) 1,725.
    d) 3,105.
    e) 9,315.

15. What will it cost to carpet a room with indoor/outdoor carpet if the room is 10 feet wide and 12 feet long? The carpet costs $12.51 per square yard.
    a) $166.80.
    b) $175.90.
    c) $184.30.
    d) $189.90.
    e) $192.20.

16. Sally has three pieces of material. The first piece is 1 yard, 2 feet, and 6 inches long; the second piece is 2 yard, 1 foot, and 5 inches long; and the third piece is 4 yards, 2 feet, and 8 inches long. How much material does Sally have?
    a) 7 yards, 1 foot, and 8 inches.
    b) 8 yards, 4 feet, and 4 inches.
    c) 8 yards and 11 inches.
    d) 9 yards and 7 inches.
    e) 10 yards.

17. A vitamin's expiration date has passed. It was supposed to contain 500 mg of Calcium, but it has lost 325 mg of Calcium. How many mg of Calcium are left?
    a) 135 mg.
    b) 175 mg.
    c) 185 mg.
    d) 200 mg.
    e) 220 mg.

18. You have orders to give a patient 20 mg of a certain medication. The medication is stored as 4 mg per 5-mL dose. How many milliliters will need to be given?
    a) 15 mL.
    b) 20 mL.
    c) 25 mL.
    d) 30 mL.
    e) 35 mL.

19. You need a 1680 ft^3 aquarium, exactly, for your fish. The pet store has four choices of aquariums. The length, width, and height are listed on the box, but not the volume. Which of the following aquariums would fit your needs?
    a) 12 ft by 12 ft by 12 ft.
    b) 13 ft by 15 ft by 16 ft.
    c) 14 ft by 20 ft by 6 ft.
    d) 15 ft by 16 ft by 12 ft.
    e) 15 ft by 12 ft by 12 ft.

20. Sabrina's boss states that she will increase Sabrina's salary from $12,000 to $14,000 per year if Sabrina enrolls in business courses at a local community college. What percent increase in salary will result from Sabrina taking the business courses?
    a) 15%.
    b) 16.7%.
    c) 17.2%.
    d) 85%.
    e) 117%.

21. Jim works for $15.50 per hour at a health care facility. He is supposed to get a $0.75 per hour raise after one year of service. What will be his percent increase in hourly pay?

    a) 2.7%.
    b) 3.3%.
    c) 133%.
    d) 4.8%.
    e) 105%.

22. Edmond has to sell his BMW. He bought the car for $49,000, but sold it at 20% less. At what price did Edmond sell the car?

    a) $24,200.
    b) $28,900.
    c) $35,600.
    d) $37,300.
    e) $39,200.

23. At a company fish fry, half of those in attendance are employees. Employees' spouses make up a third of the attendance. What is the percentage of the people in attendance who are neither employees nor employees' spouses?

    a) 10.5%.
    b) 16.7%.
    c) 25%.
    d) 32.3%.
    e) 38%.

24. If Sam can do a job in 4 days that Lisa can do in 6 days and Tom can do in 2 days, how long would the job take if Sam, Lisa, and Tom worked together to complete it?

    a) 0.8 days.
    b) 1.09 days.
    c) 1.23 days.
    d) 1.65 days.
    e) 1.97 days.

25. Sarah needs to make a cake and some cookies. The cake requires 3/8 cup of sugar, and the cookies require 3/5 cup of sugar. Sarah has 15/16 cups of sugar. Does she have enough sugar, or how much more does she need?

    a) She has enough sugar.
    b) She needs 1/8 of a cup of sugar.
    c) She needs 3/80 of a cup of sugar.
    d) She needs 4/19 of a cup of sugar.
    e) She needs 1/9 of a cup of sugar.

Arithmetic Reasoning Practice Test Answer Key

1. **Answer: Option (d)**
   Explanation: The original price of the dishwasher is given as $450. Since it is on a 15% sale, the price of dishwasher becomes 0.85* 450 = $382.5 [Please note that we have multiplied by 0.85 because this item is on 15% sale. 15% = 0.15. When an item is on 15% sale, it means that you have to pay for 100-15 ➔ 85% of the actual amount] (20% = 0.20)
   The person buying this dishwasher is an employee of this store, so he gets an additional 20% discount on this item, So, the final amount which he needs to pay becomes 0.8* 382.5 = $306 [Note that we have multiplied by 0.80 because it is on further 20% sale. When an item is on 20% sale, it means that you have to pay for 100% - 20% ➔ 80% of the actual amount]

2. **Answer: Option (d)**
   Explanation: Hotel chares a tax of 0.3% i.e. 0.3/100 = 0.003. Multiplying it with $55 gives us the amount of tax amount which hotel has charged to this traveler.
   $55* 0.003 = $0.165
   Note that the given answer choices are in cents and our answer is in dollars. We convert our answer in to cents by multiplying it with 100. It becomes 16.5 cents. The nearest possible option 17 cents which is Option (c).

3. **Answer: Option (d)**
   Explanation: The best way to answer this question is by considering all the answer choices one by one. We start with option (a) and see if it's correct. Grace has a total of 16 jellybeans, and she takes out 4. It is quite possible that she took all the green or all blue jellybeans, and missing out the red colored jellybeans; therefore, option (a) doesn't ensure us that she took out a jellybean of each color. Considering option (b) and (c), we see that even if Grace takes out 8 or 12 jellybeans, she still can't be sure if she has got all colors or not i.e. it is quite possible that she took out all 8 red ones, or may be all 8 red ones and 4 green ones, and still missing out on blue jellybeans.
   Thus, in order to be completely sure that she has taken out jellybeans of every color, she must take out at least 13 or more jellybeans. Since we are asked about the minimum number, we choose option (d).

4. **Answer: Option (c)**
   Explanation: This is a tricky question. We are given with the sales tax percentage and the actual amount of the book. First of all, we need to find out the amount we would be charged for this including sales tax, and then we need to subtract it from 100, to find out the change we will receive from them.
   8.5% tax on $80 becomes 0.085*80 = $6.8
   So, the total amount that we will be charged becomes 80+ 6.8 = $86.8
   Subtracting it from $100 to find the change, we get 100 – 86.8 = $13.40

5. **Answer: Option (a)**
   Explanation: From the given information in the question, we get to know that the pens are sold in packs of 6 at \$2.35 per pack, and we need to buy $\frac{240}{6}$ = 40 packs. Therefore, the total amount required for 240 pens is 40*2.35 = \$94.

   Also, the staplers are sold in sets of 2 at \$12.95 per set, and we need to buy $\frac{6}{2}$ = 3 sets of staplers. Therefore, the total amount for staplers equals 3*12.95 = \$38.85
   Total cost = \$94 + \$38.85 ➜ \$132.85

6. **Answer: Option (b)**
   Explanation: Let these two cyclists be A and B. Cyclist A is travelling at a speed of 6 miles per hour. Cyclist B is travelling at 10 miles per hour. Cyclist A started cycling 3 hours before cyclist B, so in these 3 hours, he had already travelled 6*3 = 18 miles. Now, lets check the distances covered by each cyclist for every hour.

   After 1 Hour ➜   Cyclist A = 18+6 = 24 miles
                    Cyclist B = 10 miles

   After 2 Hours ➜   Cyclist A = 24+6 = 30 miles
                    Cyclist B = 10+10 = 20 miles

   After 3 Hours ➜   Cyclist A = 30+6 = 36 miles
                    Cyclist B = 20+10 = 30 miles

   After 4 Hours ➜   Cyclist A = 36+6 = 42 miles
                    Cyclist B = 30+10 = 40 miles

   After 4.5 Hours ➜   Cyclist A = 42+3 = 45 miles (We have added 3 here because we are considering distance covered by cyclist A in half hour i.e. 6/2)
                    Cyclist B = 40 + 5 = 45 miles (We have added 5 here because we are considering distance covered by cyclist B in half hour i.e. 10/2)
   Therefore, after 4.5 hours, both cyclists would have covered the same distance.

7. **Answer: Option (b)**
   Explanation: We need to calculate the individual work rates of each of the three given persons.

   Jim can fill the pool in 30 minutes i.e. in one minute, he can fill $\frac{1}{30}$ of the pool.

   Sue can fill the pool in 45 minutes i.e. in one minute, Sue can fill $\frac{1}{45}$ of the pool.

   Tony can fill the pool in $1\frac{1}{2}$ hour [90 minutes], i.e. in one minute, he can fill $\frac{1}{90}$ of the pool.

   So, if Jim, Sue and Tony work together for 1 minute, they can fill $\frac{1}{30} + \frac{1}{45} + \frac{1}{90} = \frac{1}{15}$ of the pool. Therefore, in order to fill the pool completely working together, they would need 15 minutes.

8. **Answer: Option (d)**

   Explanation: In a given sample of 100 women aged over 35, 8 have been married at least twice. In order to find out the number of women at least married twice, in a sample of 5000 women, we write the following ratio:

Sample Space :	Aged Above 35
100-women :	8 married at least twice
5000-women :	'x' married at least twice

   Cross multiplying, we get x*100 = 8*5000
   x =40000/100 ➔ 400

9. **Answer: Option (e)**

   Explanation: The total distance which needs to be covered is 28 miles. Total time which John has to reach there is 30 minutes i.e. 0.5 hour.
   As we know that speed $= \frac{Distance}{Time} = \frac{28\ miles}{0.5\ hours} = 56$ miles/hour

10. **Answer: Option (a)**

    Explanation: Steven can mix 20 drinks in 5 minutes, which means that in one minute, he can mix $\frac{20}{5} = 4$ drinks.

    Sue can mix 20 drinks in 10 minutes which means that Sue can mix $\frac{20}{10} = 2$ drinks per minute.

    Jack can mix 20 drinks in 15 minutes which means that he can mix $\frac{20}{15} = 1.33$ drinks per minute.

    Therefore, if Steven, Sue and Jack work together for one minute, they can mix 4+2+1.33 = 7.33 drinks per minutes. In order to mix a total of 20 drinks working together, they will need $\frac{20}{7.33} = 2.72$ minutes.
    In order to find the exact seconds, we multiply our answer by 60. This gives us 60*2.72 = 163.7 seconds. We know that 163.7 correspond to 2 minutes and 44 seconds (approx).

11. **Answer: Option (d)**

    Explanation: From the statement of the question, it is clear that we need string that is at least 40 inches long (i.e. 36 inch waist and 4 inches for knot) but not longer than 42 inches.
    Let's examine the length of strings available in answer options.
    Option (a) = 3 feet = 36 inches Incorrect
    Option (b) = 3(3/4) feet = 45 inches Incorrect
    Option (c) = 3(5/8) feet = 42.5 inches Incorrect
    Option (d) = 3 (1/3) feet = 40 inches **Correct**
    Option (e) = 2(1/2) feet = 30 inches Incorrect

12. Answer: Option (a)

Explanation: In order to find the percentage change, we use the following formula.

Percentage Change $= \frac{Final\ value\ -\ Original\ Value}{Original\ Value} * 100$

Therefore, percentage increase becomes, $\frac{19-12}{12} * 100 = 58\%$

13. Answer: Option (c)

Explanation: It's a tricky question. First of all, you must note that one plane is flying toward north, and the other one is flying towards west. The total distance between these two cannot be calculated by simply adding their individual distances. We need to use Pythagoras theorem to solve this question. Both airplanes left the airport at same time 1:00 pm and we looking for how much apart they would be after two hours at 3:00 pm.

Plane flying toward north has a speed of 150 miles per hour, so in two hours, it would have covered 300 miles.

Plane flying towards west has a speed of 200 miles per hours, so it would have covered 400 miles in two hours.

Using Pythagoras Theorem, We find the distance between these two planes as:

Distance $= \sqrt{(300)^2 + (400)^2} = 500$ miles

14. Answer: Option (e)

Explanation: The number of people on Thursday is 345. Every next day the number of people triples. On Friday, it becomes 3*345 = 1035

On Saturday, the number of people who came to this festival became 3 * 1035 =3105

On Sunday, the number of people who came to this festival became 3 * 3105 = 9315

15. Answer: Option (a)

Explanation: It is important to note that the rate of the carpet is given is per sq. yard and the dimensions of the room are given in feet. So, we need to convert the width and length of the room in yards, and then calculate the total area of the room. We know that 1 foot = 0.33 yards

10 feet = 3.33 yards

12 feet = 4 yards

Area of the room = 4*3.33 = 13.32 sq yards

So, the total cost to carpet this room equals 13.32 * 12.51 ➔ $166.6

16. Answer: Option (d)

Explanation: First of all, we add the inches, feet and yards individually.

Inches: 6 + 5+ 8 = 19 inches

Feet = 2 + 1 + 2 = 5 Feet

Yards = 1 + 2 + 4 = 7 yards

As we know that there are 12 inches in 1 foot, so 19 inches becomes 1 foot and 7 inches. Therefore, we add one more to 5 feet, which makes it 6 feet.

Also, we know that 1 foot = 0.33 yards, so 6 feet = 2 yards.

This makes the total length equal to 9 yards and 7 inches. [9 yards because 7 yards calculated in the first step plus 2 yards from 6 feet conversion to yards.]

17. Answer: Option (b)

Explanation: The amount of calcium actually required was 500 mg in that vitamin, but it has lost 325mg of calcium in it. Therefore, it has got 500-325 = 175 mg calcium left in it after expiration.

18. Answer: Option (c)

Explanation: There are 4mg of medication in 5 mL dose. We need to give 20 mg to the patient and $\frac{20}{4} = 5$ so we multiply the dose by 5 to give our desired amount of medication to the patient. Therefore, 5* 5mL = 25 mL

19. Answer: Option (c)

Explanation: We know that the volume is given my formula length* width * height. In order to find the correct volume of the aquariums given in the answer options, we multiply their respective length, width and heights to see, which on equals to 1680.
Option (a) = 12*12*12 = 1728
Option (b) = 13*15*16 = 3120
Option (c) = 14*20*6 = 1680 which is our required answer. No need to check further options.

20. Answer: Option (b)

Explanation: If she takes the business courses, her salary would increase from $12000 to $14000. We know that

Percentage Change = $\frac{Final\ value - Original\ Value}{Original\ Value}*100$ ➔ $\frac{14000-12000}{12000}*100$

$\frac{2000}{12000}*100 = 16.7\%$

21. Answer: Option (d)

Explanation: His new hourly salary would become $15.50+$0.75 = $16.25

Percentage change = $\frac{Final\ value - Original\ Value}{Original\ Value}*100$

$\frac{16.25-15.50}{15.50}*100$

$\frac{0.75}{15.50}*100 = 4.8\%$

22. Answer: Option (e)

Explanation: Price of Edmond's car was $49000 but he had to sell it at 20% less. This means that the price at which he sold his car was 80% of the actual price. Therefore, 0.8*49000 = $39200

23. Answer: Option (b)

Explanation: The easiest way to solve these types of questions is to imagine a constant number. Let's say there are 100 people in the fish fry company, such that one half of the people are employee i.e. 100/2 = 50 employees.

Similarly, the spouses of the employees make one third of the attendance i.e. $\frac{100}{3} = 33.3$

Now, the remaining people are 100- 50 – 33.3 = 16.7 %

(Note: It is not possible that there are 33.3 or 16.7 person in the restraint. The number of people is always a whole number. But in this case while solving this question, we have used percentage approximation)

24. Answer: Option (b)

Explanation: First of all, we need to calculate the individual work rate for each of the given persons.

Sam can do that job in 4 days means that he can do ¼ of that job in a single day.

Lisa can do that same job in 6 days means that she can complete $\frac{1}{6}$ of the job in one day.

Tom can complete that job in 2 days, means that he can complete ½ of that job in one day.

So, if Sam, Lisa, and Tom work together for one day, they can complete $(\frac{1}{4} + \frac{1}{6} + \frac{1}{2}) = 0.917$ job in a single day.

In order to complete 1 job working together, they would need 1/0.917 = 1.09 Days

25. Answer: Option (c)

Explanation: Cake requires $\frac{3}{8} = 0.375$ cup of sugar, whereas, cookies require $\frac{3}{5} = 0.6$ cup of sugar. This makes a total of 0.375+0.6 = 0.975 cup of sugar.

Sarah has got $\frac{15}{16} = 0.9375$ cup of sugar.

Therefore, it is clear that Sarah needs more sugar than she already has got. The exact amount of sugar required can be calculated by subtracting total sugar from required sugar.
i.e. 0.975-0.9375 = 0.0375

Therefore, Option (c) is correct. [$\frac{3}{80} = 0.0375$]

Chapter 3: Word Knowledge

The military considers clear and concise communication so important that it is taught and graded at all levels of leadership training. If you are planning a military career, you will be tested on your verbal skills as you move through the ranks.

The good news is that most individuals have been exposed to all of the vocabulary words used on the subtest by the time they have reached the tenth grade. This doesn't mean that you are going to recognize every single word. It *does* mean, however, that you won't be expected to know advanced Latin or graduate science terminology.

This section of the test gives you 25 questions to answer in 5 minutes. This may seem like a disproportionate amount of time – it comes out to about 12 seconds per question – but don't worry! We're going to arm you with all of the knowledge you'll need in order to work quickly and efficiently through this section.

As an extra challenge to this section, the questions are formatted so the word has to be matched without context. You will typically be given a single word in all capital letters, then you must choose from the answer choices which word matches or has the same meaning. For example:

       Garner most nearly means:
         a) Create.
         b) Propose.
         c) Demonstrate.
         d) Gather.

The correct answer is: d) Gather

You will note that as we work through this section, not all questions will be formatted this way and that is for a reason. Words can be tricky and there is no shortcut to learning to understand them, or even refreshing what you might have learned years ago. The biggest mistake one can make is thinking they will just memorize a bunch of vocabulary words. This is a wasted effort. First of all, it is very unlikely you will retain that information long enough from rote memorization. Secondly, it would take endless hours to memorize enough of them. Finally, you would still be missing the key elements that allow you to figure out the meaning of a word without even knowing its definition OR knowing what it certainly does not mean which allows you to eliminate wrong answer choices.

VOCABULARY BASIC TRAINING

The first step in getting ready for this section of the AFOQT consists of reviewing the basic techniques used to determine the meanings of words you are not familiar with. The good news is that you have been using various degrees of these techniques since you first began to speak. Sharpening these skills will help you with the paragraph comprehension subtest.

Following each section you will find a practice drill. Use your scores on these to determine if you need to study a particular subject matter further. At the end of each section, you will find a Practice Drill to test your Knowledge.

The questions found on the practice drills are not given in the two formats found on the Word Knowledge subtest; rather they are designed to <u>reinforce</u> the skills needed to score well on the Word Knowledge subtest.

Context Clues

Although you won't get any context to reference words on the AFOQT, for training purposes we will start with words in context so you can start to see how to break-down a word into its meaning. Your ability to observe sentences closely is extremely useful when it comes to understanding new vocabulary words.

Types of Context

There are two different types of context that can help you understand the meaning of unfamiliar words: **sentence context** and **situational context**. Regardless of which context is present, these types of questions are not really testing your knowledge of vocabulary; they are testing your ability to comprehend the meaning of a word through its usage.

> **Situational context** is the basis of the Paragraph Comprehension subtest and will be discussed in chapter two.
>
> **Sentence context** occurs in the sentence containing the vocabulary word. To figure out words using sentence context clues, you should first determine the most important words in the sentence.
>
> > For Example: I had a hard time reading her <u>illegible</u> handwriting.
> >
> > > a) Neat.
> > > b) Unsafe.
> > > c) Sloppy.
> > > d) Educated.
>
> Already, you know that this sentence is discussing something that is hard to read. Look at the word that **illegible** is describing: **handwriting**. Based on context clues, you can tell that illegible means that her handwriting is hard to read.

Next, look at the choices. Choice **a) Neat** is obviously wrong, because neat handwriting would not be difficult to read. Choice **b) Unsafe** and **d) Educated** don't make sense. Therefore, choice **c) Sloppy** is the best answer choice.

Types of Clues

There are four types of clues that can help you understand the context, which in turn helps you define the word. They are **restatement**, **positive/negative**, **contrast**, and **specific detail**.

Restatement clues occur when the definition of the word is clearly stated in the sentence.

For Example: The dog was <u>dauntless</u> in the face of danger, braving the fire to save the girl.
   a) Difficult.
   b) Fearless.
   c) Imaginative.
   d) Pleasant.

Demonstrating **bravery** in the face of danger would be **fearless,** choice **b)**. In this case, the context clues tell you exactly what the word means.

Positive/negative clues can tell you whether a word has a positive or negative meaning.

For Example: The magazine gave a great review of the fashion show, stating the clothing was **sublime**.
   a) Horrible.
   b) Exotic.
   c) Bland
   d) Gorgeous.

The sentence tells us that the author liked the clothing enough to write a **great** review, so you know that the best answer choice is going to be a positive word. Therefore, you can immediately rule out choices **a)** and **c)** because they are negative words. **Exotic** is a neutral word; alone, it doesn't inspire a **great** review. The most positive word is gorgeous, which makes choice **d) Gorgeous** the best answer.

The following sentence uses both restatement and positive/negative clues:

"Janet suddenly found herself <u>destitute</u>, so poor she could barely afford to eat."

The second part of the sentence clearly indicates that destitute is a negative word; it also restates the meaning: very poor.

Contrast clues include the opposite meaning of a word. Words like **but, on the other hand,** and **however** are tip-offs that a sentence contains a contrast clue.

For Example: Beth did not spend any time preparing for the test, but Tyron kept a <u>rigorous</u> study schedule.
   a) Strict.
   b) Loose.
   c) Boring.
   d) Strange.

In this case, the word **but** tells us that Tyron studied in a different way than Beth. If Beth did not study very hard, then Tyron did study hard for the test. The best answer here, therefore, is choice **a) Strict**.

Specific detail clues give a precise detail that can help you understand the meaning of the word.
   For Example: The box was heavier than he expected and it began to become <u>cumbersome</u>.
   a) Impossible.
   b) Burdensome.
   c) Obligated.
   d) Easier.

Start by looking at the specific details of the sentence. Choice **d)** can be eliminated right away because it is doubtful it would become **easier** to carry something that is **heavier**. There are also no clues in the sentence to indicate he was **obligated** to carry the box, so choice **c)** can also be disregarded. The sentence specifics, however, do tell you that the package was cumbersome because it was heavy to carry; something heavy to carry is a burden, which is **burdensome**, choice **b)**.

It is important to remember that more than one of these clues can be present in the same sentence. The more there are, the easier it will be to determine the meaning of the word, so look for them.

Denotation and Connotation

As you know, many English words have more than one meaning. For example, the word **quack** has two distinct definitions: the sound a duck makes; and a person who publicly pretends to have a skill, knowledge, education, or qualification which they do not possess.

The **denotations** of a word are the dictionary definitions.

The **connotations** of a word are the implied meaning(s) or emotion which the word makes you think.

For Example:

"Sure," Pam said excitedly, "I'd just love to join your club; it sounds so exciting!"

Now, read this sentence:

"Sure," Pam said sarcastically, "I'd just love to join your club; it sounds so exciting!"

Even though the two sentences only differ by one word, they have completely different meanings. The difference, of course, lies in the words "excitedly" and "sarcastically."

Look back to the underlined word – **reinforce** - in the second paragraph of page 13. Can you think of several words that could be used and the sentence have the same meaning?

Comme

Practice Drill: Vocabulary Basic Training

Use context clues to determine the meaning of each underlined word.

1. His story didn't seem very <u>realistic</u>; even though it was a documentary.
   a) Believable.
   b) Humorous.
   c) Poetic.
   d) Exciting.

2. Listening to music too loudly, especially through headphones, can <u>impair</u> your hearing.
   a) Damage.
   b) Heighten.
   c) Use.
   d) Ensure.

3. Kelly's game happened to <u>coincide</u> with the Sue's recital.
   a) Happen before.
   b) Occur at the same time.
   c) Occur afterward.
   d) Not happen.

4. The weather has been very extreme lately; thankfully, today it's much more <u>temperate</u>.
   a) Troubling.
   b) Beautiful.
   c) Cold.
   d) Moderate.

5. He knew he couldn't win the race after falling off his bike, so he had to <u>concede</u>.
   a) Continue.
   b) Give up.
   c) Challenge.
   d) Be thankful.

6. The editor, preferring a more <u>terse</u> writing style, cut 30% of the words from the article.
   a) Elegant.
   b) Factual.
   c) Descriptive.
   d) Concise.

7. Victor Frankenstein spent the last years of his life chasing his <u>elusive</u> monster, which was always one step ahead.
    a) Unable to be compared.
    b) Unable to be captured.
    c) Unable to be forgotten.
    d) Unable to be avoided.

8. Certain <u>passages</u> were taken from the book for the purpose of illustration.
    a) Excerpts.
    b) Contents.
    c) Paragraphs.
    d) Tables.

9. The investigator searched among the <u>ruins</u> for the cause of the fire.
    a) Terminal.
    b) Foundation.
    c) Rubble.
    d) Establishment.

10. To make her novels more engaging, Cynthia was known to <u>embellish</u> her writing with fictitious details.
    a) Add to.
    b) Detract.
    c) Isolate.
    d) Disavow.

11. Robert's well-timed joke served to <u>diffuse</u> the tension in the room and the party continued happily.
    a) Refuse.
    b) Intensify.
    c) Create.
    d) Soften.

12. I had a difficult time understanding the book because the author kept <u>digressing</u> to unrelated topics.
    a) Deviating, straying.
    b) Regressing, reverting.
    c) Changing the tone.
    d) Expressing concisely.

13. The senator <u>evaded</u> almost every question.
   a) Avoided.
   b) Answered indirectly.
   c) Refused to answer directly.
   d) Deceived.

14. Sammie hasn't come out of her room all afternoon, but I would <u>surmise</u> that it is because she is upset about not being able to go to the mall.
   a) Confirm.
   b) Surprise.
   c) Believe.
   d) Guess.

15. The details can be worked out later; what's important is that the company follows the <u>crux</u> of the argument, which is that everyone be paid equally.
   a) Overall tone.
   b) Specific fact.
   c) Main point.
   d) Logic, reasoning.

Use context clues to choose the best word to complete the sentence.

16. Mr. Collins _____ tomatoes so vehemently that he felt ill just smelling them.
   a) Resented.
   b) Disliked.
   c) Detested.
   d) Hated.

17. We were rolling on the ground with laughter during the _____ new movie.
   a) Comical.
   b) Humorous.
   c) Amusing.
   d) Hilarious.

18. Tina's parents made us feel right at home during our visit to their house with their generous _____ .
   a) Unselfishness.
   b) Politeness.
   c) Hospitality.
   d) Charity.

19. Although his mother was not happy that he broke the window, she was pleased that he was _____ about it.

    a) Honest.

    b) Trustworthy.

    c) Authentic.

    d) Decent.

20. The soldiers _____ to their feet immediately when then officer walked into the room.

    a) Stood.

    b) Leapt.

    c) Rose.

    d) Skipped.

Practice Drill: Vocabulary Basic Training – Answers

1. **a) Believable**. Realistic means accurate, truthful, and believable.

2. **a) Damage**. This is the only logical choice.

3. **b) Occur at the same time**. According to information in the sentence, the game was scheduled at the same time as the recital.

4. **d) Moderate**. The context says that the weather has been "extreme." It does not say if the weather has been extremely hot or cold; therefore, choices **b) Beautiful** and **c) Cold** can be ruled out. The sentence also indicates a change from negative to positive making moderate the best choice.

5. **b) Give up**. The speaker of the sentence knows they cannot win, so choice **b)** is the best choice.

6. **d) Concise**. Terse means concise, using no unnecessary words. The main clue is that the editor cut words from the article, reducing its wordiness.

7. **b) Unable to be captured**. Elusive means evasive, difficult to capture.

8. **a) Excerpt**. An excerpt is a passage or quote from a book, article, or other publication

9. **c) Rubble** is synonymous with ruin.

10. **a) Add to**. To embellish is to add details to a story to make it more appealing.

11. **d) Soften**. The clues *tension* and *continue happily* tell you that **d)** is the best choice

12. **a) To deviate, stray**. To digress means to deviate; to stray from the main subject in writing or speaking.

13. **a) To avoid**. To evade means to avoid by cleverness. The senator avoids answering the question by changing the subject.

14. **d) Guess**. The speaker is guessing why Samantha is upset based on circumstances; she has not actually given a reason.

15. c) Main point. Crux means the central or main point, especially of a problem. The main context clue is that the speaker isn't concerned with the details but is focused on getting agreement on the main point.

16. c) Detested. The knowledge that Mr. Collins feels ill just smelling tomatoes suggests that his hatred for tomatoes is intense; therefore, the best choice will be the most negative. To **dislike** tomatoes – choice **b)** – is the most neutral word, so this choice can be ruled out. **Resented** is a word that generally applies to people or their actions, ruling out choice **a)**. Given the choice between **c)** and **d),** the most negative is **c) Detested**.

17. d) Hilarious. The movie must be extremely funny for the audience to have this sort of reaction, and, while all of the answer choices are synonyms for funny, the only one that means extremely funny is choice **d) Hilarious**.

18. c) Hospitality. Although all four choices describe different types of kindness, **unselfishness** – choice **a)** – can be ruled out because it has the same basic meaning as the adjective, generous. Choice **d) Charity** is a kindness usually associated with those less fortunate; since nothing in the context indicates this type of relationship, this choice can also be eliminated. Left with choices **b) Politeness** and **c) Hospitality**, hospitality best describes the kindness of welcoming someone into your home.

19. a) Honest. Again we have a case in which all of the word choices are synonyms for the word honest. In this case, the most neutral word is the best choice. Choice **b) Trustworthy**, **c) Authentic**, and **d) Decent** do not make as much sense as the most basic synonym, **honest**.

20. b) Leapt. The word immediately is the main clue. **a) Stood** and **c) Rose** are neutral words that do not convey a sense of urgency. Choice **b) Leapt** is the only word that implies the immediacy demanded by the sentence context.

ROOTS, PREFIXES, and SUFFIXES

You just got done with what could be called a "warm up" exercise, and now we will get into the tougher material you need to know specifically for the AFOQT. Although you are not expected to know every word in the English language, you are expected to have the ability to use deductive reasoning to find the choice that is the best match for the word in question, which is why we are going to explain how to break a word into its parts of meaning

prefix – root – suffix

One trick in dividing a word into its parts is to first divide the word into its **syllables**. To show how syllables can help you find roots and affixes, we'll use the word **descendant,** which means one who comes from an ancestor. Start by dividing the word into its individual syllables; this word has three: **de-scend-ant**. The next step is to look at the beginning and end of the word, and then determine if these syllables are prefixes, suffixes, or possible roots. You can then use the meanings of each part to guide you in defining the word. When you divide words into their specific parts, they do not always add up to an exact definition, but you will see a relationship between their parts.

Note: This trick won't always work in every situation, because not all prefixes, roots, and suffixes have only one syllable. For example, take the word **monosyllabic** (which ironically means "one syllable"). There are five syllables in that word, but only three parts. The prefix is "mono," meaning "one." The root "syllab" refers to "syllable," while the suffix "ic" means "pertaining to." Therefore, we have one very long word which means "pertaining to one syllable."

The more familiar you become with these fundamental word parts, the easier it will be to define unfamiliar words. Although the words found on the Word Knowledge subtest are considered vocabulary words learned by the tenth grade level of high school, some are still less likely to be found in an individual's everyday vocabulary. The root and affixes list in this chapter uses more common words as examples to help you learn them more easily. Don't forget that you use word roots and affixes every day, without even realizing it. Don't feel intimidated by the long list of roots and affixes (prefixes and suffixes) at the end of this chapter, because you already know and use them every time you communicate with some else, verbally and in writing. If you take the time to read through the list just once a day for two weeks, you will be able to retain most of them and understand a high number of initially unfamiliar words.

Roots

Roots are the building blocks of all words. Every word is either a root itself or has a root. Just as a plant cannot grow without roots, neither can vocabulary, because a word must have a root to give it meaning.

For Example: The test instructions were **unclear.**

The root is what is left when you strip away all the prefixes and suffixes from a word. In this case, take away the prefix "un-", and you have the root **clear**.

Roots are not always recognizable words, because they generally come from Latin or Greek words, such as **nat**, a Latin root meaning **born**. The word native, which means a person born of a referenced placed, comes from this root, so does the word prenatal, meaning before birth. Yet, if you used the prefix **nat** instead of born, just on its own, no one would know what you were talking about.

Words can also have more than one root. For example, the word **omnipotent** means all powerful. Omnipotent is a combination of the roots **omni-**, meaning all or every, and -**potent**, meaning power or strength. In this case, **omni** cannot be used on its own as a single word, but **potent** can. Again, it is important to keep in mind that roots do not always match the exact definitions of words and they can have several different spellings, but breaking a word into its parts is still one of the best ways to determine its meaning.

Prefixes and Suffixes

Prefixes are syllables added to the beginning of a word and suffixes are syllables added to the end of the word. Both carry assigned meanings. The common name for prefixes and suffixes is **affixes**. Affixes do not have to be attached directly to a root and a word can often have more than one prefix and/or suffix. Prefixes and suffixes can be attached to a word to completely change the word's meaning or to enhance the word's original meaning. Although they don't mean much to us on their own, when attached to other words affixes can make a world of difference.

We can use the word **prefix** as an example:

Fix means to place something securely.
Pre means before.
Prefix means to place something before or in front.

An example of a suffix:

> **Femin** is a root. It means female, woman.
> **-ism** means act, practice or process.
> **Feminism** is the defining and establishing of equal political, economic, and social rights for women.

Unlike prefixes, **suffixes** can be used to change a word's part of speech.

> For example, take a look at these sentences:
> > Randy raced to the finish line.
> > Shana's costume was very racy.

In the first sentence, raced is a verb. In the second sentence, racy is an adjective. By changing the suffix from **-ed** to **-y**, the word race changes from a verb into an adjective, which has an entirely different meaning.

Although you cannot determine the meaning of a word by a prefix or suffix alone, you *can* use your knowledge of what root words mean to eliminate answer choices; indicating if the word is positive or negative can give you a partial meaning of the word.

Practice Drill: Roots, Prefixes, and Suffixes

Try to find the root in each of the underlined words.

1. The bridge was out, so the river was <u>impassable</u>.
   - a) Im-
   - b) -pass-
   - c) -a-
   - d) –able

2. I am usually on time, but my husband is <u>chronically</u> late.
   - a) Chron-
   - b) -chronical-
   - c) -ally-
   - d) -ic

3. The only way to succeed is by <u>striving</u> to do your best.
   - a) Str-
   - a) Striv-
   - b) Strive-
   - c) -ing

4. We drifted along lazily on the <u>tranquil</u> river.
   - a) Tra-
   - b) -qui-
   - c) Tranq-
   - d) -uil

5. A <u>pediatrician</u> is a doctor who takes care of children.
   - a) Ped-
   - b) -ia-
   - c) -tri-
   - d) -cian

Choose the word that shares the same root as the given word.

6. Audible
   a) Auditorium.
   b) Because.
   c) Dribble.
   d) Bagel.

7. Nominate
   a) Eaten.
   b) Minute.
   c) Hated.
   d) Synonym.

8. Disappoint
   a) Disappear.
   b) Appointment.
   c) Interest.
   d) Potato.

9. Dilute
   a) Flute.
   b) Dictate.
   c) Pollute.
   d) Hesitate.

10. Sympathy
   a) System.
   b) Empathy.
   c) Pattern.
   d) Rhythm.

11. Science
   a) Conscious.
   b) Once.
   c) Alien.
   d) Parasite.

12. Incline
   a) Recline.
   b) Independent.
   c) Cluster.
   d) Twine.

For each question below, use the Latin word root to determine underlined word's meaning.

13. An amiable person is:
   a) Talkative, loud.
   b) Truthful, honest.
   c) Highly educated.
   d) Friendly, good-natured.

14. A lucid argument:
   a) Is very clear and intelligible.
   b) Is loosely held together, tenuous.
   c) Frequently digresses.
   d) Errs repeatedly in its logic.

15. A complacent person:
   a) Frequently makes mistakes, but does not accept responsibility.
   b) Likes to pick fights.
   c) Is contented to a fault, self-satisfied.
   d) Is known to tell lies, embellish the truth.

16. To exacerbate a problem means:
   a) To solve it.
   b) To analyze it.
   c) To lessen it.
   d) To worsen it.

17. To measure the veracity of something is to measure its:
   a) Value or worth.
   b) Truthfulness.
   c) Weight.
   d) Life force.

18. Something that is eloquent is:
   a) Dull, trite, hackneyed.
   b) Expressed in a powerful and effective manner.
   c) Very old, antiquated.
   d) Equally divided or apportioned.

19. To indict someone is to:
   a) Pick a fight with that person.
   b) Stop or block that person from doing something.
   c) Charge that person with a crime.
   d) Love that person dearly.

20. A <u>quiescent</u> place is:

    a) Very isolated.

    b) Tumultuous, chaotic.

    c) Sacred.

    d) Still, at rest.

21. An individual with <u>equanimity</u>:

    a) Has a violent temper.

    b) Is very stubborn.

    c) Enjoys the company of others.

    d) Is even-tempered and composed.

What are the affixes in each word?

22. Disease

    a) Dis-

    b) -ise-

    c) -eas-

    d) -ase

23. Uncomfortable

    a) Un-

    b) Un-, -com-

    c) -fort-

    d) Un-, -able

24. Disrespected

    a) Re-, -spect, -ed

    b) Dis-, -ed

    c) Dis-, re-, -ed

    d) Respect-, -ed

25. Impressive

    a) Im-, -ive

    b) -ive

    c) Press-, -ive

    d) Impre-, -ive

26. Predated

    a) Pre-

    b) Pre-, -d

    c) Pre-, -ed

    d) –d

Using your knowledge of prefixes and root words, try to determine the following words' meanings.

27. To take <u>precaution</u> is to:

    a) Prepare before doing something.

    b) Remember something that happened earlier.

    c) Become aware of something for the first time.

    d) Try to do something again.

28. To <u>reorder</u> a list is to:

    a) Use the same order again.

    b) Put the list in a new order.

    c) Get rid of the list.

    d) Find the list.

29. An <u>antidote</u> to a disease is:

    a) Something that is part of the disease.

    b) Something that works against the disease.

    c) Something that makes the disease worse.

    d) Something that has nothing to do with the disease.

30. Someone who is <u>multiethnic</u>:

    a) Likes only certain kinds of people.

    b) Lives in the land of his or her birth.

    c) Is from a different country.

    d) Has many different ethnicities.

31. Someone who is <u>misinformed</u> has been:

    a) Taught something new.

    b) Told the truth.

    c) Forgotten.

    d) Given incorrect information.

Choose the best answer to each question. (Remember you are looking for the closest meaning.)

32. <u>Exorbitant</u> means:

a) Belonging to a group.

b) To orbit.

c) Beneath conscious awareness.

d) Far beyond what is normal or reasonable.

33. <u>Denunciation</u> means:

a) To denounce or openly condemn.

b) Critical, of or like a condemnation.

c) One who denounces or openly condemns another.

d) The act of denouncing or openly condemning.

34. <u>Metamorphosis</u> means:

a) To transform.

b) One who has changed.

c) A transformation.

d) Tending to change frequently.

35. To <u>reconcile</u> means:

a) To reestablish a close relationship between.

b) To move away from.

c) To undermine.

d) To surpass or outdo.

36. <u>Didactic</u> means:

a) A teacher or instructor.

b) Intended to instruct, moralizing.

c) To preach or moralize.

d) The process of instructing.

37. <u>Unilateral</u> means:

a) To multiply.

b) Understated.

c) Literal.

d) One-sided.

38. <u>Subordinate</u> means:

a) Under someone else's authority or control.

b) Organized according to rank; hierarchical.

c) Something ordinary or average, without distinction.

d) Repeated frequently to aid memorization.

39. <u>Incisive</u> means:

     a) Insight.

     b) Worthy of consideration.

     c) Penetrating.

     d) To act forcefully.

40. <u>Intermittent</u> means:

     a) Badly handled.

     b) Occurring at intervals

     c) Greatly varied.

     d) A number between one and ten.

41. <u>Miscreant</u> means:

     a) Someone who is unconventional.

     b) Someone who lacks creativity.

     c) A very naive person.

     d) An evil person or villain.

Practice Drill: Roots, Prefixes, and Suffixes - Answers

1. **b) –pass-**

2. **a) Chron-**

3. **c) Strive-**

4. **b) –qui-.** *Quies* is a Latin root meaning rest or quiet.

5. **a) Ped-.** *Ped* is a Latin root meaning child or education. You might recognize that the suffix **-cian** refers to what someone does, such as physician or beautician. The suffix **-iatr** relates to doctors, as you can see in the words psychiatry and podiatry. Both suffixes support the root of the word.

6. **a) Auditorium.** From the Latin root **aud,** meaning hearing or listening.

7. **d) Synonym.** The words nominate and synonym share the root, **nom,** meaning name. Remember, roots are not necessarily going to be in the same position in other words.

8. **b) Appointment.** Greek root **poie,** meaning to make.

9. **c) Pollute.** Both dilute and pollute come from the root **lut,** meaning to wash.

10. **b) Empathy.** The words sympathy and empathy come from the Greek root **path,** meaning feeling, suffering, or disease.

11. **a) Conscious.** Science and conscious share the Latin root **sci,** which means to know.

12. **a) Recline.** Incline and recline both share the Greek root *clin,* meaning to lean toward or bend.

13. **d).** The root **am** means love. Amiable means friendly, agreeable, good natured, likeable, or pleasing.

14. **a).** The root **luc/lum/lus** means light. Lucid means very clear, easy to understand, intelligible.

15. **c).** The root **plac** means to please. Complacent means contented to a fault; self-satisfied.

16. **d).** The root **ac** means sharp, bitter. Exacerbate is to increase the severity, violence, or bitterness of.

17. **b).** The root **ver** means truth. Veracity means truth or truthfulness.

18. **b).** The root **loc/log/loqu** means word or speech. Eloquent means expressed in a powerful, fluent, and persuasive manner.

19. **c).** The root **dic/dict/dit** means to say, tell, or use words. To indict means to formally accuse of or charge with a crime.

20. d). The root **qui** means quiet. Quiescent means inactive, quiet, or at rest.

21. d). The root **equ** means equal or even. Equanimity means calmness of temperament, even-temperedness, or patience and composure, especially under stress.

22. a) Dis-. The prefix **dis-** means away from, deprive of, reversal, or not. If someone has a **disease** they are not well.

23. d) Un-, -able. The prefix **un-** means not. The suffix **-able** means ability or worthy of. **Uncomfortable** means not able to be in a state of comfort.

24. c) Dis-, re-, -ed. The prefix **dis-** means away from, reversal, or not. The prefix **re-** means back or again. The suffix **-ed** indicates that the word is in the past tense. **Disrespected** means showed a lack of respect towards.

25. a) Im-, -ive. The prefix **im-** means in, into, or within. The suffix **-ive** means having the nature of. **Impressive** means having the ability inspire an internal feeling of awe.

26. c) Pre-, -ed. The prefix **pre-** means before. The suffix **-ed** indicates that the word is in the past tense. **Predated** means came before the date.

27. a) Prepare before doing something. **Pre-** means before; **caution** means to be careful or take heed.

28. b) Put the list in a new order. *Re-* means again. In this case, order means organize. Reorder then means to organize the list again or to put the list into a different order.

29. b) Something that works against the disease. The prefix **anti-** means against. An **antidote** is something that works against a disease or a poison.

30. d) Has many different ethnicities. The prefix **multi-** means many. Someone who is **multiethnic** has relatives from many different ethnic groups.

31. d) Given incorrect information. **Mis-** means opposite, and to be **informed** is to have the correct information.

32. d) Far beyond what is normal or reasonable. The prefix **ex-** means out, out of, away from.

33. a) The act of denouncing or openly condemning. The prefix **de-** means against, the root **nounc** means to state or declare, and the noun suffix **-tion** means the act or state of.

34. c) A transformation. The prefix **meta-** means change, while the root **morph** means shape or form, and the **noun** suffix **-sis** means the process of. **Metamorphosis** means a marked change of form or a transformation.

35. a) Means to reestablish a relationship. The prefix **re-** means back or again and, the root **con** means with. Together they mean back together again or reestablishing a relationship.

36. b) Intended to instruct or moralize. The adjective suffix **-ic** means pertaining or relating to, having the quality of. Only choices **b)** and **d)** define a quality, and choice **d)** would require an additional suffix.

37. d) One-sided. The prefix **uni-** means one.

38. a) Under someone else's authority or control. The prefix **sub-** means under, beneath or below.

39. c) Penetrating. The adjective suffix **-ive** means having the nature of.

40. b) Occurring at intervals. The prefix **inter-** means between or among.

41. d) An evil person or villain. The prefix **mis-** means bad, evil, or wrong. The suffix **–ant** means an agent or something that performs the action.

SYNONYMS and ANTONYMS

Synonyms are groups of words that mean the same, or almost the same, thing as each other. The word synonym comes from the Greek roots **syn-,** meaning same, and **-nym,** meaning name. **Hard, difficult, challenging,** and **arduous** are synonyms of one another.

Antonyms are sets of words that have opposite, or nearly opposite, meanings of one another. The word antonym comes from the Greek roots **ant-,** meaning opposing, and **–nym** (name). **Hard** and **easy** are antonyms.

Synonyms do not always have exactly the same meanings, and antonyms are not always exact opposites. For example, scalding is an adjective that means burning. Boiling water can be described as scalding or as hot. **Hot** and **scalding** are considered synonyms, even though the two words do not mean exactly the same thing; something that is scalding is considered to be extremely hot.

In the same manner, antonyms are not always exact opposites. **Cold** and **freezing** are both antonyms of scalding. Although freezing is closer to being an exact opposite of scalding, cold is still considered an antonym. Antonyms can often be recognized by their prefixes and suffixes.

Here are rules that apply to prefixes and suffixes of antonyms:

- **Many antonyms can be created simply by adding prefixes.** Certain prefixes, such as *a-, de-, non-,* and *un-,* can be added to words to turn them into antonyms. **Atypical** is an antonym of **typical,** and **nonjudgmental** is an antonym of **judgmental.**

- **Some prefixes and suffixes are antonyms of one another.** The prefixes **ex-** (out of) and **in- /il-/im-/ir-** (into) are antonyms, and are demonstrated in the antonym pair **exhale/inhale.** Other prefix pairs that indicate antonyms include **pre-/post-, sub-/super-,** and **over-/under-.** The suffixes **-less,** meaning without, and **-ful,** meaning full of, often indicate that words are antonyms as well. For example: **meaningless** and **meaningful** are antonyms.

Practice Drill: Synonyms and Antonyms

In each sentence or group of sentences, choose whether the underlined words are synonyms, antonyms, or neither.

1. I think Mrs. Robinson is honest, but Jordan thinks she's treacherous.

2. Marley is making a stew for the class potluck, while Tara is cooking a roast.

3. The doctors agreed that the disease was not terminal. This came as welcome news to the man's family, who feared it might be life-threatening.

4. My grandfather built his house on the side of a mountain. He erected the house with his own two hands in the 1960s.

5. I always assumed Lisa was sociable; at the dance, however, she seemed rather bashful.

6. Many animals prey on rabbits, so rabbits tend to move cautiously. Lions do not have any natural predators, so they walk very boldly.

7. Our basement was full of old junk, so we gathered up all the trash and put it in bags.

8. Most people in the class were excited to go on a field trip, but Janet was unenthusiastic.

9. Terrah likes English class the most, while Durrell prefers Spanish.

10. The villagers ran for safety during the dangerous storm.

Choose the best answer choice for the following questions.

11. Awe is most dissimilar to:
    a) Contempt.
    b) Reverence.
    c) Valor.
    d) Distortion.

12. Intricate is most similar to:
    a) Delicate.
    b) Costly.
    c) Prim.
    d) Complex.

13. Skeptic is most dissimilar to:
   a) Innovator.
   b) Friend.
   c) Politician.
   d) Believer.

14. Hypothetical is most dissimilar to:
   a) Uncritical.
   b) Actual.
   c) Specific.
   d) Imaginary.

15. Enhance is most dissimilar to:
   a) Diminish.
   b) Improve.
   c) Digress.
   d) Deprive.

16. Manipulate is most similar to:
   a) Simplify.
   b) Deplete.
   c) Nurture.
   d) Handle.

17. Subjective is most dissimilar to:
   a) Invective.
   b) Objectionable.
   c) Unbiased.
   d) Obedient.

18. Succinct is most dissimilar to:
   a) Distinct.
   b) Laconic.
   c) Feeble.
   d) Verbose.

19. Enthusiastic is most similar to:
   a) Adamant.
   b) Available.
   c) Cheerful.
   d) Eager.

20. <u>Adequate</u> is most similar to:
   a) Sufficient.
   b) Mediocre.
   c) Proficient.
   d) Average.

21. <u>Uniform</u> is most dissimilar to:
   a) Dissembling.
   b) Diverse.
   c) Bizarre.
   d) Slovenly.

22. <u>Ecstatic</u> is most similar to:
   a) Inconsistent.
   b) Positive.
   c) Wild.
   d) Thrilled.

Practice Drill: Synonyms and Antonyms - Answers

1. **Antonyms.**

2. **Neither**.

3. **Synonyms.**

4. **Synonyms.**

5. **Antonyms.**

6. **Antonyms.**

7. **Synonyms.**

8. **Antonyms.**

9. **Neither.**

10. **Neither.**

11. **a) Contempt**. To be **awe** of something is to admire it; to have **contempt** for something is to consider it worthless.

12. **d) Complex**. Intricate means having many elaborately arranged elements; **complex** means complicated or involved.

13. **d) Believer**. A **skeptic** is someone who doubts; a **believer** is one who thinks something is true.

14. **b) Actual**. To be **hypothetical** is to be contingent on being tested; to be **actual** is to exist in fact.

15. **a) Diminish**. To **enhance** is to increase; to **diminish** is to decrease.

16. **d) Handle**. To **manipulate** is to manage or to **handle** in a governing manner.

17. **c) Unbiased**. To be **subjective** is to be influenced by one's own emotions or beliefs without regard to evidence presented; to be **unbiased** is to be objective or impartial.

18. d) Verbose. To be **succinct** is to be brief and to the point; to be **verbose** is to use excessive words, to be wordy.

19. d) Eager. Enthusiastic bother mean showing great earnestness.

20. a) Sufficient. If something is **adequate**, it is considered to be **sufficient**.

21. b) Diverse. To be **uniform** is to be consistent or the same as others; to be **diverse** is to have variety.

22. d) Thrilled. A person who is **ecstatic** is delighted or **thrilled**.

REVIEW

Remember that roots are the basic unit of meaning in words. When you read a word that is unfamiliar to you, divide the word into syllables and look for the root by removing any prefixes and suffixes.

You have also learned that prefixes and suffixes are known collectively as **affixes**. Although affixes are not words by themselves, they are added to roots or words to change the meaning of roots or change a word's part of speech. **Prefixes** that change or enhance the meanings of words, and are found at the beginning of words. **Suffixes** change or enhance the meanings of words and/or change parts of speech and are found at the end of words.

You have also learned that **synonyms** are words that have the same or almost the same meaning, while **antonyms** are words that have opposite or nearly opposite meanings. Synonyms and antonyms of a word will always share the same part of speech. That is, a synonym or antonym of a verb has to be a verb; a synonym or antonym of an adjective has to be an adjective; and so forth. We also learned that not all words have synonyms or antonyms, and that synonyms do not always have exactly the same meaning, just as antonyms do not have to be exact opposites.

Tips

Use words that you are very familiar with as examples when you study word roots. The more familiar the word is to you, the easier it will be for you to remember the meaning of the root word. Use words that create a vivid picture in your imagination.

Be sure to look at all parts of the word to determine meaning.

Remember the power of elimination on an exam. Use your knowledge of word roots to eliminate incorrect answers. The more you narrow down your choices, the better your chances of choosing the correct answer. You have to do so quickly of course, but even eliminating one wrong answer before guessing greatly increases your chances.

Roots do not always match the exact definitions of words. Another important thing to keep in mind is that sometimes one root will have several different spellings.

Affixes do not have to be attached directly to a root. A word can often have more than one affix, even more than one prefix or suffix. For instance, the word **unremarkably** has two prefixes (un- and re-) and two suffixes (-able and -ly).

Root or Affix	Meaning	Examples
a, ac, ad, af, ag, al, an, ap, as, at	to, toward, near, in addition to, by	aside, accompany, adjust, aggression, allocate, annihilate, affix, associate, attend, adverb
a-, an-	not, without	apolitical, atheist, anarchy, anonymous, apathy,
ab, abs	away from, off	absolve, abrupt, absent
-able, -ible	Adjective: worth, ability	solvable, incredible
acer, acid, acri	bitter, sour, sharp	acerbic, acidity, acrid, acrimony
act, ag	do, act, drive	active, react, agent, active, agitate
acu	sharp	acute, acupuncture, accurate
-acy, -cy	Noun: state or quality	privacy, infancy, adequacy, intimacy, supremacy
-ade	act, product, sweet drink	blockade, lemonade
aer, aero	air, atmosphere, aviation	aerial, aerosol, aerodrome
ag, agi, ig, act	do, move, go	agent, agenda, agitate, navigate, ambiguous, action
-age	Noun: activity, or result of action	courage, suffrage, shrinkage, tonnage
agri, agro	pertaining to fields or soil	agriculture, agroindustry
-al	Noun: action, result of action	referral, disavowal, disposal, festival
-al, -ial, -ical	Adjective: quality, relation	structural, territorial, categorical
alb, albo	white, without pigment	albino, albeit
ali, allo, alter	other	alias, alibi, alien, alloy, alter, alter ego, altruism
alt	high, deep	altimeter, altitude
am, ami, amor	love, like, liking	amorous, amiable, amicable, enamored
ambi	both	ambidextrous
ambul	to walk	ambulatory, amble, ambulance, somnambulist
-an	Noun: person	artisan, guardian, historian, magician
ana, ano	up, back, again, anew	anode, anagram
-ance, -ence	Noun: action, state, quality or process	resistance, independence, extravagance, fraudulence
-ancy, -ency	Noun: state, quality or capacity	vacancy, agency, truancy, latency
andr, andro	male, characteristics of men	androcentric, android

ang	angular	angle
anim	mind, life, spirit, anger	animal, animate, animosity
ann, annu, enni	yearly	annual, annual, annuity, anniversary, perennial
-ant, -ent	Noun: an agent, something that performs the action	disinfectant, dependent, fragrant
-ant, -ent, -ient	Adjective: kind of agent, indication	important, dependent, convenient
ante	before	anterior, anteroom, antebellum, antedate, antecedent antediluvian
anthrop	man	anthropology, misanthrope, philanthropy
anti, ant	against, opposite	antisocial, antiseptic, antithesis, antibody, antinomies, antifreeze, antipathy
anti, antico	old	antique, antiquated, antiquity
apo, ap, aph	away from, detached, formed	apology, apocalypse
aqu	water	aqueous
-ar, -ary	Adjective: resembling, related to	spectacular, unitary
arch	chief, first, rule	archangel, architect, archaic, monarchy, matriarchy, patriarchy
-ard, -art	Noun: characterized	braggart, drunkard, wizard
aster, astr	star	aster, asterisk, asteroid, astronomy, astronaut
-ate	Noun: state, office, function	candidate, electorate, delegate
-ate	Verb: cause to be	graduate, ameliorate, amputate, colligate
-ate	Adjective: kind of state	inviolate
-ation	Noun: action, resulting state	specialization, aggravation, alternation
auc, aug, aut	to originate, to increase	augment , author, augment, auction
aud, audi, aur, aus	to hear, listen	audience, audio, audible, auditorium, audiovisual, audition, auricular
aug, auc	increase	augur, augment, auction
aut, auto	self	automobile, automatic, automotive, autograph, autonomous, autoimmune
bar	weight, pressure	barometer
be	on, around, over, about, excessively,	berate, bedeck, bespeak, belittle, beleaguer

	make, cause, name, affect	
belli	war	rebellion, belligerent, casus belli, bellicose
bene	good, well, gentle	benefactor, beneficial, benevolent, benediction, beneficiary, benefit
bi, bine	two	biped, bifurcate, biweekly, bivalve, biannual
bibl, bibli, biblio	book	bibliophile, bibliography, Bible
bio, bi	life	biography, biology biome, biosphere
brev	short	abbreviate, brevity, brief
cad, cap, cas, ceiv, cept, capt, cid, cip	to take, to seize, to hold	receive, deceive, capable, capacious, captive, accident, capture, occasion, concept, intercept, forceps, except, reciprocate
cad, cas	to fall	cadaver, cadence, cascade
-cade	procession	motorcade
calor	heat	calorie, caloric, calorimeter
capit, capt	head	decapitate, capital, captain, caption
carn	flesh	carnivorous, incarnate, reincarnation, carnal
cat, cata, cath	down, with	catalogue, category, catheter
caus, caut	burn, heat	caustic, cauldron, cauterize
cause, cuse, cus	cause, motive	because, excuse, accusation
ceas, ced, cede, ceed, cess	to go, to yield, move, go, surrender	succeed, proceed, precede, recede, secession, exceed, succession
cent	hundred	centennial, century, centipede
centr, centri	center	eccentricity, centrifugal, concentric, eccentric
chrom	color	chrome, chromosome, polychrome, chromatic
chron	time	chronology, chronic, chronicle, synchronize
cide, cis, cise	to kill, to cut, cut down	homicide, incision, circumcision, scissors
circum	around	circumnavigate, circumflex, circumstance, circumference, circumvent, circulatory
cit	call, start	incite, citation, cite
civ	citizen	civic, civil, civilian, civilization

clam, claim	cry out	exclamation, clamor, proclamation, reclamation, acclaim
clin	lean, bend	decline, inclination
clud, clus claus	to close, shut	include, exclude, clause, claustrophobia, enclose, exclusive, reclusive, conclude
co, cog, col, coll, con, com, cor	with, together	cohesiveness, collaborate, convene, commitment, compress, contemporary, converge, compact, convenient, conjoin, combine, correct
cogn, gnos	to know	recognize, cognizant, diagnose, incognito, prognosis
com, con	fully	complete, compel, conscious, condense, confess, confirm
contr, contra, counter	against, opposite	contradict, counteract, contravene, contrary, counterspy, contrapuntal
cord, cor, cardi	heart	cordial, concord, discord, courage, encourage
corp	body	corporation, corporal punishment, corpse, corpulent
cort	correct	escort, cortege
cosm	universe, world	cosmos, microcosm, cosmopolitan, cosmonaut
cour, cur, curr, curs	run, course	occur, excursion, discourse, courier, course
crat, cracy	rule	autocrat, aristocrat, theocracy, technocracy
cre, cresc, cret, crease	grow	create, crescent, accretion, increase
crea	create	creature, recreation, creation
cred	believe	creed, credo, credence, credit, credulous, incredulous, incredible
cresc, cret, crease, cru	rise, grow	crescendo, concrete, increase, decrease, accrue
crit	separate, choose	critical, criterion, hypocrite
cur, curs	run	current, concurrent, concur, incur, recur, occur, courier, precursor, cursive
cura	care	curator, curative, manicure
cycl, cyclo	wheel, circle, circular	Cyclops, unicycle, bicycle, cyclone, cyclic
de-	from, down, away, to do the opposite,	detach, deploy, derange, decrease, deodorize, devoid,

	reverse, against	deflate, degenerate
dec, deca	ten, ten times	decimal, decade, decimate, decathlon
dec, dign	suitable	decent decorate dignity
dei, div	God	divinity, divine, deity, divination, deify
dem, demo	people, populace, population	democracy, demography, demagogue, epidemic
dent, dont	tooth	dental, denture, orthodontist, periodontal
derm	skin, covering	hypodermic, dermatology, epidermis, taxidermy
di-, dy-	two, twice, double	divide, diverge
dia	through, across, between	diameter, diagonal, dialogue dialect, dialectic, diagnosis, diachronic
dic, dict, dit	say, speak	dictation, dictionary, dictate, dictator, Dictaphone, edict, predict, verdict, contradict, benediction
dis, dif	not, opposite of, reverse, separate, deprive of, away	dismiss, differ, disallow, disperse, dissuade, divide, disconnect, disproportion, disrespect, distemper, disarray
dit	give	credit, audit
doc, doct	teach, prove	docile, doctor, doctrine, document, dogma, indoctrinate
domin	master, that which is under control	dominate, dominion, predominant, domain
don	give	donate, condone
dorm	sleep	dormant, dormitory
dox	thought, opinion, praise	orthodox, heterodox, paradox, doxology
-drome	run, step	syndrome, aerodrome
duc, duct	to lead, pull	produce, abduct, product, transducer, viaduct, aqueduct, induct, deduct, reduce, induce
dura	hard, lasting	durable, duration, endure
dynam	power	dynamo, dynamic, dynamite, hydrodynamics
dys-	bad, abnormal, difficult, impaired, unfavorable	dysfunctional, dyslexia
e-	not, missing, out, fully, away, computer network related	emit, embed, eternal, ether, erase, email

ec-	out of, outside	echo, eclipse, eclectic, ecstasy
eco-	household, environment, relating to ecology or economy	ecology, economize, ecospheres
ecto-	outside, external	ectomorph, ectoderm, ectoplasm
-ed	Verb: past tense	dressed, faded, patted, closed, introduced
-ed	Adjective: having the quality or characteristics of	winged, moneyed, dogged, tiered
-en	Verb: to cause to become	lengthen, moisten, sharpen
-en	Adjective: material	golden, woolen, silken
en-, em-	put into, make, provide with, surround with	enamor, embolden, enslave, empower, entangle
-ence, -ency	Noun: action or process, quality or state	reference, emergency, dependence, eminence, latency
end-	inside, within	endorse, endergonic, endoskeleton, endoscope,
epi-	upon, close to, over, after, altered	epicenter, epilogue, epigone
equi-	equal	equidistant, equilateral, equilibrium, equinox, equation, equator
-er, -ier	Adjective: comparative	better, brighter, sooner, hotter, happier
-er, -or	Noun: person or thing that does something	flyer, reporter, player, member, fryer, collector, concentrator
-er, -or	Verb: action	ponder, dishonor, clamor
erg	work, effect	energy, erg, allergy, ergometer
-ery	collective qualities, art, practice, trade, collection, state, condition	snobbery, bakery, greenery, gallery, slavery
-es, -ies	Noun: plural of most nouns ending in -ch, -s, -sh, -o and -z and some in -f and -y	passes, glasses, ladies, heroes
-es, -ies	Verb: third person singular present indicative of verbs that end in -ch, -s, -sh, - and some in -y	blesses, hushes, fizzes, defies
-ess	female	actress, goddess, poetess
-est, -iest	Adjective or Adverb: superlative	latest, strongest, luckiest
ev-, et-	time, age	medieval, eternal

ex-	out of, away from, lacking, former	exit, exhale, exclusive, exceed, explosion, ex-mayor
exter-, extra-, extro-	outside of, beyond	external, extrinsic, extraordinary, extrapolate, extraneous, extrovert
fa, fess	speak	fable, fabulous, fame, famous, confess, profess
fac, fact, fec, fect, fic, fas, fea	do, make	difficult, fashion, feasible, feature, factory, effect, manufacture, amplification, confection
fall, fals	deceive	fallacy, falsify, fallacious
femto	quadrillionth	femtosecond
fer	bear, carry	ferry, coniferous, fertile, defer, infer, refer, transfer
fic, feign, fain, fit, feat	shape, make, fashion	fiction, faint, feign
fid	belief, faith	confide, diffident, fidelity
fid, fide, feder	faith, trust	confidante, fidelity, confident, infidelity, infidel, federal, confederacy,
fig	shape, form	effigy, figure, figment
fila, fili	thread	filigree, filament, filter, filet, filibuster
fin	end, ended, finished	final, finite, finish, confine, fine, refine, define, finale
fix	repair, attach	fix, fixation, fixture, affix, prefix, suffix
flex, flect	bend	flex, reflex, flexible, flexor, inflexibility, reflect, deflect, circumflex
flict	strike	affliction, conflict, inflict
flu, fluc, fluv, flux	flow	influence, fluid, flue, flush, fluently, fluctuate, reflux, influx
-fold	Adverb: in a manner of, marked by	fourfold
for, fore	before	forecast, fortune, foresee
forc, fort	strength, strong	effort, fort, forte, fortifiable, fortify, forte, fortitude
form	shape, resemble	form, format, conform, formulate, perform, formal, formula
fract, frag, frai	break	fracture, infraction, fragile, fraction, refract, frail
fuge	flee	subterfuge, refuge, centrifuge
-ful	Noun: an amount or quantity that fills	mouthful

-ful	Adjective: having, giving, marked by	fanciful
fuse	pour	confuse, transfuse
-fy	make, form into	falsify, dandify
gam	marriage	bigamy, monogamy, polygamy
gastr, gastro	stomach	gastric, gastronomic, gastritis, gastropod
gen	kind	generous
gen	birth, race, produce	genesis, genetics, eugenics, genealogy, generate, genetic, antigen, pathogen
geo	earth	geometry, geography, geocentric, geology
germ	vital part	germination, germ, germane
gest	carry, bear	congest, gestation
giga	billion	gigabyte, gigaflop
gin	careful	gingerly
gloss, glot	tongue	glossary, polyglot, epiglottis
glu, glo	lump, bond, glue	glue, agglutinate, conglomerate
gor	to gather, to bring together	category, categorize
grad, gress, gree	to gather, to bring together, step, go	grade, degree, progress, gradual, graduate, egress
graph, gram, graf	write, written, draw	graph, graphic, autograph, photography, graphite, telegram, polygraph, grammar, biography, lithograph, graphic
grat	pleasing	congratulate, gratuity, grateful, ingrate
grav	heavy, weighty	grave, gravity, aggravate, gravitate
greg	herd	gregarious, congregation, segregate
hale, heal	make whole, sound	inhale, exhale, heal, healthy, healthiness
helio	sun	heliograph, heliotrope, heliocentric
hema, hemo	blood	hemorrhage, hemoglobin, hemophilia, hemostat
her, here, hes	stick	adhere, cohere, cohesion, inherent, hereditary, hesitate
hetero	other, different	heterodox, heterogeneous, heterosexual, heterodyne

hex, ses, sex	six	hexagon, hexameter, sestet, sextuplets
homo	same	homogenize, homosexual, homonym, homophone
hum, human	earth, ground, man	humus, exhume, humane
hydr, hydra, hydro	water	dehydrate, hydrant, hydraulic, hydraulics, hydrogen, hydrophobia
hyper	over, above	hyperactive, hypertensive, hyperbolic, hypersensitive, hyperventilate, hyperkinetic
hypn	sleep	hypnosis, hypnotherapy
-ia	Noun: names, diseases	phobia
-ian, an	Noun: related to, one that is	pedestrian, human
-iatry	Noun: art of healing	psychiatry
-ic	Adjective: quality, relation	generic
-ic, ics	Noun: related to the arts and sciences	arithmetic, economics
-ice	Noun: act	malice
-ify	Verb: cause	specify
ignis	fire	ignite, igneous, ignition
-ile	Adjective: having the qualities of	projectile
in, im	into, on, near, towards	instead, import
in, im, il, ir	not	illegible, irresolute, inaction, inviolate, innocuous, intractable, innocent, impregnable, impossible, imposter
infra	beneath	infrared, infrastructure
-ing	Noun: material made for, activity, result of an activity	flooring, swimming, building
-ing	Verb: present participle	depicting
-ing	Adjective: activity	cohering
inter	between, among	international, intercept, interject, intermission, internal, intermittent,
intra	within, during, between layers, underneath	intramural, intranet

intro	into, within, inward	interoffice, introvert, introspection, introduce
-ion	Noun: condition or action	abduction
-ish	Adjective: having the character of	newish
-ism	Noun: doctrine, belief, action or conduct	formalism
-ist	Noun: person or member	podiatrist
-ite	Noun: state or quality	graphite
-ity, ty	Noun: state or quality	lucidity, novelty
-ive	Noun: condition	native
-ive, -ative, -itive	Adjective: having the quality of	festive, cooperative, sensitive
-ize	Verb: cause	fantasize
jac, ject	throw	reject, eject, project, trajectory, interject, dejected, inject, ejaculate, adjacent
join, junct	join	adjoining, enjoin, juncture, conjunction, injunction, conjunction
judice	judge	prejudice
jug, junct, just	to join	junction, adjust, conjugal
juven	young	juvenile, rejuvenate
labor	work	laborious, belabor
lau, lav, lot, lut	wash	launder, lavatory, lotion, ablution, dilute
lect, leg, lig	choose, gather, select, read	collect, legible, eligible
leg	law	legal, legislate, legislature, legitimize
-less	Adjective: without, missing	motiveless
levi	light	alleviate, levitate, levity
lex, leag, leg	law	legal, college, league
liber, liver	free	liberty, liberal, liberalize, deliverance
lide	strike	collide, nuclide
liter	letters	literary, literature, literal, alliteration, obliterate
loc, loco	place, area	location, locally, locality, allocate, locomotion
log, logo, ology	word, study, say, speech, reason,	catalog, prologue, dialogue, zoology, logo

	study	
loqu, locut	talk, speak	eloquent, loquacious, colloquial, circumlocution
luc, lum, lun, lus, lust	light	translucent, luminary, luster, lunar, illuminate, illustrate
lude	play	prelude
-ly	Adverb: in the manner of	fluently
macr-, macer	lean	emaciated, meager
magn	great	magnify, magnificent, magnanimous, magnate, magnitude, magnum
main	strength, foremost	mainstream, mainsail, domain, remain
mal	bad, badly	malformation, maladjusted, dismal, malady, malcontent, malfunction, malfeasance, maleficent
man, manu	hand, make, do	manual, manage, manufacture, manacle, manicure, manifest, maneuver, emancipate, management
mand	command	mandatory, remand, mandate
mania	madness	mania, maniac, kleptomania, pyromania
mar, mari, mer	sea, pool	marine, marsh, maritime, mermaid
matri	mother	matrimony, maternal, matriarchate, matron
medi	half, middle, between, halfway	mediate, medieval, Mediterranean, mediocre
mega	great, million	megaphone, megaton, megabyte, megalopolis
mem	recall, remember	memo, commemoration, memento, memoir, memorable
ment	mind	mental, mention
-ment	Noun: condition or result	document
meso	middle	mesomorph, mesosphere
meta	beyond, change	metaphor, metamorphosis, metabolism,
meter	measure	meter, voltammeter, barometer, thermometer
metr	admeasure, apportion	metrics, asymmetric, parametric, telemetry
micro	small, millionth	microscope, microfilm, microwave, micrometer,
migra	wander	migrate, emigrant, immigrate
mill, kilo	thousand	millennium, kilobyte, kiloton

milli	thousandth	millisecond, milligram, millivolt
min	little, small	minute, minor, minuscule
mis	wrong, bad, badly	misconduct, misinterpret, misnomer, mistake
mit, miss	send	emit, remit, submit, admit, commit, permit, transmit, omit, intermittent, mission, missile
mob, mov, mot	move	motion, remove, mobile, motor
mon	warn, remind	monument, admonition, monitor, premonition
mono	one	monopoly, monotype, monologue, mononucleosis,
mor, mort	mortal, death	mortal, immortal, mortality, mortician, mortuary
morph	shape, form	amorphous, dimorphic, metamorphosis, morphology, polymorphic, morpheme, amorphous
multi	many, much	multifold, multilingual, multiply, multitude, multipurpose, multinational
nano	billionth	nanosecond
nasc, nat, gnant, nai	to be born	nascent, native, pregnant, naive
nat, nasc	to be from, to spring forth	innate, natal, native, renaissance
neo	new	neolithic, neologism, neophyte, neonate
-ness	Noun: state, condition, quality	kindness
neur	nerve	neuritis, neuropathic, neurologist, neural, neurotic
nom	law, order	autonomy, astronomy, gastronomy, economy
nom, nym	name	nominate, synonym
nomen, nomin	name	nomenclature, nominate, ignominious
non	nine	nonagon
non	not	nonferrous, nonsense, nonabrasive, nondescript
nov	new	novel, renovate, novice, nova, innovate
nox, noc	night	nocturnal, equinox
numer	number	numeral, numeration, enumerate, innumerable
numisma	coin	numismatics
nunci, nunc, nounc	speak, declare, warn	pronounce, announcement

ob, oc, of, op	toward, against, in the way	oppose, occur, offer, obtain
oct	eight	octopus, octagon, octogenarian, octave
oligo	few, little	Oligocene, oligosaccharide, oligotrophic, oligarchy
omni	all, every	omnipotent, omniscient, omnipresent, omnivorous
onym	name	anonymous, pseudonym, antonym, synonym
oper	work	operate, cooperate, opus
-or	Noun: condition or activity	valor, honor, humor, minor
ortho	straight, correct	orthodox, orthodontist, orthopedic, unorthodox
-ory	Noun: place for, serves for	territory, rectory
-ous, -eous, -ose, -ious	Adjective: having the quality of, relating to	adventurous, courageous, verbose, fractious
over	excessive, above	overwork, overall, overwork
pac	peace	pacifist, pacify, pacific ocean
pair, pare	arrange, assemblage, two	repair, impair, compare, prepare
paleo	old	Paleozoic, Paleolithic,
pan	all	Pan-American, pan-African, panacea, pandemonium
para	beside	paradox, paraprofessional, paramedic, paraphrase, parachute
pat, pass, path	feel, suffer	patient, passion, sympathy, pathology
pater, patr	father	paternity, patriarch, patriot, patron, patronize
path, pathy	feeling, suffering	pathos, sympathy, antipathy, apathy, telepathy
ped, pod	foot	pedal, impede, pedestrian, centipede, tripod,
pedo	child	orthopedic, pedagogue, pediatrics
pel, puls	drive, push, urge	compel, dispel, expel, repel, propel, pulse, impulse, pulsate, compulsory, expulsion, repulsive
pend, pens, pond	hang, weigh	pendant, pendulum, suspend, appendage, pensive, append
per	through, intensive	persecute, permit, perspire, perforate, persuade
peri	around	periscope, perimeter, perigee, periodontal

phage	eat	macrophage, bacteriophage
phan, phas, phen, fan, phant, fant	show, make visible	phantom, fantasy
phe	speak	blaspheme, cipher, phenomenon, philosopher
phil	love	philosopher, philanthropy, philharmonic, bibliophile
phlegma	inflammation	phlegm, phlegmatic
phobia, phobos	fear	phobia, claustrophobia, homophobia
phon	sound	telephone, phonics, phonograph, phonetic, homophone, microphone, symphony, euphonious
phot, photo	light	photograph, photoelectric, photogenic, photosynthesis, photon
pict	paint, show, draw	picture, depict
plac, plais	please	placid, placebo, placate, complacent
pli, ply	fold	reply, implicate, ply
plore	cry out, wail	implore, exploration, deploring
plu, plur, plus	more	plural, pluralist, plus
pneuma, pneumon	breath	pneumatic, pneumonia,
pod	foot, feet	podiatry, tripod
poli	city	metropolis, police, politics, Indianapolis, megalopolis, acropolis
poly	many	polytheist, polygon, polygamy, polymorphous
pon, pos, pound	place, put	postpone, component, opponent, proponent, expose, impose, deposit, posture, position, expound, impound
pop	people	population, populous, popular
port	carry	porter, portable, transport, report, export, import, support, transportation
portion	part, share	portion, proportion
post	after, behind	postpone, postdate
pot	power	potential, potentate, impotent
pre, pur	before	precede

prehendere	seize, grasp	apprehend, comprehend, comprehensive, prehensile
prin, prim, prime	first	primacy, primitive, primary, primal, primeval, prince, principal
pro	for, forward	propel
proto	first	prototype, protocol, protagonist, protozoan,
psych	mind, soul	psyche, psychiatry, psychology, psychosis
punct	point, dot	punctual, punctuation, puncture, acupuncture,
pute	think	dispute, computer
quat, quad	four	quadrangle, quadruplets
quint, penta	five	quintet, quintuplets, pentagon, pentane, pentameter
quip	ship	equip, equipment
quir, quis, quest, quer	seek, ask	query, inquire, exquisite, quest
re	back, again	report, realign, retract, revise, regain
reg, recti	straighten	regiment, regular, rectify, correct, direct, rectangle
retro	backwards	retrorocket, retrospect, retrogression, retroactive
ri, ridi, risi	laughter	deride, ridicule, ridiculous, derision, risible
rog, roga	ask	prerogative, interrogation, derogatory
rupt	break	rupture, interrupt, abrupt, disrupt
sacr, sanc, secr	sacred	sacred, sacrosanct, sanction, consecrate, desecrate
salv, salu	safe, healthy	salvation, salvage, salutation
sanct	holy	sanctify, sanctuary, sanction, sanctimonious, sacrosanct
sat, satis	enough	saturate, satisfy
sci, scio, scientia	know	science, conscious, omniscient
scope	see, watch	telescope, microscope, kaleidoscope, periscope, stethoscope
scrib, script	write	scribe, scribble, inscribe, describe, subscribe, prescribe, manuscript

se	apart, move away from	secede
sect, sec	cut	intersect, transect, dissect, secant, section
sed, sess, sid	sit	sediment, session, obsession, possess, preside, president, reside, subside
semi	half, partial	semifinal, semiconscious, semiannual, semimonthly, semicircle
sen, scen	old, grow old	senior, senator, senile, senescence, evanescent
sent, sens	feel, think	sentiment, consent, resent, dissent, sentimental, sense, sensation, sensitive, sensory, dissension
sept	seven	septet, septennial
sequ, secu, sue	follow	sequence, consequence, sequel, subsequent, prosecute, consecutive, second, ensue, pursue
serv	save, serve, keep	servant, service, subservient, servitude, preserve, conserve, reservation, deserve, conservation, observe
-ship	Noun: status, condition	relationship, friendship
sign, signi	sign, mark, seal	signal, signature, design, insignia, significant
simil, simul	like, resembling	
sist, sta, stit	stand, withstand, make up	assist, insist, persist, circumstance, stamina, status, state, static, stable, stationary, substitute
soci	to join, companions	sociable, society
sol, solus	alone	solo, soliloquy, solitaire, solitude, solitary, isolate
solv, solu, solut	loosen, explain	solvent, solve, absolve, resolve, soluble, solution, resolution, resolute, dissolute, absolution
somn	sleep	insomnia, somnambulist
soph	wise	philosophy, sophisticated
spec, spect, spi, spic	look, see	specimen, specific, spectator, spectacle, aspect, speculate, inspect, respect, prospect, retrospective, introspective, expect, conspicuous
sper	render favorable	prosper
sphere	ball, sphere	sphere, stratosphere, hemisphere, spheroid
spir	breath	spirit, conspire, inspire, aspire, expire, perspire, respiration
stand, stant, stab, stat, stan, sti, sta,	stand	stature, establish, stance

stead		
-ster	person	mobster, monster
strain, strict, string, stige	bind, pull, draw tight	stringent, strict, restrict, constrict, restrain, boa constrictor
stru, struct, stroy, stry	build	construe, structure, construct, instruct, obstruct, destruction, destroy, industry, ministry
sub, suc, suf, sup, sur, sus	under, below, from, secretly, instead of	sustain, survive, support, suffice, succeed, submerge, submarine, substandard, subvert
sume, sump	take, use, waste	consume, assume, sump, presumption
super, supra	over, above	superior, suprarenal, superscript, supernatural, superimpose
syn, sym	together, at the same time	sympathy, synthesis, synchronous, syndicate
tact, tang, tag, tig, ting	touch	tactile, contact, intact, intangible, tangible, contagious, contiguous, contingent
tain, ten, tent, tin	hold, keep, have	retain, continue, content, tenacious
tect, teg	cover	detect, protect, tegument
tele	distance, far, from afar	telephone, telegraph, telegram, telescope, television, telephoto, telecast, telepathy, telepathy
tem, tempo	time	tempo, temporary, extemporaneously, contemporary, pro tem, temporal
ten, tin, tain	hold	tenacious, tenant, tenure, untenable, detention, retentive, content, pertinent, continent, obstinate, contain, abstain, pertain, detain
tend, tent, tens	stretch, strain	tendency, extend, intend, contend, pretend, superintend, tender, extent, tension, pretense
tera	trillion	terabyte, teraflop
term	end, boundary, limit	exterminate, terminal
terr, terra	earth	terrain, terrarium, territory, terrestrial
test	to bear witness	testament, detest, testimony, attest, testify
the, theo	God, a god	monotheism, polytheism, atheism, theology
therm	heat	thermometer, theorem, thermal, thermos bottle, thermostat, hypothermia

thesis, thet	place, put	antithesis, hypothesis, synthesis, epithet
tire	draw, pull	attire, retire, entire
tom	cut	atom (not cutable), appendectomy, tonsillectomy, dichotomy, anatomy
tor, tors, tort	twist	torture, retort, extort, distort, contort, torsion, tortuous, torturous
tox	poison	toxic, intoxicate, antitoxin
tract, tra, trai, treat	drag, draw, pull	attract, tractor, traction, extract, retract, protract, detract, subtract, contract, intractable
trans	across, beyond, change	transform, transoceanic, transmit, transportation, transducer
tri	three	tripod, triangle, trinity, trilateral
trib	pay, bestow	tribute, contribute, attribute, retribution, tributary
tribute	give	contribute, distribute, tributary
turbo	disturb	turbulent, disturb, turbid, turmoil
typ	print	type, prototype, typical, typography, typewriter, typology, typify
ultima	last	ultimate, ultimatum
umber, umbraticum	shadow	umbra, penumbra, (take) umbrage, adumbrate
un	not, against, opposite	unceasing, unequal
uni	one	uniform, unilateral, universal, unity, unanimous, unite, unison, unicorn
-ure	Noun: act, condition, process, function	exposure, conjecture, measure
vac	empty	vacate, vacuum, evacuate, vacation, vacant, vacuous
vade	go	evade, invader
vale, vali, valu	strength, worth	equivalent, valiant, validity, evaluate, value, valor
veh, vect	to carry	vector, vehicle, convection, vehement
ven, vent	come	convene, intervene, venue, convenient, avenue, circumvent, invent, convent, venture, event, advent, prevent
ver, veri	true	very, aver, verdict, verity, verify, verisimilitude

95

verb, verv	word	verify, veracity, verbalize, verve
vert, vers	turn, change	convert, revert, advertise, versatile, vertigo, invert, reversion, extravert, introvert, diversion, introvert, convertible, reverse, controversy
vi	way	viable, vibrate, vibrant
vic, vicis	change, substitute	vicarious, vicar, vicissitude
vict, vinc	conquer	victor, evict, convict, convince, invincible
vid, vis	see	video, evident, provide, providence, visible, revise, supervise, vista, visit, vision, review, indivisible
viv, vita, vivi	alive, life	revive, survive, vivid, vivacious, vitality, vital, vitamins, revitalize
voc, voke	call	vocation, avocation, convocation, invocation, evoke, provoke, revoke, advocate, provocative, vocal
vol	will	malevolent, benevolent, volunteer, volition
volcan	fire	volcano, vulcanize, Vulcan
volv, volt, vol	turn about, roll	revolve, voluble, voluminous, convolution, revolt, evolution
vor	eat greedily	voracious, carnivorous, herbivorous, omnivorous, devour
-ward	Adverb: in a direction or manner	homeward
-wise	Adverb: in the manner of, with regard to	clockwise, bitwise
with	against	withhold, without, withdraw, forthwith
-y	Noun: state, condition, result of an activity	society, victory
-y	Adjective: marked by, having	hungry, angry, smeary, teary
zo	animal	zoo (zoological garden), zoology, zodiac, protozoan

Chapter 4: Mathematics Knowledge

The Math Knowledge section tests various concepts in numbers and operations, algebra, geometry, data analysis, statistics, and probability. In this test section, you will be provided with 25 questions to answer within a 22-minute time limit, which gives you a little less than a minute to solve each problem. This seems like less time than it actually is, so don't worry! Before taking the AFOQT, you want to make sure that you have a good understanding of the math areas covered. You will need to sharpen your skills, but don't worry – we'll provide you with the knowledge that you'll need to know for the test.

As also mentioned in the Arithmetic Reasoning section, the practice questions here are combined for the obvious reason that the concepts are tied together and most effectively studied as a single concept. Don't focus on how the questions are formatted slightly different, the mathematical fundamentals are identical and that's what it always comes down to. The only difference in the Arithmetic Reasoning section is to not get distracted by the excess information and to read quickly.

Math Concepts Tested

You have a much better chance of getting a good Math Knowledge score if you know what to expect. The test covers math up to and including the first semester of Algebra II as well as fundamental geometry. You will not be given any formulas, such as those required for geometry calculations, so you need to make sure that you have studied them so they are fresh in your mind.

Here is a breakdown of areas covered:

Numbers and Operations
Absolute values, inequalities, probabilities, exponents, and radicals.

Algebra and Functions
Basic equation solving, simultaneous equations, binomials & polynomials, and inequalities.

Geometry and Measurement
Angle relationships, area and perimeter of geometric shapes, and volume.

Math skills that you won't need:
- Working with bulky numbers or endless calculations.
- Working with imaginary numbers or the square roots of negative numbers.
- Trigonometry or calculus.

Important Note: You are not allowed to use a calculator for any section of the AFOQT.

The Most Common Mistakes

Here is a list of the four most commonly- made mistakes concerning mathematics, starting with the most common.

1. Answer is the wrong sign (positive / negative).

2. Order of Operations not following when solving.

3. Misplaced decimal.

4. Solution is not what the question asked for.

These are the basics that individuals tend to overlook when they only have a minute or less to do their calculations. This is why it is so important that you pay attention right from the start of the problem. You may be thinking, "But, those are just common sense." Exactly! Remember, even simple mistakes still result in an incorrect answer.

Strategies

Review the Basics: First and foremost, practice your basic skills such as sign changes, order of operations, simplifying fractions, and equation manipulation. These are the skills you will use the most on almost every problem on the Math Knowledge and the Arithmetic tests sections. Remember when it comes right down to it, there are still only four math operations used to solve any math problem, which are adding, subtracting, multiplying and dividing; the only thing that changes is the order they are used to solve the problem.

Although accuracy counts more than speed; **Don't Waste Time** stuck on a question! Remember, you only have 22 minutes to answer 25 questions for this section test. This is why your knowledge of the basics is so important. If you have to stop and think about what 9 * 6 equals, or use your fingers to add 13 + 8, then you need to spend time on these fundamentals before going on to the concepts. There are minute tests at the end of this chapter. If you can complete those tests in the time specified, the time required for you to calculate the more complex problems during the test will decrease greatly.

Make an Educated Guess: If necessary, eliminate at least one answer choice as most probably incorrect and guess which one is most likely correct from the remaining choices.

Math Formulas, Facts, and Terms that You Need to Know

The next few pages will cover the various math subjects (starting with the basics, but in no particular order) along with worked examples. Use this guide to determine the areas in which you need more review and work these areas first. You should take your time at first and let your brain recall the math necessary to solve the problems, using the examples given to remember these skills.

Order of Operations

PEMDAS – **P**arentheses/**E**xponents/**M**ultiply/**D**ivide/**A**dd/**S**ubtract

Perform the operations within parentheses first, and then any exponents. After those steps, perform all multiplication and division. (These are done from left to right, as they appear in the problem) Finally, do all required addition and subtraction, also from left to right as they appear in the problem.

> **Example**: Solve $(-(2)^2 - (4 + 7))$.
> $(-4 - 11) = -\textbf{15}$.
>
> **Example**: Solve $((5)^2 \div 5 + 4 * 2)$.
> $25 \div 5 + 4 * 2$.
>
> $5 + 8 = \textbf{13}$.

Positive & Negative Number Rules

$(+) + (-)$ = Subtract the two numbers. Solution gets the sign of the larger number.

$(-) + (-)$ = Negative number.

$(-) * (-)$ = Positive number.

$(-) * (+)$ = Negative number.

$(-) / (-)$ = Positive number.

$(-) / (+)$ = Negative number.

Greatest Common Factor (GCF)

The greatest factor that divides two numbers.

> **Example**: The GCF of 24 and 18 is 6. 6 is the largest number, or greatest factor, that can divide both 24 and 18.

Geometric Sequence

Each term is equal to the previous term multiplied by x.

> **Example**: 2, 4, 8, 16.
>
> $x = \textbf{2}$.

Fractions

Adding and subtracting fractions requires a common denominator.

Find a common denominator for:

$$\frac{2}{3} - \frac{1}{5}$$

$$\frac{2}{3} - \frac{1}{5} = \frac{2}{3}\left(\frac{5}{5}\right) - \frac{1}{5}\left(\frac{3}{3}\right) = \frac{10}{15} - \frac{3}{15} = \frac{7}{15}$$

To add mixed fractions, work first the whole numbers, and then the fractions.

$$2\frac{1}{4} + 1\frac{3}{4} = 3\frac{4}{4} = 4$$

To subtract mixed fractions, convert to single fractions by multiplying the whole number by the denominator and adding the numerator. Then work as above.

$$2\frac{1}{4} - 1\frac{3}{4} = \frac{9}{4} - \frac{7}{4} = \frac{2}{4} = \frac{1}{2}$$

To multiply fractions, convert any mixed fractions into single fractions and multiply across; reduce to lowest terms if needed.

$$2\frac{1}{4} * 1\frac{3}{4} = \frac{9}{4} * \frac{7}{4} = \frac{63}{16} = 3\frac{15}{16}$$

To divide fractions, convert any mixed fractions into single fractions, flip the second fraction, and then multiply across.

$$2\frac{1}{4} \div 1\frac{3}{4} = \frac{9}{4} \div \frac{7}{4} = \frac{9}{4} * \frac{4}{7} = \frac{36}{28} = 1\frac{8}{28} = 1\frac{2}{7}$$

Probabilities

A probability is found by dividing the number of desired outcomes by the number of possible outcomes. (The piece divided by the whole.)

Example: What is the probability of picking a blue marble if 3 of the 15 marbles are blue?

3/15 = 1/5. The probability is **1 in 5** that a blue marble is picked.

Prime Factorization

Expand to prime number factors.

Example: $104 = 2 * 2 * 2 * 13$.

Absolute Value

The absolute value of a number is its distance from zero, not its value.

So in $|x| = a$, "x" will equal "$-a$" as well as "a."

Likewise, $|3| = 3$, and $|-3| = 3$.

Equations with absolute values will have two answers. Solve each absolute value possibility separately. All solutions must be checked into the original equation.

> **Example:** Solve for x:
> $|2x - 3| = x + 1$.
>
> Equation One: $2x - 3 = -(x + 1)$.
> $\qquad\qquad\quad\ 2x - 3 = -x - 1$.
> $\qquad\qquad\quad\ 3x = 2$.
> $\qquad\qquad\quad\ x = 2/3$.
>
> Equation Two: $2x - 3 = x + 1$.
> $\qquad\qquad\quad\ x = 4$.

Mean, Median, Mode

Mean is a math term for "average." Total all terms and divide by the number of terms.

> Find the mean of 24, 27, and 18.
> $24 + 27 + 18 = 69 \div 3 = 23$.

Median is the middle number of a given set, found after the numbers have all been put in numerical order. In the case of a set of even numbers, the middle two numbers are averaged.

> What is the median of 24, 27, and 18?
> 18, **24**, 27.
>
> What is the median of 24, 27, 18, and 19?
>
> 18, 19, 24, 27 ($19 + 24 = 43$. $43/2 = 21.5$).

Mode is the number which occurs most frequently within a given set.

> What is the mode of 2, 5, 4, 4, 3, 2, 8, 9, 2, 7, 2, and 2?
>
> The mode would be **2** because it appears the most within the set.

Exponent Rules

Rule	Example
$x^0 = 1$	$5^0 = 1$
$x^1 = x$	$5^1 = 5$
$x^a \cdot x^b = x^{a+b}$	$5^2 * 5^3 = 5^5$
$(xy)^a = x^a y^a$	$(5 * 6)^2 = 5^2 * 6^2 = 25 * 36$
$(x^a)^b = x^{ab}$	$(5^2)^3 = 5^6$
$(x/y)^a = x^a/y^a$	$(10/5)^2 = 10^2/5^2 = 100/25$
$x^a/y^b = x^{a-b}$	$5^4/5^3 = 5^1 = 5$ (remember $x \neq 0$)
$x^{1/a} = \sqrt[a]{x}$	$25^{1/2} = \sqrt[2]{25} = 5$
$x^{-a} = \dfrac{1}{x^a}$	$5^{-2} = \dfrac{1}{5^2} = \dfrac{1}{25}$ (remember $x \neq 0$)
$(-x)^a$ = positive number if "a" is even; negative number if "a" is odd.	

Roots

Root of a Product: $\sqrt[n]{a \cdot b} = \sqrt[n]{a} \cdot \sqrt[n]{b}$

Root of a Quotient: $\sqrt[n]{\dfrac{a}{b}} = \dfrac{\sqrt[n]{a}}{\sqrt[n]{b}}$

Fractional Exponent: $\sqrt[n]{a^m} = a^{m/n}$

Literal Equations

Equations with more than one variable. Solve in terms of one variable first.

Example: Solve for y: $4x + 3y = 3x + 2y$.

Step 1 – Combine like terms: $3y - 2y = 4x - 2x$.

Step 2 – Solve for y: $\mathbf{y = 2x}$.

Midpoint

To determine the midpoint between two points, simply add the two x coordinates together and divide by 2 (midpoint x). Then add the y coordinates together and divide by 2 (midpoint y).

$$\left(\frac{x_1 + x_2}{2}, \frac{y_1 + y}{2} \right)$$

102

Inequalities

Inequalities are solved like linear and algebraic equations, except the sign must be reversed when dividing by a negative number.

Example: $-7x + 2 < 6 - 5x$.

Step 1 – Combine like terms: $-2x < 4$.

Step 2 – Solve for x. (Reverse the sign): $x > -2$.

Solving compound inequalities will give you two answers.

Example: $-4 \leq 2x - 2 \leq 6$.

Step 1 – Add 2 to each term to isolate x: $-2 \leq 2x \leq 8$.

Step 2: Divide by 2: $-1 \leq x \leq 4$.

Solution set is **[-1, 4]**.

Algebraic Equations

When simplifying or solving algebraic equations, you need to be able to utilize all math rules: exponents, roots, negatives, order of operations, etc.

1. Add & Subtract: Only the coefficients of like terms.

   Example: $5xy + 7y + 2yz + 11xy - 5yz = 16xy + 7y - 3yz$.

2. Multiplication: First the coefficients then the variables.

   Example: Monomial * Monomial.

   $(3x^4y^2z)(2y^4z^5) = 6x^4y^6z^6$.

   (A variable with no exponent has an implied exponent of 1.)

   Example: Monomial * Polynomial.

   $(2y^2)(y^3 + 2xy^2z + 4z) = 2y^5 + 4xy^4z + 8y^2z$.

Example: Binomial * Binomial.

$(5x + 2)(3x + 3)$.

First: $5x * 3x = 15x^2$.

Outer: $5x * 3 = 15x$.

Inner: $2 * 3x = 6x$.

Last: $2 * 3 = 6$.

Combine like terms: $15x^2 + 21x + 6$.

Example: Binomial * Polynomial.

$(x + 3)(2x^2 - 5x - 2)$.

First term: $x(2x^2 - 5x - 2) = 2x^3 - 5x^2 - 2x$.

Second term: $3(2x^2 - 5x - 2) = 6x^2 - 15x - 6$.

Added Together: $2x^3 + x^2 - 17x - 6$.

Distributive Property

When a variable is placed outside of a parenthetical set, it is *distributed* to all of the variables within that set.

$5(2y - 3x) = 10y - 15x$ [Can also be written as $(2y - 3x)5$].

$2x(3y + 1) + 6x = 6xy + 2x + 6x = 6xy + 8x$.

Fundamental Counting Principle

(The number of possibilities of an event happening) * (the number of possibilities of another event happening) = the total number of possibilities.

Example: If you take a multiple choice test with 5 questions, with 4 answer choices for each question, how many test result possibilities are there?

Solution: Question 1 has 4 choices; question 2 has 4 choices; etc.

$4 * 4 * 4 * 4 * 4$ (one for each question) = **1024 possible test results**.

Linear Systems

There are two different methods can be used to solve multiple equation linear systems:

Substitution Method: This solves for one variable in one equation and substitutes it into the other equation. **Example**: Solve: $3y - 4 + x = 0$ and $5x + 6y = 11$.

1. Step 1: Solve for one variable:
   $3y - 4 = 0$.
   $3y + x = 4$.
   $x = 4 - 3y$.

2. Step 2: Substitute into the second equation and solve:
   $5(4 - 3y) + 6y = 11$.
   $20 - 15y + 6y = 11$.
   $20 - 9y = 11$.
   $-9y = -9$.
   $y = 1$.

3. Step 3: Substitute into the first equation:
   $3(1) - 4 + x = 0$.
   $-1 + x = 0$.
   $x = 1$.

   Solution: $x = 1, y = 1$.

Addition Method: Manipulate one of the equations so that when it is added to the other, one variable is eliminated. **Example**: Solve: $2x + 4y = 8$ and $4x + 2y = 10$.

1. Step 1: Manipulate one equation to eliminate a variable when added together: $-2(2x + 4y = 8)$.
   $-4x - 8y = -16$.
   $(-4x - 8y = -16) + (4x + 2y = 10)$.
   $-6y = -6$.
   $y = 1$.

2. Step 2: Plug into an equation to solve for the other variable:
   $2x + 4(1) = 8$.
   $2x + 4 = 8$.
   $2x = 4$.
   $x = 2$.

   Solution: $x = 2, y = 1$.

Quadratics

Factoring: Converting $ax^2 + bx + c$ to factored form. Find two numbers that are factors of c and whose sum is b. **Example**: Factor: $2x^2 + 12x + 18 = 0$.

1. Step 1: If possible, factor out a common monomial: $2(x^2 - 6x + 9)$.

2. Step 2: Find two numbers that are factors of 9 and which equal -6 when added:
   $2(x \quad)(x \quad)$.
   $\quad\;\; -3 \;\;, -3$

3. Step 3: Fill in the binomials. Be sure to check your answer signs.
   $2(x - 3)(x - 3)$.

4. Step 4: To solve, set each to equal 0.
   $x - 3 = 0$. So, $x = 3$.

Difference of squares:

$$a^2 - b^2 = (a + b)(a - b).$$

$$a^2 + 2ab + b^2 = (a + b)(a + b).$$

$$a^2 - 2ab + b^2 = (a - b)(a - b).$$

Geometry

- **Acute Angle**: Measures less than 90°.

- **Acute Triangle**: Each angle measures less than 90°.

- **Obtuse Angle**: Measures greater than 90°.

- **Obtuse Triangle**: One angle measures greater than 90°.

- **Adjacent Angles**: Share a side and a vertex.

- **Complementary Angles**: Adjacent angles that sum to 90°.

- **Supplementary Angles**: Adjacent angles that sum to 180°.

- **Vertical Angles**: Angles that are opposite of each other. They are always congruent (equal in measure).

- **Equilateral Triangle**: All angles are equal.

- **Isosceles Triangle**: Two sides and two angles are equal.

- **Scalene**: No equal angles.

- **Parallel Lines**: Lines that will never intersect. Y **ll** X means line Y is parallel to line X.

- **Perpendicular Lines**: Lines that intersect or cross to form 90° angles.

- **Transversal Line**: A line that crosses parallel lines.

- **Bisector**: Any line that cuts a line segment, angle, or polygon exactly in half.

- **Polygon**: Any enclosed plane shape with three or more connecting sides (ex. a triangle).

- **Regular Polygon**: Has all equal sides and equal angles (ex. square).

- **Arc**: A portion of a circle's edge.

- **Chord**: A line segment that connects two different points on a circle.

- **Tangent**: Something that touches a circle at only one point without crossing through it.

- **Sum of Angles**: The sum of angles of a polygon can be calculated using $(n-1)180^{o}$, when n = the number of sides.

Regular Polygons

Polygon Angle Principle: S = The sum of interior angles of a polygon with n-sides.

$S = (n - 2)180$.

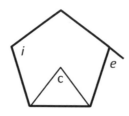

The measure of each central angle (c) is $360°/n$.
The measure of each interior angle (i) is $(n - 2)180°/n$.
The measure of each exterior angle (e) is $360°/n$.

To compare areas of similar polygons: $A_1/A_2 = (\text{side}_1/\text{side}_2)^2$.

Triangles

The angles in a triangle add up to $180°$.

Area of a triangle = $\frac{1}{2} * b * h$, or $\frac{1}{2}bh$.

Pythagoras' Theorem: $a^2 + b^2 = c^2$.

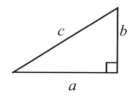

Trapezoids

Four-sided polygon, in which the bases (and only the bases) are parallel.
Isosceles Trapezoid – base angles are congruent.

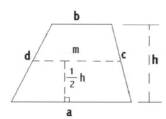

Area and Perimeter of a Trapezoid

$$m = \frac{1}{2}(a + b)$$

$$Area = \frac{1}{2}h*(a + b) = m*h$$

$$Perimeter = a + b + c + d = 2m + c + d$$

If m is the median then: $m \, \| \, \overline{AB}$ and $m \, \| \, CD$

108

Rhombus

Four-sided polygon, in which all four sides are congruent and opposite sides are parallel.

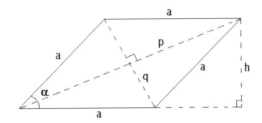

Area and Perimeter of a Rhombus

$$Perimeter = 4a$$

$$Area = a^2 \sin \alpha = a * h = \frac{1}{2}pq$$

$$4a^2 = p^2 + q^2$$

Rectangle

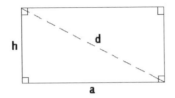

Area and Perimeter of a Rectangle

$$d = \sqrt{a^2 + h^2}$$

$$a = \sqrt{d^2 - h^2}$$

$$h = \sqrt{d^2 - a^2}$$

$$Perimeter = 2a + 2h$$

$$Area = a \cdot h$$

Square

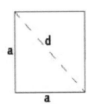

Area and Perimeter of a Square

$$d = a\sqrt{2}$$

$$Perimeter = 4a = 2d\sqrt{2}$$

$$Area = a^2 = \frac{1}{2}d^2$$

Circle

Area and Perimeter of a Circle

$$d = 2r$$

$$Perimeter = 2\pi r = \pi d$$

$$Area = \pi r^2$$

Cube

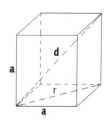

Area and Volume of a Cube

$$r = a\sqrt{2}$$

$$d = a\sqrt{3}$$

$$Area = 6a^2$$

$$Volume = a^3$$

Cuboid

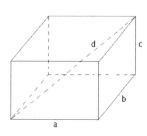

Area and Volume of a Cuboid

$$d = \sqrt{a^2 + b^2 + c^2}$$

$$A = 2(ab + ac + bc)$$

$$V = abc$$

Cylinder

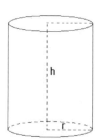

Area and Volume of a Cylinder

$$d = 2r$$

$$A_{surface} = 2\pi rh$$

$$A_{base} = 2\pi r^2$$

$$Area = A_{surface} + A_{base}$$

$$= 2\pi r\,(h + r)$$

$$Volume = \pi r^2 h$$

Mathematics Knowledge Practice Test Questions

1. If Lynn can type a page in p minutes, how many pages can she do in 5 minutes?
    a) 5/p.
    b) $p - 5$.
    c) $p + 5$.
    d) $p/5$.
    e) $1 - p + 5$.

2. If Sally can paint a house in 4 hours, and John can paint the same house in 6 hours, then how long will it take for both of them to paint the house together?
    a) 2 hours and 24 minutes.
    b) 3 hours and 12 minutes.
    c) 3 hours and 44 minutes.
    d) 4 hours and 10 minutes.
    e) 4 hours and 33 minutes.

3. The sales price of a car is $12,590, which is 20% off the original price. What is the original price?
    a) $14,310.40.
    b) $14,990.90.
    c) $15,290.70.
    d) $15,737.50.
    e) $16,935.80.

4. Solve the following equation for a: $2a \div 3 = 8 + 4a$.
    a) -2.4.
    b) 2.4.
    c) 1.3.
    d) -1.3.
    e) 0.

5. If $y = 3$, then what is $y^3(y^3 - y)$?
    a) 300.
    b) 459.
    c) 648.
    d) 999.
    e) 1099.

6. The average of three numbers is v. If one of the numbers is z and another is y, then what is the remaining number?
   a) $ZY - V$.
   b) $Z/V - 3 - Y$.
   c) $Z/3 - V - Y$.
   d) $3V - Z - Y$.
   e) $V - Z - Y$.

7. Mary is reviewing her algebra quiz. She has determined that one of her solutions is incorrect. Which one is it?
   a) $2x + 5(x - 1) = 9$; $x = 2$.
   b) $p - 3(p - 5) = 10$; $p = 2.5$.
   c) $4y + 3y = 28$; $y = 4$.
   d) $5w + 6w - 3w = 64$; $w = 8$.
   e) $t - 2t - 3t = 32$; $t = 8$.

8. What simple interest rate will Susan need to secure in order to make $2,500 in interest on a $10,000 principal over 5 years?
   a) 4%.
   b) 5%.
   c) 6%.
   d) 7%.
   e) 8%.

9. Which of the following is not a rational number?
   a) -4.
   b) $1/5$.
   c) $0.8333333...$
   d) 0.45.
   e) $\sqrt{2}$.

10. Find $0.12 \div 1$.
   a) 12.
   b) 1.2.
   c) .12.
   d) .012.
   e) .0012.

11. $(9 \div 3) * (8 \div 4)$ equals:
   a) 1.
   b) 6.
   c) 72.
   d) 576.
   e) 752.

12. Describe the following sequence in mathematical terms: 144, 72, 36, 18, and 9.
   a) Descending arithmetic sequence.
   b) Ascending arithmetic sequence.
   c) Descending geometric sequence.
   d) Ascending geometric sequence.
   e) Miscellaneous sequence.

13. Which of the following is not a whole number followed by its square?
   a) 1, 1.
   b) 6, 36.
   c) 8, 64.
   d) 10, 100.
   e) 11, 144.

14. There are 12 more apples than oranges in a basket of 36 apples and oranges. How many apples are in the basket?
   a) 12.
   b) 15.
   c) 24.
   d) 28.
   e) 36.

15. Which of the following correctly identifies 4 consecutive odd integers, where the sum of the middle two integers is equal to 24?
   a) 5, 7, 9, 11.
   b) 7, 9, 11, 13.
   c) 9, 11, 13, 15.
   d) 11, 13, 15, 17.
   e) 13, 15, 17, 19.

16. What is the next number in the sequence? 6, 12, 24, 48, ___.
    a) 72.
    b) 96.
    c) 108.
    d) 112.
    e) 124.

17. What is the volume of a cylinder with a diameter of 1 foot and a height of 14 inches?
    a) 2104.91 cubic inches.
    b) 1584 cubic inches.
    c) 528 cubic inches.
    d) 904.32 cubic inches.
    e) 264 cubic inches.

18. What is the volume of a cube whose width is 5 inches?
    a) 15 cubic inches.
    b) 25 cubic inches.
    c) 64 cubic inches.
    d) 100 cubic inches.
    e) 125 cubic inches.

19. If a discount of 25% off the retail price of a desk saves Mark $45, what was desk's original price?
    a) $135.
    b) $160.
    c) $180.
    d) $210.
    e) $215.

20. A customer pays $1,100 in state taxes on a newly-purchased car. What is the value of the car if state taxes are 8.9% of the value?
    a) $9.765.45.
    b) $10,876.90.
    c) $12,359.55.
    d) $14,345.48.
    e) $15,745.45.

21. How long will Lucy have to wait before for her $2,500 invested at 6% earns $600 in simple interest?

    a) 2 years.
    b) 3 years.
    c) 4 years.
    d) 5 years.
    e) 6 years.

22. If $r = 5z$ and $15z = 3y$, then r equals:

    a) y.
    b) $2y$.
    c) $5y$.
    d) $10y$.
    e) $15y$.

23. What is 35% of a number if 12 is 15% of a number?

    a) 5.
    b) 12.
    c) 28.
    d) 33.
    e) 62.

24. A computer is on sale for $1,600, which is a 20% discount off the regular price. The regular price is?

    a) $1800.
    b) $1900.
    c) $2000.
    d) $2100.
    e) $2200.

25. A car dealer sells an SUV for $39,000, which represents a 25% profit over the cost. What was the cost of the SUV to the dealer?

    a) $29,250.
    b) $31,200.
    c) $32,500.
    d) $33,800.
    e) $33,999.

Mathematics Knowledge Practice Test Answer Key

1. Answer: Option(a)
Explanation: From the given information in the question, Lynn writes one page in 'p' minutes. Now, we are asked about the number of pages Lynn can write in 5 minutes. The simplest way to solve this question is by writing it in ratio form I.e.

1 page ➜ 'p' minutes
X pages ➜ 5 minutes
Cross multiplying the above equations, we get 5*1 =x*p
Therefore, x = 5/p (Which means that he can type 5/p pages in 5 minutes)

2. Answer: Option (a)
Explanation: Sally can paint a house in 4 hours means that in one hour, Sally paints ¼ of the house. Similarly, John can paint a house in 6 hours, which means that he paints $\frac{1}{6}$ of the house in 1 hour. If both Sally and John work together for one hour, they can paint (1/4 + 1/6) = 5/12 of the house. In order to paint the house completely, they would need 12/5 hours. Please note that 12/5 = 2.4 hours.

If we multiply 2.4 with 60, we can find out the exact number of minutes they are taking. 2.4 * 60 = 144 minutes. From the given answer options, only answer (a) correspond to 144 minutes (i.e. 2 hours and 24 minutes).

3. Answer: Option (d)
Explanation: The sales price of the car is 20% off the original price (20% discount) which means that the given price of $12590 is 80% of the original price. Let's say that 'x' is the original price of the car, then

(80/100)*x = 12590 (i.e. 80% of 'x' equals $12590)
Solving the above equation, x = 12590*(100/80) ➜ $15,737 Option (d)

4. Answer: Option (a)
Explanation: We re-write this equation as $\frac{2a}{3}$ = 8+4a. Now, we multiply by 3 on both sides. The equation becomes 2a = 24 + 12a ➜ -24 = 10a ➜ **a= -2.4** Option (a)

5. Answer: Option (c)
Explanation: It's a relatively simple question. The value of 'y' is given as 3. We know that 3^3 = 27. So, the expression becomes 27 * (27-3) = 27*24 ➜ **648** Option (c)

6. Answer: Option (d)
Explanation: Let's suppose that the unknown number is 'w'. So, the average of three numbers becomes,
$$\frac{W+Z+Y}{3} = V$$

Multiplying by '3' on both sides, we get
w+z+y = 3v
W= 3v-z-y
So, the unknown number equals 3V- Z -Y

7. Answer: Option (e)
Explanation: In these types of questions, we have to check each answer option to find out the desired answer. In this particular question, we are looking for the option which gives INCORRECT answer. (It's very important that you read the statement of the question correctly)

Option(a) ➜ 2(2) + 5(2-1) = 4+ 5 =9 Which gives the correct answer.
Option (b)➜ 2.5- 3(2.5 -5) = 10 which gives the correct answer.
Option (c)➜ 4(4)+ 3(4) = 28 which gives the correct answer
Option (d) ➜ 5(8) + 6(8) -3(8) = 64 which gives the correct answer
Option (e) ➜ 8 – 2(8) – 3(8) = -32 $\neq$ 32. Option (e) gives us incorrect answer, therefore, we choose this option.

8. Answer: Option (b)
Explanation: The principal amount is given as $10,000 and the total interest generated on this amount in 5 years is $2500. If we suppose that 'x' is the percentage of interest per year, then the equation becomes,
5 * (x/100) * 10000 = 2500
Solving for 'x', we get x = 5%.

9. Answer: Option (e)
Explanation: A rational number is the one which can be written in form of a simple fraction. If we observe closely, only option (e) gives us a number which cannot be written in form of a fraction.

10. Answer: Option (c)
Explanation: Any number divided by '1' gives the same number as a result. Therefore, 0.12/1 = 0.12

11. Answer: Option (b)
Explanation: This is a very simple question. All you need to know is PEMDAS rule. First of all, we solve what is within the parenthesis, and then we multiply the answers of each parenthesis.
9 divided by 3 equals 3.
8 divided by 4 equals 2.
We multiply 3 and 2 to get our final answer: 3*2 = 6

12. Answer: Option (c)
Explanation: From the given sequence of numbers, we note that the numbers start from the highest and gradually decrease (144 > 72 > 36 18 > 9). Because of this decreasing order, we are sure that these numbers are in descending order. Also, we note that every next number in this sequence is obtained by dividing the previous number by 2. Therefore, it is Descending Geometric Sequence. (Some students might confuse it with geometric sequence with arithmetic sequence but please note that, for a sequence to be arithmetic, the difference between any two consecutive numbers in that sequence must be the same.)

13. Answer: Option (e)
Explanation: We know that $11^2 = 121$ ➜ $121 \neq 144$.
Option (e) is 11, 144. Since we are to choose the option in which a whole number is not followed by its square, and we know that $11^2 = 121$ instead of 144, we select option(e).

14. Answer: Option (c)
Explanation: Let's suppose that there are 'x' oranges in the basket. From the given statement of the question, the number of apples is 12 more than the number of oranges i.e. x+12. Also, its given that the total number of apples and oranges is 36. Writing this information in form of an equation, it becomes:
x+ x+12 = 36
2x= 36-12
x= 24/2
x= 12
Number of apples = x + 12 ➜ 12+12 = 24 Option (c)

15. Answer: Option (c)
Explanation: We need to take care of two things in order to answer this question. Firstly, the numbers should be consecutive odd numbers. All given options meet this criterion. Secondly, we need to look for the option in which the middle two numbers give us a sum of 24. Only option (c) has numbers such that the sum of middle two is 24 (i.e. 11 + 13 = 24).

16. Answer: Option (b)
Explanation: If we observe closely, we note that every next number in this sequence is obtained by multiplying the previous number by 2. i.e.
48 = 24*2
24= 12*2
12= 6*2

Therefore, in order to find the next number in the sequence, we multiply 48 by 2.
48*2 = 96

17. Answer: Option (b)
Explanation: We know that the volume of a cylinder is given by the formula $V= \pi r^2 h$
Important thing to note in this question is that the diameter of the cylinder in given instead of its radius. Also, its given in feet instead of inches. So, we first convert it into inches i.e. 1 foot = 12 inches diameter. So, the radius becomes $12/2 = 6$ inches.
Now, putting in the values of radius and height in the formula, we get
$V= (3.14)(6)^2(14) = 1584$ cubic inches.

18. Answer: Option (e)
Explanation: We are given with the width of the cube. As we know that all sides of the cube are equal to each other, we say that the length and height of this cube is also 5.
So, the volume of this cube becomes;
Volume = Length * Width * Height = 5 * 5 * 5 = 125

19. Answer: Option (c)
Explanation: From the given information in the question, we know that 25% of the actual price of desk is $45. If we write this in form of an equation, it becomes;
$(25/100) * x = \$45$ (25% of 'x' equals $45)
$x= 45/0.25$ ➔ $180
Therefore, the actual price of the desk equals to $180.

20. Answer: Option (c)
Explanation: Let's suppose that the actual value of the taxes is 'x'. 8.9% of this value equals $1100. Writing this in form of an equation, we get:
$(8.9/100)* x = 1100$
$x=1100/ 0.089$ ➔ $12359

21. Answer: Option (c)
Explanation: We know that:
In this given question, principal amount is $2500, interest is $600, and rate is 0.06.
Interest = Principal Amount * Rate * Time
Putting values in this formula, we get
$600 = 2500 * 0.06 * Time$
Time = 600/ (2500*0.07) ➔ 4
Therefore, time required = **4 years**.

22. Answer: Option (a)
Explanation: We are given with two equations in this question. Firstly, it's given that r = 5z. Secondly, its given that 15z = 3y, and we are asked about the value of 'r' in terms of 'y'. If we divide the second equation by '3', we get 5z = y, but from the first equation (i.e. r = 5z), we know that 5z = r.
So, we conclude that r = 5z = y ➔ r = y

23. Answer: Option(c)
Explanation: This is a tricky question. We need to find 35% of a number but this number is unknown. But we are given with that fact that 12 is 15% of that number. So, we first find out that 12 is 15% of what number? In order to find that out, we write the following equation:

$0.15 * x = 12$

$x = 12/0.15 \rightarrow 80$

Now, we need to find 35% of 80. This can be easily found by multiplying 80 by (35/100) i.e. $80 * 0.35 = 28$

24. Answer: Option (c)
Explanation: From the statement of the question, it is clear that when we take 20% off the price of computer, it costs $1600. This means that $1600 equals 80% of the actual price of the computer. Writing this in form of an equation;

$0.8 * x = \$1600$

$x = 1600/0.8$

$x = \$2000$ where 'x' is the actual price of the computer.

25. Answer: Option (b)
Explanation: First of all, you should know that 25% profit on the actual price means that we have multiplied the original price by 1.25 i.e. (1+ 0.25). So, in order to find the actual price of SUV, we divide it by 1.25. This gives us $39000/1.25 \rightarrow \$31200$ which is the original price of the SUV.

Chapter 5: Instrument Comprehension

The instrument comprehension section will test your ability to understand basic aviation instrumentation by providing two dials, a compass and artificial horizon, and then requiring you to identify an image of an aircraft that correlates to what is shown on the dials. It might seem difficult since you may not have any previous flight experience, but once you understand the dials, most find this section to be relatively easy and straightforward.

Let's review the dials first, then we'll explain how the questions are formatted and how you need to use the dials to answer the questions. In each question, you will be presented two dials that look just like this:

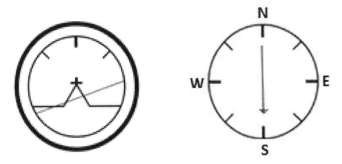

The dial on the left is your artificial horizon. This dial can be kind of confusing the first time you see it. In the aritical horizon pictured above, the dial indicates that the aircraft is in a slight climb and banking right. What makes this confusing to people, is that it is the "horizon" that moves in the dial. The easiest way to explain it is to imagine it is the view from the aircraft. Here's how it works: the line with a triangle in the middle with the "plus sign" is intended to be the wings and nose of the aircraft. Now, think of that in relation to the diagnoal line cutting across the dial, sloping to downward to the left. That sloping line is the horizon. As the aircraft climbs upward, the horizon will dip below level, just like it would be viewed from the cockpit. Then, as the aircraft banks right, visualize in your mind the wings of the aircraft turning in relation to the horizon. After you try a few, it becomes easier and easier to immediatley visualize.

The dial on the right likely needs no explanation. It is a simple compass indicating the direction of travel of the aircraft. We will come back to this feature later, as it is a great way to quickly and easily eliminate wrong answers.

Now that you've been introduced to both dials, let's review the artificial horizon some more by going over some examples.

In this example, the horizon is flat and level at the center point. That means there is no climb or dive, and the aircrafts wings are flat and level as represented by the image of the plane.

In the above artificial horizon, the aircraft is in a dive. As you can see, the horizon has moved above the fusalage silhouette (the line with the triangle representing the aircraft). Try to imagine you are looking through the windshield of a plane as it starts to dive. As the nose tips down, the horizon will move upward in your field of vision. That's exactly what the artificial horizon reprsents.

Similar to an aircraft diving, is if it is climbing. Again, imagine sitting in the cockpit as the plane climbs. In your field of vision, the horizon would go down, down, down as the nose turns up. Again, that's exactly what the artificial horizon is doing in the dial.

Banking is where most people get confused. Most people who experience frustration with this are typically visualizing the angle of the horizon as the angle of the wings. This happens because the dial is from the perspective of the pilot in the aircraft, but on the AFOQT exam, the images you are shown are from outside the aircraft and could be viewed from the front, back, or sides. There inlies the challenge, to imagine the perspective of the pilot and translate that into the image you are shown. As you can see in the above example, the horizon is slopes down to the right, but the wings of the plane are turns leftward as it banks left. Again, visualize sitting in the aircraft as it banks and how the horizon would appear in relation to the windshield.

Here is a final example that throws you one last curveball. In this example, the aircraft appears to be coming towards you. If the aircraft is coming towards you, the artificial horizon will appear to tilt the same way as the wings because your perspective is mirrored to the direction of travel. If you get confused, remember to first think about what direction the aircraft is banking (to it's own right or it's own left), then correlate that to the image of the aircraft.

Now, let's put it all together in an example of an actual test question. The questions will appear on the exam much like the one below:

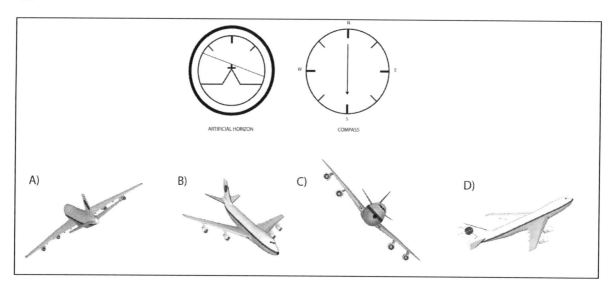

As we mentioned earlier, we are coming back to the compass. This is the easiest way to eliminate wrong answer choices, and sometimes immediately find the correct answer. You always want to reference the artificial horizon just to double check (sometimes options on the test are very similar), but it is fastest and easiest to start with the compass. In this example, we see the aircraft is heading South. On the exam, the direction of travel is simply that "South" is coming towards you, "North" is flying away, "East" is to the right, and "West" is to the left. Almost too easy, right? In this example, the compass indicates "South" and looking at the choices, there is only one aircraft heading directly towards you, which is choice C. Just to double check, the artificial horizon dial indicates that the aircraft is neither diving nor climbing, but is banking relatively hard to the left. Choice C confirms that, as that aircraft is shown to be neither climbing nor diving and is indeed banking hard to the left. The answer is C.

Now that you've got a decent grasp on the fundamentals and have seen how the parts of the puzzle fit together, it's time to get some practice in. Keep in mind that on the actual test, you will have 6 minutes to answer 20 questions. That's about 20 seconds per question which might seem fast, but once you have some practice under your belt, you'll be able to recognize the correct answer in just a few seconds leaving you ample time to double check all the answer choices before moving on to the next question. **Always look at all of the answer choices before selecting your answer!**

Instrument Comprehension Practice Test

1.

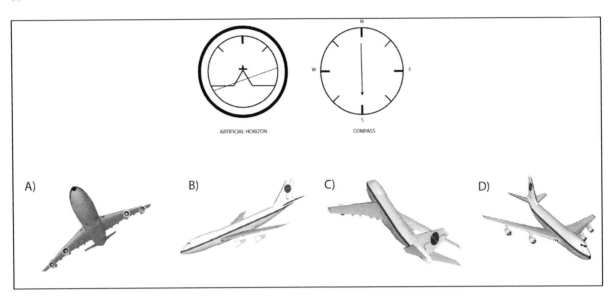

2.

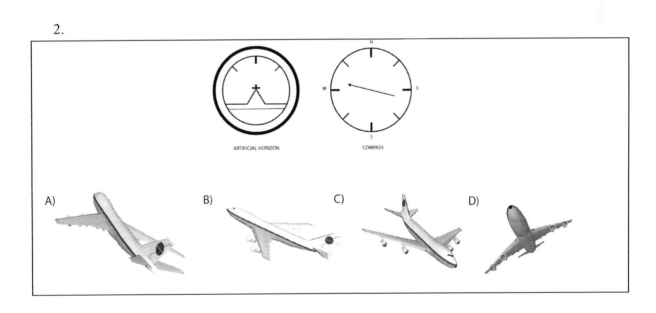

3.

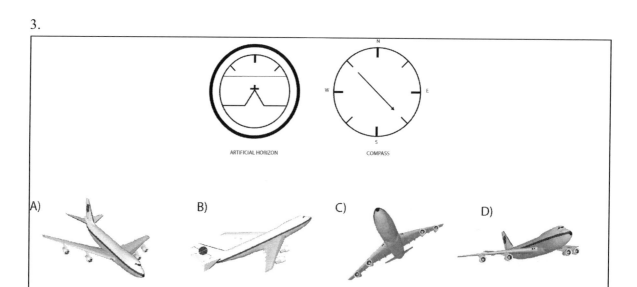

4.

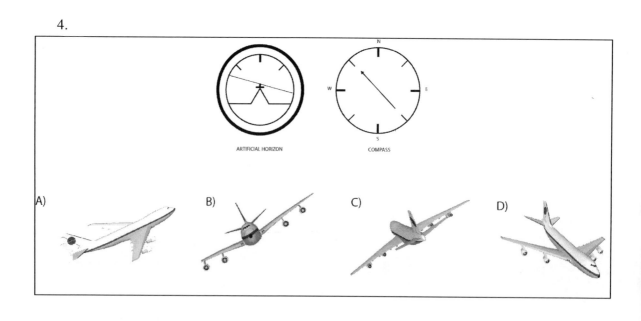

5.

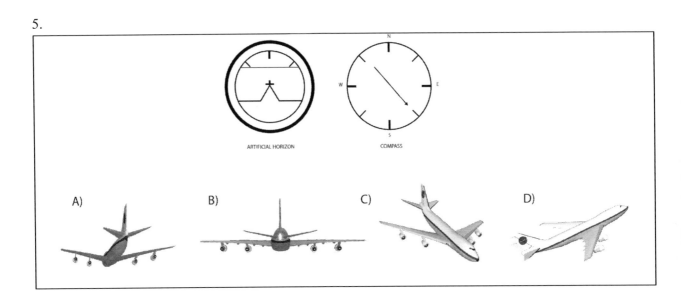

6.

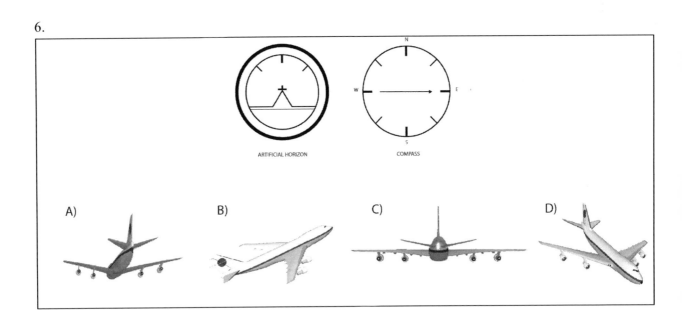

7.

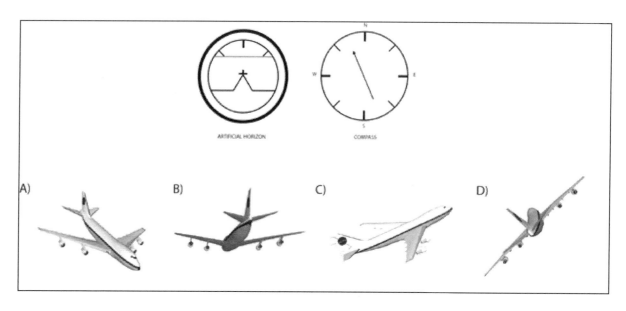

8.

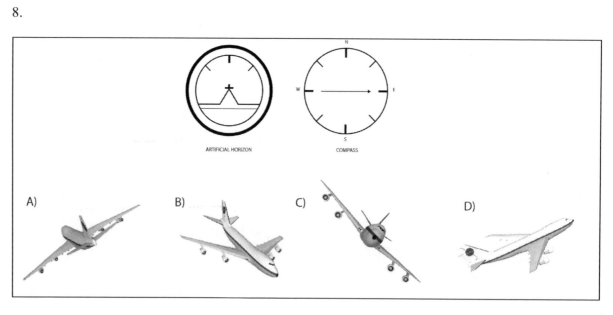

9.

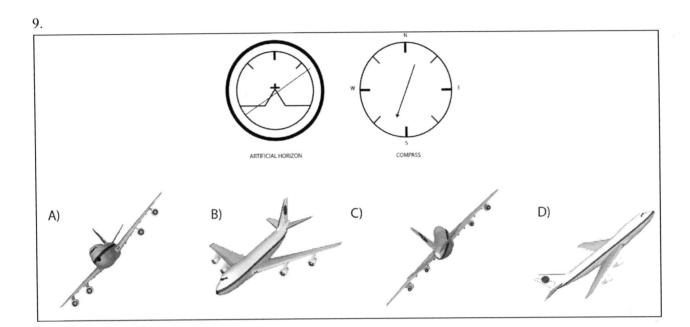

10.

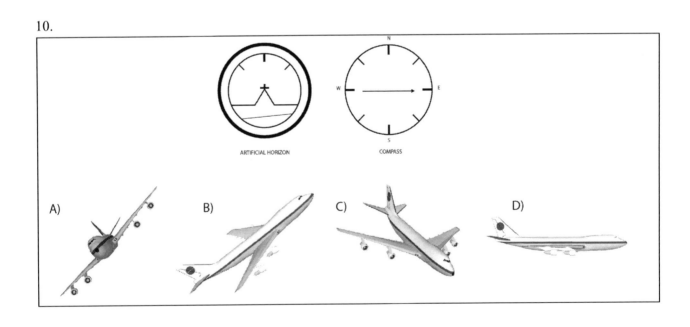

11.

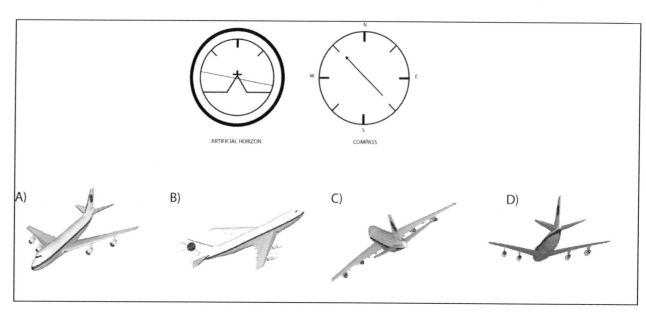

12.

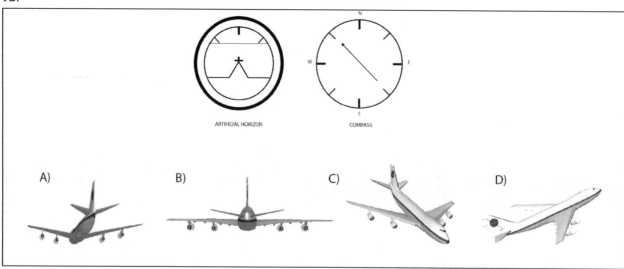

13.

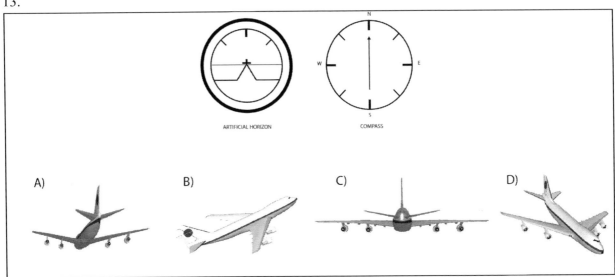

14.

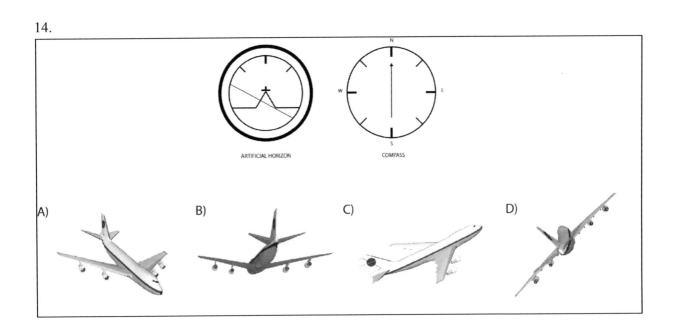

131

15.

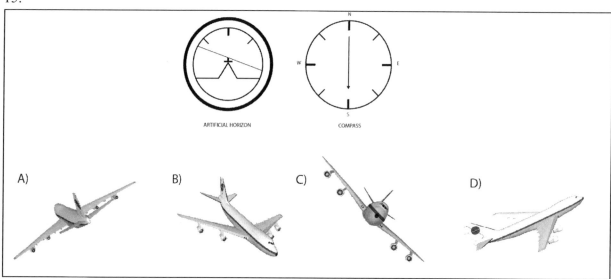

16.

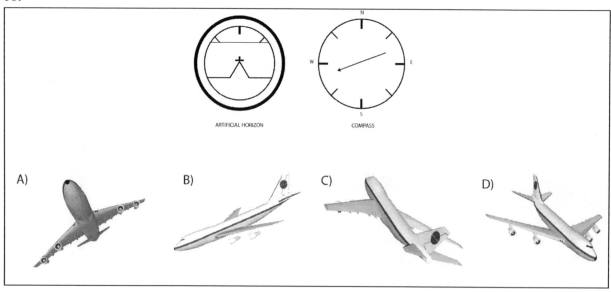

132

17.

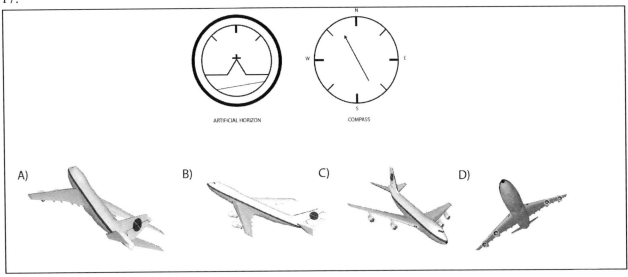

18.

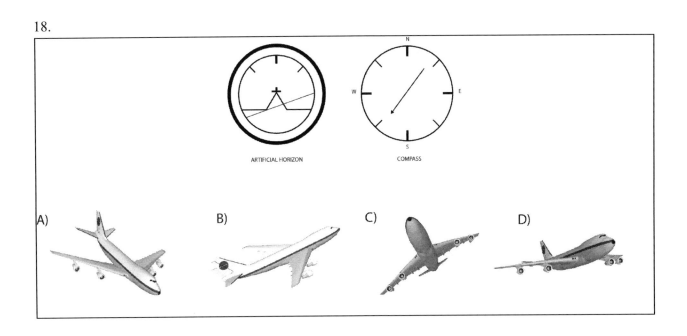

19.

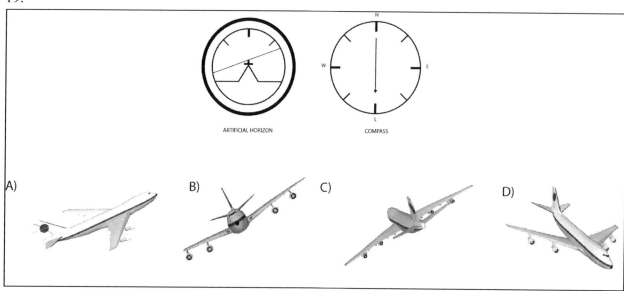

20.

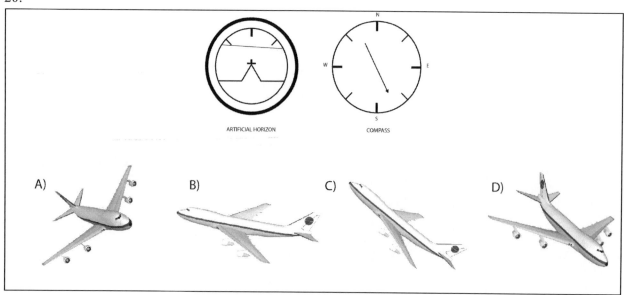

ANSWER KEY:

1. A
2. B
3. A
4. C
5. C
6. B
7. B
8. D
9. A
10. B
11. C
12. A
13. C
14. D
15. C
16. B
17. A
18. C
19. B
20. D

Chapter 6: Block Counting

The Block Counting section is relatively straight forward, but can be challenging for some people. You will be shown a shape with different stacked blocks. Some of the blocks will have a number on them, and your objective is to determine how many other blocks touch the block indicated. The challenge is that you must visualize in three dimensionally how these blocks move through the entire structure. Most mistakes come from counting a block twice on accident.

Let's look at an example. In the below image, you can see five numbered blocks. If you were asked to count how many blocks touch block #3, what would your answer be?

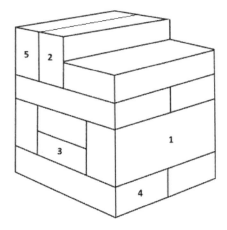

The correct answer is 5, however, some people will have landed on six. Why is this? People who have difficulty visualizing 3D images might have counted block #4 twice because they will count blocks on one side of the shape that run past the block in the question, then count blocks from the other side of the shape they can see. The block below is the same as the one in the example, but with the blocks on one side shaded.

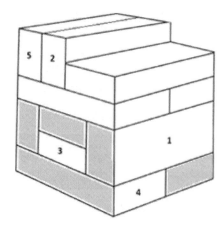

The mistake is counting the "other side" of block 4 as shown below with the hash marks. You have to keep in mind which blocks you have already counted and try to visualize the shapes moving past each other and how they connect.

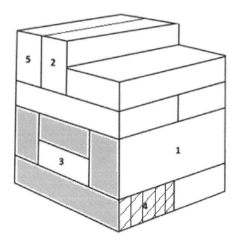

While this section is straightforward, it can be challenging. To make it even more so, keep in mind you have only 3 minutes to complete 20 questions. That is a mere 9 seconds per question! Practice now and see how you do. If you struggle with this section, don't forget that accuracy is just as important as speed. It does no good to answer 20 questions incorrectly when you could have only answered 10, but gotten them all correct.

If you struggle with this section, the only way to get better is to practice, practice, practice. Use the example questions and make your own numbers for individual blocks and practice counting around them to sharpen your skills, then go back and work on speed on the practice test.

Block Counting Practice Test

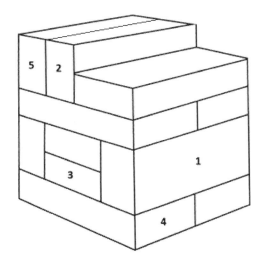

1. Block 1 is touched by _____ other blocks?
    - a. 2
    - b. 4
    - c. 6
    - d. 7
    - e. 8

2. Block 2 is touched by _____ other blocks?
    - a. 2
    - b. 3
    - c. 4
    - d. 5
    - e. 6

3. Block 4 is touched by _____ other blocks?
    - a. 3
    - b. 5
    - c. 6
    - d. 4
    - e. 2

4. Block 5 is touched by _____ other blocks?
    - a. 2
    - b. 3
    - c. 4
    - d. 5
    - e. 6

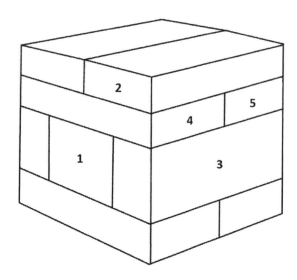

5. Block 1 is touched by _____ other blocks?
   a. 2
   b. 4
   c. 6
   d. 7
   e. 8

6. Block 2 is touched by _____ other blocks?
   a. 2
   b. 3
   c. 4
   d. 5
   e. 6

7. Block 4 is touched by _____ other blocks?
   a. 3
   b. 5
   c. 6
   d. 4
   e. 2

8. Block 3 is touched by _____ other blocks?
   a. 2
   b. 3
   c. 4
   d. 5
   e. 6

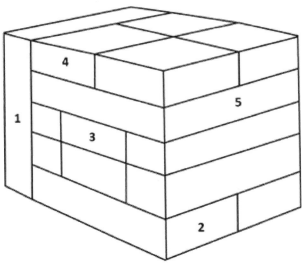

9. Block 1 is touched by _____ other blocks?
   a. 2
   b. 4
   c. 6
   d. 7
   e. 8

10. Block 2 is touched by _____ other blocks?
   a. 2
   b. 3
   c. 4
   d. 6
   e. 5

11. Block 3 is touched by _____ other blocks?
   a. 6
   b. 5
   c. 3
   d. 4
   e. 2

12. Block 5 is touched by _____ other blocks?
   a. 7
   b. 6
   c. 4
   d. 5
   e. 8

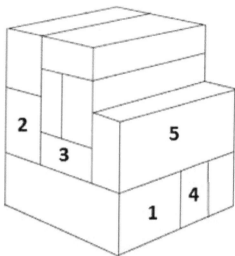

13. Block 1 is touched by _____ other blocks?
    a. 2
    b. 4
    c. 6
    d. 7
    e. 8

14. Block 2 is touched by _____ other blocks?
    a. 2
    b. 3
    c. 4
    d. 6
    e. 5

15. Block 3 is touched by _____ other blocks?
    a. 7
    b. 5
    c. 3
    d. 4
    e. 6

16. Block 5 is touched by _____ other blocks?
    a. 7
    b. 6
    c. 4
    d. 5
    e. 8

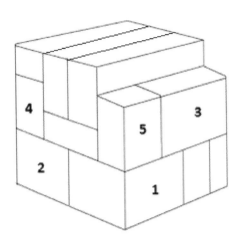

17. Block 1 is touched by _____ other blocks?
    a. 5
    b. 4
    c. 6
    d. 7
    e. 8

18. Block 2 is touched by _____ other blocks?
    a. 2
    b. 5
    c. 4
    d. 6
    e. 7

19. Block 3 is touched by _____ other blocks?
    a. 6
    b. 5
    c. 3
    d. 4
    e. 2

20. Block 5 is touched by _____ other blocks?
    a. 7
    b. 6
    c. 4
    d. 5
    e. 8

Block Counting Answer Key

1. C
2. C
3. D
4. B
5. C
6. B
7. C
8. D
9. D
10. E
11. A
12. E
13. B
14. D
15. A
16. D
17. A
18. B
19. A
20. C

Chapter 7: Table Reading

In the Table Reading section, the objective is simple enough. For each question, you are given an X & Y coordinate. Find that intersection on the table and identify the number located there. Of all the sections on the AFOQT where time is a factor, none compare to Table Reading. You will only have 7 minutes to complete 40 questions, an absurdly short amount of time at only 10.5 seconds per question.

The general concept is easy enough, any 6th grader could understand how to read a simple chart. So how do you prepare for this section to overcome the obstacle of time? Practice is of course important, but using a systematic approach is imperative. Have you ever tried counting backwards from 100 to 0 while someone is yelling random numbers in your ear? The Table Reading section is similar to that. You will see so many numbers, it becomes extraordinarily easy to forget what the coordinates were you needed and have to go back and reference the question again. By doing that, you would have already wasted 5-10 seconds minimum, which is one more question you now do not have time to answer.

Your goal is to not worry about time at all until the last 30 seconds. As you practice, force yourself to focus ONLY on the question at hand. Do not think about how much time has gone by, how many questions you have left, if you made a mistake on the last question, etc. The real test of this section is to see if, as an officer in the US Air Force, you possess the capability to stay calm under pressure, maintain your bearing, and stay focused.

As mentioned, don't worry about time until the last 30 seconds or so. When that time hits, go ahead and mark an answer for all remaining questions. There is no "wrong answer penalty" on the AFOQT, so you should never, ever leave a question blank on any section of this exam.

Let's get started on practice so you can get a feel for this section. Do not overwhelm yourself with this section. It is not possible to substantially speed up your time any more than after the first 10-15 practice questions you try. It is simply a function of time and it takes more than 10.5 seconds to read the question, scroll through the table, find the answer, and mark your answer choice. Rushing is counter-productive. Your goal with this practice round is just to familiarize yourself with the format, then move on. Do NOT take this practice test untimed! You want to know approximately how many questions you can answer in 7 minutes normally, so that you can better track your progress on test day and not lose track of time.

For purposes of this practice test, you will be presented 10 questions per page with the exact same graph for reference. Get a timer ready, and give it a try. Your goal should be to have 100% correct of questions you are able to attempt before you have to start filling in before time runs out.

Table Reading Practice Test

X - Value

Y \ X	-16	-15	-14	-13	-12	-11	-10	-9	-8	-7	-6	-5	-4	-3	-2	-1	0	1	2	3	4	5	6	7	8	9	10	11	12	13	14	15	16
16	7	3	5	2	8	10	9	9	10	11	12	12	13	14	15	15	16	17	18	19	19	20	21	22	22	23	24	25	26	26	27	28	29
15	30	29	29	28	27	26	25	25	24	23	22	21	21	20	19	18	17	17	16	15	14	13	13	12	11	10	9	9	8	9	3	5	6
14	7	23	4	5	11	7	23	39	30	29	7	23	39	29	26	15	45	7	23	9	36	30	29	7	24	3	9	36	7	23	11	21	24
13	8	14	18	47	4	8	14	20	7	23	8	14	20	31	28	7	24	8	14	23	10	7	23	55	34	6	23	10	8	14	20	55	34
12	3	9	19	46	19	3	9	15	8	14	3	9	15	32	30	55	34	3	9	29	16	8	14	9	42	2	29	16	3	9	15	9	42
11	6	23	11	98	21	6	23	28	3	9	6	23	41	34	31	9	42	6	23	14	44	3	9	6	19	1	14	44	6	23	86	6	19
10	2	29	17	58	11	16	7	18	6	23	10	17	18	13	18	6	19	8	19	66	20	6	23	11	21	29	26	15	3	9	19	5	24
9	1	14	15	54	3	14	12	13	2	29	16	16	17	18	19	20	20	21	22	23	24	2	29	26	27	31	28	7	6	23	32	32	33
8	9	11	11	44	3	9	36	5	1	14	44	48	22	43	29	44	48	22	43	7	23	1	14	11	21	32	30	55	2	29	7	23	29
7	10	9	54	24	6	23	10	11	9	11	46	50	34	44	23	46	50	34	44	8	14	9	11	38	40	34	31	9	1	14	8	14	14
6	21	5	81	4	2	29	16	17	10	9	48	51	91	44	14	48	51	91	44	3	9	10	9	22	22	22	7	24	9	11	3	9	11
5	23	13	24	45	1	14	44	15	29	26	15	45	2	3	9	44	55	17	6	4	23	13	13	12	11	15	55	34	10	9	6	23	24
4	25	33	35	36	38	40	11	11	31	28	7	24	41	6	23	23	26	28	31	33	18	7	33	23	26	28	9	42	36	38	41	55	34
3	27	19	20	21	22	22	9	54	32	30	55	34	13	2	29	16	7	18	64	22	22	12	34	16	7	18	6	19	10	17	18	9	42
2	29	14	13	13	12	11	5	81	34	31	23	11	11	1	14	7	24	44	48	22	43	13	36	14	12	13	2	29	16	16	17	6	19
1	31	28	7	24	30	29	13	24	3	22	29	17	5	9	11	55	34	46	50	34	44	15	37	13	2	29	16	16	17	20	9	54	12
0	32	30	55	34	7	23	21	23	26	28	3	9	36	38	41	9	42	48	51	91	44	17	39	23	9	81	16	15	14	13	5	81	81
-1	34	31	9	42	8	14	11	16	7	18	6	23	10	17	18	6	19	38	40	7	23	19	40	21	22	22	24	24	9	11	13	24	24
-2	7	33	25	38	3	9	3	14	12	13	2	29	16	16	17	20	21	22	22	8	14	36	22	13	12	11	34	34	10	9	7	24	24
-3	12	34	41	18	6	23	7	33	7	23	9	81	16	15	14	13	13	12	11	3	9	13	12	34	31	9	42	64	86	15	55	34	5
-4	13	36	52	39	2	29	12	34	8	14	23	24	28	31	33	3	9	36	26	6	23	9	36	3	33	3	9	36	63	89	9	42	42
-5	15	37	14	22	1	14	13	36	3	9	29	7	18	64	22	6	23	10	7	6	8	48	22	43	18	6	23	10	3	11	6	19	22
-6	17	39	21	40	9	11	15	37	6	23	14	22	26	30	7	2	29	16	24	6	46	50	34	44	8	2	29	16	35	36	30	29	31
-7	19	40	15	40	10	9	17	39	3	9	11	7	33	41	12	1	14	44	34	23	48	51	91	44	16	1	14	44	20	21	7	23	33
-8	36	22	4	41	7	33	19	40	26	10	9	12	34	41	13	36	33	35	36	38	40	20	3	9	36	23	26	28	3	9	36	38	41
-9	38	44	55	41	12	34	36	22	7	18	64	13	36	23	15	37	19	20	21	22	22	13	6	23	10	16	7	18	6	23	10	17	18
-10	40	36	7	42	13	36	5	81	3	9	36	15	37	29	17	39	14	13	13	12	11	3	2	29	16	14	12	13	2	29	16	16	17
-11	42	47	18	42	15	37	13	24	3	23	10	17	39	14	19	40	3	3	9	36	54	6	1	14	44	3	9	36	23	26	28	29	5
-12	44	48	22	43	17	39	22	1	2	29	16	19	40	11	36	22	24	6	23	10	81	2	21	23	26	28	31	33	7	24	1	14	48
-13	46	50	34	44	19	40	23	26	1	14	44	36	22	41	54	55	34	2	29	16	24	3	11	16	7	18	64	22	55	34	9	11	25
-14	48	51	91	44	36	22	16	7	18	6	23	10	17	18	81	9	42	1	14	44	28	3	9	36	38	41	43	46	9	42	10	9	1
-15	50	53	15	16	22	3	14	12	13	2	29	16	16	17	24	6	19	11	16	7	18	6	23	10	17	18	18	18	6	19	16	6	22
-16	51	27	5	45	54	15	3	54	10	11	24	20	4	89	6	55	4	2	14	12	13	2	29	16	16	17	18	19	5	20	20	4	33

	X	Y		A	B	C	D	E
1	-16	3		7	17	27	86	5
2	-4	15		21	81	97	77	70
3	14	10		23	81	73	46	19
4	-15	1		74	40	81	62	28
5	15	-12		39	14	25	44	13
6	6	-5		77	12	8	22	18
7	-10	4		90	11	13	41	58
8	6	-9		6	82	61	82	12
9	-5	-16		75	5	20	71	45
10	-14	-6		66	7	94	21	55

	-16	-15	-14	-13	-12	-11	-10	-9	-8	-7	-6	-5	-4	-3	-2	-1	0	1	2	3	4	5	6	7	8	9	10	11	12	13	14	15	16
16	7	3	5	2	8	10	9	9	10	11	12	12	13	14	15	15	16	17	18	19	19	20	21	22	22	23	24	25	26	26	27	28	29
15	30	29	29	28	27	26	25	25	24	23	22	21	21	20	19	18	17	17	16	15	14	13	13	12	11	10	9	9	8	9	3	5	6
14	7	23	4	5	11	7	23	39	30	29	7	23	39	29	26	15	45	7	23	9	36	30	29	7	24	3	9	36	7	23	11	21	24
13	8	14	18	47	4	8	14	20	7	23	8	14	20	31	28	7	24	8	14	23	10	7	23	55	34	6	23	10	8	14	20	55	34
12	3	9	19	46	19	3	9	15	8	14	3	9	15	32	30	55	34	3	9	29	16	8	14	9	42	2	29	16	3	9	15	9	42
11	6	23	11	98	21	6	23	28	3	9	6	23	41	34	31	9	42	6	23	14	44	3	9	6	19	1	14	44	6	23	86	6	19
10	2	29	17	58	11	16	7	18	6	23	10	17	18	13	18	6	19	8	19	66	20	6	23	11	21	29	26	15	3	9	19	5	24
9	1	14	15	54	3	14	12	13	2	29	16	16	17	18	19	20	20	21	22	23	24	2	29	26	27	31	28	7	6	23	32	32	33
8	9	11	11	44	3	9	36	5	1	14	44	48	22	43	29	44	48	22	43	7	23	1	14	11	21	32	30	55	2	29	7	23	29
7	10	9	54	24	6	23	10	11	9	11	46	50	34	44	23	46	50	34	44	8	14	9	11	38	40	34	31	9	1	14	8	14	14
6	21	5	81	4	2	29	16	17	10	9	48	51	91	44	14	48	51	91	44	3	9	10	9	22	22	22	7	24	9	11	3	9	11
5	23	13	24	45	1	14	44	15	29	26	15	45	2	3	9	44	55	17	6	4	23	13	13	12	11	15	55	34	10	9	6	23	24
4	25	33	35	36	38	40	11	11	31	28	7	24	41	6	23	23	26	28	31	33	18	7	33	23	26	28	9	42	36	38	41	55	34
3	27	19	20	21	22	22	9	54	32	30	55	34	13	2	29	16	7	18	64	22	22	12	34	16	7	18	6	19	10	17	18	9	42
2	29	14	13	13	12	11	5	81	34	31	23	11	11	1	14	7	24	44	48	22	43	13	36	14	12	13	2	29	16	16	17	6	19
1	31	28	7	24	30	29	13	24	3	22	29	17	5	9	11	55	34	46	50	34	44	15	37	13	2	29	16	16	17	20	9	54	12
0	32	30	55	34	7	23	21	23	26	28	3	9	36	38	41	9	42	48	51	91	44	17	39	23	9	81	16	15	14	13	5	81	81
-1	34	31	9	42	8	14	11	16	7	18	6	23	10	17	18	6	19	38	40	7	23	19	40	21	22	22	24	24	9	11	13	24	24
-2	7	33	25	38	3	9	3	14	12	13	2	29	16	16	17	20	21	22	22	8	14	36	22	13	12	11	34	34	10	9	7	24	24
-3	12	34	41	18	6	23	7	33	7	23	9	81	16	15	14	13	13	12	11	3	9	13	12	34	31	9	42	64	86	15	55	34	5
-4	13	36	52	39	2	29	12	34	8	14	23	24	28	31	33	3	9	36	26	6	23	9	36	3	33	3	9	36	63	89	9	42	42
-5	15	37	14	22	1	14	13	36	3	9	29	7	18	64	22	6	23	10	7	6	8	48	22	43	18	6	23	10	3	11	6	19	22
-6	17	39	21	40	9	11	15	37	6	23	14	22	26	30	7	2	29	16	24	6	46	50	34	44	8	2	29	16	35	36	30	29	31
-7	19	40	15	40	10	9	17	39	3	9	11	7	33	41	12	1	14	44	34	23	48	51	91	44	16	1	14	44	20	21	7	23	33
-8	36	22	4	41	7	33	19	40	26	10	9	12	34	41	13	36	33	35	36	38	40	20	3	9	36	23	26	28	3	9	36	38	41
-9	38	44	55	41	12	34	36	22	7	18	64	13	36	23	15	37	19	20	21	22	22	13	6	23	10	16	7	18	6	23	10	17	18
-10	40	36	7	42	13	36	5	81	3	9	36	15	37	29	17	39	14	13	13	12	11	3	2	29	16	14	12	13	2	29	16	16	17
-11	42	47	18	42	15	37	13	24	3	23	10	17	39	14	19	40	3	3	9	36	54	6	1	14	44	3	9	36	23	26	28	29	5
-12	44	48	22	43	17	39	22	1	2	29	16	19	40	11	36	22	24	6	23	10	81	2	21	23	26	28	31	33	7	24	1	14	48
-13	46	50	34	44	19	40	23	26	1	14	44	36	22	41	54	55	34	2	29	16	24	3	11	16	7	18	64	22	55	34	9	11	25
-14	48	51	91	44	36	22	16	7	18	6	23	10	17	18	81	9	42	1	14	44	28	3	9	36	38	41	43	46	9	42	10	9	1
-15	50	53	15	16	22	3	14	12	13	2	29	16	16	17	24	6	19	11	16	7	18	6	23	10	17	18	18	18	6	19	16	6	22
-16	51	27	5	45	54	15	3	54	10	11	24	20	4	89	6	55	4	2	14	12	13	2	29	16	16	17	18	19	5	20	20	4	33

Y - Value

	X	Y
11	6	16
12	-4	11
13	-11	5
14	10	-3
15	6	-12
16	8	7
17	-9	0
18	-12	-3
19	12	-2
20	4	-5

A	B	C	D	E
22	19	32	62	21
68	87	41	81	3
14	89	68	73	50
75	42	82	44	47
53	15	25	21	85
96	74	87	40	4
73	23	43	93	6
6	14	32	30	64
45	24	18	8	10
36	8	95	40	34

X - Value

Y \ X	-16	-15	-14	-13	-12	-11	-10	-9	-8	-7	-6	-5	-4	-3	-2	-1	0	1	2	3	4	5	6	7	8	9	10	11	12	13	14	15	16
16	7	3	5	2	8	10	9	9	10	11	12	12	13	14	15	15	16	17	18	19	19	20	21	22	22	23	24	25	26	26	27	28	29
15	30	29	29	28	27	26	25	25	24	23	22	21	21	20	19	18	17	17	16	15	14	13	13	12	11	10	9	9	8	9	3	5	6
14	7	23	4	5	11	7	23	39	30	29	7	23	39	29	26	15	45	7	23	9	36	30	29	7	24	3	9	36	7	23	11	21	24
13	8	14	18	47	4	8	14	20	7	23	8	14	20	31	28	7	24	8	14	23	10	7	23	55	34	6	23	10	8	14	20	55	34
12	3	9	19	46	19	3	9	15	8	14	3	9	15	32	30	55	34	3	9	29	16	8	14	9	42	2	29	16	3	9	15	9	42
11	6	23	11	98	21	6	23	28	3	9	6	23	41	34	31	9	42	6	23	14	44	3	9	6	19	1	14	44	6	23	86	6	19
10	2	29	17	58	11	16	7	18	6	23	10	17	18	13	18	6	19	8	19	66	20	6	23	11	21	29	26	15	3	9	19	5	24
9	1	14	15	54	3	14	12	13	2	29	16	16	17	18	19	20	20	21	22	23	24	2	29	26	27	31	28	7	6	23	32	32	33
8	9	11	11	44	3	9	36	5	1	14	44	48	22	43	29	44	48	22	43	7	23	1	14	11	21	32	30	55	2	29	7	23	29
7	10	9	54	24	6	23	10	11	9	11	46	50	34	44	23	46	50	34	44	8	14	9	11	38	40	34	31	9	1	14	8	14	14
6	21	5	81	4	2	29	16	17	10	9	48	51	91	44	14	48	51	91	44	3	9	10	9	22	22	22	7	24	9	11	3	9	11
5	23	13	24	45	1	14	44	15	29	26	15	45	2	3	9	44	55	17	6	4	23	13	13	12	11	15	55	34	10	9	6	23	24
4	25	33	35	36	38	40	11	11	31	28	7	24	41	6	23	23	26	28	31	33	18	7	33	23	26	28	9	42	36	38	41	55	34
3	27	19	20	21	22	22	9	54	32	30	55	34	13	2	29	16	7	18	64	22	22	12	34	16	7	18	6	19	10	17	18	9	42
2	29	14	13	13	12	11	5	81	34	31	23	11	11	1	14	7	24	44	48	22	43	13	36	14	12	13	2	29	16	16	17	6	19
1	31	28	7	24	30	29	13	24	3	22	29	17	5	9	11	55	34	46	50	34	44	15	37	13	2	29	16	16	17	20	9	54	12
0	32	30	55	34	7	23	21	23	26	28	3	9	36	38	41	9	42	48	51	91	44	17	39	23	9	81	16	15	14	13	5	81	81
-1	34	31	9	42	8	14	11	16	7	18	6	23	10	17	18	6	19	38	40	7	23	19	40	21	22	22	24	24	9	11	13	24	24
-2	7	33	25	38	3	9	3	14	12	13	2	29	16	16	17	20	21	22	22	8	14	36	22	13	12	11	34	34	10	9	7	24	24
-3	12	34	41	18	6	23	7	33	7	23	9	81	16	15	14	13	13	12	11	3	9	13	12	34	31	9	42	64	86	15	55	34	5
-4	13	36	52	39	2	29	12	34	8	14	23	24	28	31	33	3	9	36	26	6	23	9	36	3	33	3	9	36	63	89	9	42	42
-5	15	37	14	22	1	14	13	36	3	9	29	7	18	64	22	6	23	10	7	6	8	48	22	43	18	6	23	10	3	11	6	19	22
-6	17	39	21	40	9	11	15	37	6	23	14	22	26	30	7	2	29	16	24	6	46	50	34	44	8	2	29	16	35	36	30	29	31
-7	19	40	15	40	10	9	17	39	3	9	11	7	33	41	12	1	14	44	34	23	48	51	91	44	16	1	14	44	20	21	7	23	33
-8	36	22	4	41	7	33	19	40	26	10	9	12	34	41	13	36	33	35	36	38	40	20	3	9	36	23	26	28	3	9	36	38	41
-9	38	44	55	41	12	34	36	22	7	18	64	13	36	23	15	37	19	20	21	22	22	13	6	23	10	16	7	18	6	23	10	17	18
-10	40	36	7	42	13	36	5	81	3	9	36	15	37	29	17	39	14	13	13	12	11	3	2	29	16	14	12	13	2	29	16	16	17
-11	42	47	18	42	15	37	13	24	3	23	10	17	39	14	19	40	3	3	9	36	54	6	1	14	44	3	9	36	23	26	28	29	5
-12	44	48	22	43	17	39	22	1	2	29	16	19	40	11	36	22	24	6	23	10	81	2	21	23	26	28	31	33	7	24	1	14	48
-13	46	50	34	44	19	40	23	26	1	14	44	36	22	41	54	55	34	2	29	16	24	3	11	16	7	18	64	22	55	34	9	11	25
-14	48	51	91	44	36	22	16	7	18	6	23	10	17	18	81	9	42	1	14	44	28	3	9	36	38	41	43	46	9	42	10	9	1
-15	50	53	15	16	22	3	14	12	13	2	29	16	16	17	24	6	19	11	16	7	18	6	23	10	17	18	18	18	6	19	16	6	22
-16	51	27	5	45	54	15	3	54	10	11	24	20	4	89	6	55	4	2	14	12	13	2	29	16	16	17	18	19	5	20	20	4	33

	X	Y
21	15	1
22	-13	4
23	12	15
24	-14	-10
25	-5	-13
26	-2	-16
27	-4	-4
28	-12	9
29	5	1
30	3	9

A	B	C	D	E
76	95	54	16	39
36	87	69	89	15
23	72	62	8	40
7	15	74	24	26
30	36	76	27	48
59	2	6	41	66
28	50	45	28	59
60	25	85	59	3
2	15	14	83	79
38	43	23	61	34

X - Value

Y \ X	-16	-15	-14	-13	-12	-11	-10	-9	-8	-7	-6	-5	-4	-3	-2	-1	0	1	2	3	4	5	6	7	8	9	10	11	12	13	14	15	16
16	7	3	5	2	8	10	9	9	10	11	12	12	13	14	15	15	16	17	18	19	19	20	21	22	22	23	24	25	26	26	27	28	29
15	30	29	29	28	27	26	25	25	24	23	22	21	21	20	19	18	17	17	16	15	14	13	13	12	11	10	9	9	8	9	3	5	6
14	7	23	4	5	11	7	23	39	30	29	7	23	39	29	26	15	45	7	23	9	36	30	29	7	24	3	9	36	7	23	11	21	24
13	8	14	18	47	4	8	14	20	7	23	8	14	20	31	28	7	24	8	14	23	10	7	23	55	34	6	23	10	8	14	20	55	34
12	3	9	19	46	19	3	9	15	8	14	3	9	15	32	30	55	34	3	9	29	16	8	14	9	42	2	29	16	3	9	15	9	42
11	6	23	11	98	21	6	23	28	3	9	6	23	41	34	31	9	42	6	23	14	44	3	9	6	19	1	14	44	6	23	86	6	19
10	2	29	17	58	11	16	7	18	6	23	10	17	18	13	18	6	19	8	19	66	20	6	23	11	21	29	26	15	3	9	19	5	24
9	1	14	15	54	3	14	12	13	2	29	16	16	17	18	19	20	20	21	22	23	24	2	29	26	27	31	28	7	6	23	32	32	33
8	9	11	11	44	3	9	36	5	1	14	44	48	22	43	29	44	48	22	43	7	23	1	14	11	21	32	30	55	2	29	7	23	29
7	10	9	54	24	6	23	10	11	9	11	46	50	34	44	23	46	50	34	44	8	14	9	11	38	40	34	31	9	1	14	8	14	14
6	21	5	81	4	2	29	16	17	10	9	48	51	91	44	14	48	51	91	44	3	9	10	9	22	22	22	7	24	9	11	3	9	11
5	23	13	24	45	1	14	44	15	29	26	15	45	2	3	9	44	55	17	6	4	23	13	13	12	11	15	55	34	10	9	6	23	24
4	25	33	35	36	38	40	11	11	31	28	7	24	41	6	23	23	26	28	31	33	18	7	33	23	26	28	9	42	36	38	41	55	34
3	27	19	20	21	22	22	9	54	32	30	55	34	13	2	29	16	7	18	64	22	22	12	34	16	7	18	6	19	10	17	18	9	42
2	29	14	13	13	12	11	5	81	34	31	23	11	11	1	14	7	24	44	48	22	43	36	14	12	13	2	29	16	17	20	9	54	12
1	31	28	7	24	30	29	13	24	3	22	29	17	5	9	11	55	34	46	50	34	44	15	37	13	2	29	16	16	17	20	9	54	12
0	32	30	55	34	7	23	21	23	26	28	3	9	36	38	41	9	42	48	51	91	44	17	39	23	9	81	16	15	14	13	5	81	81
-1	34	31	9	42	8	14	11	16	7	18	6	23	10	17	18	6	19	38	40	7	23	19	40	21	22	22	24	24	9	11	13	24	24
-2	7	33	25	38	3	9	3	14	12	13	2	29	16	16	17	20	21	22	22	8	14	36	22	13	12	11	34	34	10	9	7	24	24
-3	12	34	41	18	6	23	7	33	7	23	9	81	16	15	14	13	13	12	11	3	9	13	12	34	31	9	42	64	86	15	55	34	5
-4	13	36	52	39	2	29	12	34	8	14	23	24	28	31	33	3	9	36	26	6	23	9	36	3	33	3	9	36	63	89	9	42	42
-5	15	37	14	22	1	14	13	36	3	9	29	7	18	64	22	6	23	10	7	6	8	48	22	43	18	6	23	10	3	11	6	19	22
-6	17	39	21	40	9	11	15	37	6	23	14	22	26	30	7	2	29	16	24	6	46	50	34	44	8	2	29	16	35	36	30	29	31
-7	19	40	15	40	10	9	17	39	3	9	11	7	33	41	12	1	14	44	34	23	48	51	91	44	16	1	14	44	20	21	7	23	33
-8	36	22	4	41	7	33	19	40	26	10	9	12	34	41	13	36	33	35	36	38	40	20	3	9	36	23	26	28	3	9	36	38	41
-9	38	44	55	41	12	34	36	22	7	18	64	13	36	23	15	37	19	20	21	22	22	13	6	23	10	16	7	18	6	23	10	17	18
-10	40	36	7	42	13	36	5	81	3	9	36	15	37	29	17	39	14	13	13	12	11	3	2	29	16	14	12	13	2	29	16	16	17
-11	42	47	18	42	15	37	13	24	3	23	10	17	39	14	19	40	3	3	9	36	54	6	1	14	44	3	9	36	23	26	28	29	5
-12	44	48	22	43	17	39	22	1	2	29	16	19	40	11	36	22	24	6	23	10	81	2	21	23	26	28	31	33	7	24	1	14	48
-13	46	50	34	44	19	40	23	26	1	14	44	36	22	41	54	55	34	2	29	16	24	3	11	16	7	18	64	22	55	34	9	11	25
-14	48	51	91	44	36	22	16	7	18	6	23	10	17	18	81	9	42	1	14	44	28	3	9	36	38	41	43	46	9	42	10	9	1
-15	50	53	15	16	22	3	14	12	13	2	29	16	16	17	24	6	19	11	16	7	18	6	23	10	17	18	18	18	6	19	16	6	22
-16	51	27	5	45	54	15	3	54	10	11	24	20	4	89	6	55	4	2	14	12	13	2	29	16	16	17	18	19	5	20	20	4	33

Y - Value (row labels, left axis)

	X	Y
31	15	-14
32	-4	-9
33	1	6
34	-6	-9
35	5	7
36	-7	-5
37	4	8
38	14	10
39	5	-16
40	-11	16

A	B	C	D	E
9	93	33	45	83
51	1	36	41	43
91	63	14	26	57
71	37	91	50	64
98	9	15	15	88
67	11	25	9	28
57	9	23	15	39
19	85	92	12	43
86	2	27	76	22
45	12	88	29	10

Table Reading – Answer Key

1. C
2. A
3. E
4. E
5. B
6. D
7. B
8. C
9. A
10. D
11. E
12. C
13. A
14. B
15. D
16. D
17. B
18. A
19. E
20. B
21. C
22. A
23. D
24. A
25. B
26. C
27. D
28. E
29. B
30. C
31. A
32. C
33. A
34. E
35. B
36. D
37. C
38. A
39. B
40. E

Chapter 8: Aviation Information

While the Aviation Information (AI) subtest consists of 20 items (questions) and lasts just eight of the 210 minutes of AFOQT testing, the amount of knowledge required to obtain a good score is substantial. The AI subtest measures the applicant's knowledge of general aeronautical concepts and terminology.

There are excellent online and printed study resources, including the Federal Aviation Administration's 281-page "Airplane Flying Handbook" (in pdf format at faa.gov). Instructional videos about aeronautics, aircraft structures and instruments, airports, and other AI topics are on YouTube.

The following information and sample multiple choice questions will help the applicant prepare for the AI portion of the AFOQT, but it is suggested to supplement what you find here with other expert sources if you are serious about maximizing your score.

Types of aviation and aircraft categories

Since the early 20th century, two main types of aviation have developed: *civil* and *military*, both of which involve *fixed-wing* and *rotary-wing* aircraft. Fighter jets, bombers, airliners, and corporate jets are examples of the former, while the latter group includes helicopters, gyrocopters, and tilt-rotor flying machines.

An aircraft is a machine supported aloft by lift created by air flowing across *airfoil* surfaces, be they *wings* attached to an airplane's fuselage, a *propeller* rotated by gears connected to an engine drive shaft, or spinning helicopter *rotor blades*, or by *buoyancy*, as in the case of airships and hot air balloons.

In the United States, civilian aircraft are certified under the following categories: normal, utility, acrobatic, commuter, transport, manned free balloons, and special classes. Special Airworthiness Certificates are issued by the Federal Aviation Administration for the following categories: primary, restricted, multiple, limited, light-sport, experimental, special flight permit, and provisional.

Military aircraft are categorized by the mission they perform: air superiority, anti-submarine warfare, coastal and sea lane patrolling, electronic warfare, ground attack (close air support), interdiction, mid-air refueling, mine sweeping, reconnaissance, search and rescue, strategic bombing, surveillance, training, transport, and weather observation.

Aircraft structure and components

Fixed-wing aircraft – called airplanes, or informally, planes – have a fuselage, wings, and an empennage (tail). A nose section, including the cockpit and cabin comprise the *fuselage*. The *empennage* consists of a vertical stabilizer and an attached (hinged) *rudder* that can be moved left or right by the pilot via cockpit controls (pedals), and a horizontal *stabilizer* and hinged *elevator* that is also under the pilot's control and moves up and down. Some aircraft, like the U.S. Air Force's F-16 fighter jet, have an all-moving horizontal stabilizer-elevator called a *stabilator*.

The inboard portion of airplane wings have extendible sections called *flaps*, which are located along the trailing (aft) edge. They are used to increase the wing's surface area and deflect the airflow downward, thereby augmenting lift at reduced speeds. With flaps extended, planes can takeoff and land at a lower velocity, which requires less runway.

Some airplanes have leading-edge *slats*, which are also extended to maintain lift at relatively low airspeeds. Like flaps, slats help an airplane takeoff and land at a lower velocity, allowing for operations on shorter runways. The Air Force's C-17 strategic airlifter is an example of a military plane with slats and flaps.

On top of the wings of many turbine-powered aircraft are *spoilers*, hinged panels that move upward after landing and destroy the residual lift in order to put the plane's full weight on the landing gear and maximize tire friction on the runway, thereby enhancing deceleration.

High-performance airplanes often have one or more *air brakes* – also called *speed brakes* – to help decelerate the aircraft, and in flight, increase the rate of descent. For example, the USAF's F-15 fighter jet has a large airbrake on the top fuselage that extends after landing. Air brakes are not spoilers because they are not designed to destroy lift.

The main structural member inside each wing of an airplane is the *spar*, which runs the length of the wing. Larger wings usually have more than one spar to provide extra support. Shaped *ribs* are attached perpendicularly to the spar or spars in order to provide the wing with more structure and greater strength. A *skin* of aircraft aluminum (in most cases) is attached to the framework of spar(s) and ribs.

Airplanes that fly substantially below the speed of sound typically have wings that are *perpendicular* to the aircraft's longitudinal (nose-to-tail) axis. The wings of most jet planes are *swept* back to delay the drag associated with air compressibility at high subsonic speeds. Swept wings increase the performance of high performance airplanes.

Some military aircraft have a *delta wing* (shaped like a triangle) while others have *variable-geometry wings*. In the case of the latter, the pilot swings the wings forward to a position that is roughly perpendicular to the fuselage for takeoff and landing and flight at low airspeeds, and back when flying at high subsonic, transonic, and supersonic velocities. The Air Force's B-1B Lancer bomber is a variable-geometry airplane.

Toward the outer trailing edge of each wing is a hinged flight control surface called an *aileron* that moves up and down. Ailerons operate in a direction opposite to each other and control the plane's rolling motion around the longitudinal axis. Ailerons are used to perform banking turns.

A *trim tab* on the rear of the rudder, elevator, and one aileron (usually) act to change the aerodynamic load on the surface and reduce the need for constant pilot pressure on the control column (or joystick) and left and right pedal. Each trim tab is controlled by the pilot via a switch or wheel in the cockpit.

Regarding a source of thrust, most aircraft are powered by one or more *piston* or *turbine* engines. In terms of propulsion type, the latter group consists of *turboprop, turbojet*, and *turbofan*. Fighter aircraft have one turbojet engine or a pair of them, each equipped with an *afterburner*, which provides an increase in thrust above non-afterburner full throttle (called military power).

The pilot controls engine operation (start, ground idle, checks, throttle movement, reverse thrust, shutdown) via switches and levers in the cockpit. The number of engine controls corresponds to the number of engines. In single- and multi-engine planes with adjustable-pitch propellers, blade angle is also controlled from the cockpit via levers.

Reverse thrust is a feature of turboprop and many jet-powered aircraft, including airliners, aerial tankers, and transport planes. Reverse thrust is used after landing to shorten the ground roll, the runway distance required by the decelerating airplane. Turboprop reverse thrust involves the rotation of propeller blades (three to six, typically) to a blade angle that causes air to be forced forward (away from the plane), not backward over the wings and tail surfaces, as happens when the aircraft taxis and during takeoff, climb, cruise, descent, and landing.

Reverse thrust on jet aircraft is achieved by temporarily directing the engine exhaust forward. After landing, the pilot moves the reverse thrust levers on the cockpit throttle quadrant, which causes two rounded metallic sections on the back end of each engine – called buckets, or clamshell doors – to pneumatically move and come together. When deployed, they stop the engine exhaust from going aft and direct the hot airflow forward at an angle.

Another type of reverse thrust on some jet aircraft involve pivoting doors located roughly half way along the engine. After landing, the pilot moves the reverse thrust levers, which causes the doors (four on each engine) to open. As with the buckets/clamshell doors, the result is exhaust deflected forward, which increases aircraft deceleration greatly.

Most aircraft land on wheels – called *landing gear* – and many types of planes have retractable wheels. Wheel retraction results in less drag when the aircraft is airborne. Fixed- and rotary-wing aircraft equipped with *skis* are able to land and maneuver on surfaces covered with snow and/or ice.

Airplanes that takeoff and land on water have *floats* attached to supports that are connected to the fuselage, or a *boat-like hull* on the bottom of the fuselage. *Amphibious* aircraft can take off and land on both land and water due to retractable wheels.

Rotary-wing aircraft (the U.S. Air Force has two fleets of them) have a *fuselage, tail,* and *fin* (in most cases), and *landing gear* (e.g., skids, wheels, inflatable floats). The most common type of rotary-wing aircraft is the helicopter.

Aerodynamics forces
There are four main aerodynamic forces that act on an aircraft when it is airborne: weight, lift, thrust, and drag.

The aircraft and everything in it – pilots, passengers, fuel, cargo, etc. – have mass (weight). Because of the earth's gravitational pull, the combined mass of the aircraft and its contents acts downward. From a physics perspective, the total weight force is deemed to act through the aircraft's *center of gravity.*

Aerodynamic loads associated with flight maneuvers and air turbulence affect the aircraft's weight. Whenever an aircraft flies a curved flight path at a certain altitude, the load factor (force of gravity, or "G") exerted on the airfoils (e.g., wings, rotor blades) is greater than the aircraft's total weight.

When a pilot turns an aircraft by banking (rolling) left or right, the amount of "G" increases. Banking further in order to turn more tightly causes the machine's effective weight ("G" loading) to increase more. An airplane banked 30 degrees weighs an additional 16 percent, but at 60 degrees of bank – a very steep turn – it weighs twice as much as it does in straight and level flight in smooth air.

Gusts produced by turbulent air can quickly impose aerodynamic forces that also increase the aircraft's "G" (weight) force.

Lift is the force that counteracts an aircraft's weight and causes the machine to rise into the air and stay aloft. Lift is produced by airfoils that move through the air at a speed sufficient to create a pressure differential between the two surfaces and a resulting upward force. Lift acts perpendicular to the direction of flight through the airfoil's *center of pressure,* or *center of lift.*

Thrust is an aircraft's forward force, which is created by one or more engines (the largest plane in the world, the Antonov An-225 Mriya, has six huge turbofan jet engines). In propeller-driven airplanes and rotary-wing aircraft, the power output of the engine(s) is transformed into rotary motion via one or more transmissions (gear boxes). Generally, thrust acts parallel to the aircraft's longitudinal axis.

Drag opposes thrust; it is a rearward-acting force caused by airflow passing over the aircraft's structure and becoming disrupted. Drag acts parallel to the *relative wind* and is a function of aircraft shape and size, its velocity and angle (inclination) in relation to airflow, and the air's mass, viscosity, and compressibility.

An aircraft's *total drag* is the sum of its *profile drag, induced drag,* and *parasite drag.* When total drag is the lowest, the aircraft experiences its maximum endurance (in straight and level flight), best rate of climb, and for helicopters, minimum rate-of-descent speed for autorotation.

Profile drag is the sum of *form drag* and *skin friction.* Form drag varies with air pressure around the aircraft and its cross-sectional shape. Skin friction is a function of the roughness of the outer surface of an aircraft (due to surface imperfections, protruding rivet heads, etc.).

Induced drag is a product of lift; stationary aircraft generate no such drag. However, as lift is created during acceleration along the runway or strip (in the case of airplanes) or increased rotor rpm and angle of attack (in the case of helicopters), the resulting pressure differential between the airfoil surfaces creates an air vortex at the wing's or rotor blade's tip. The vortex moves parallel to the aircraft's longitudinal axis and expands in diameter with distance from the airfoil. The effect of each vortex is a retarding aerodynamic force called induced drag.

Parts of an aircraft that do not contribute to the production of lift create *parasite drag* when the machine is moving. On airplanes, such components include the nose section and fuselage, landing gear, engine pylons and cowlings, vertical stabilizer, and rudder. On helicopters, the cockpit and cabin, landing skids or wheels, externally mounted engines (on some types), tail boom, and fin create parasite drag.

Scientific principles of relevance to aeronautics
Bernoulli's Principle
In 1738, a Swiss scientist named Daniel Bernoulli published a book entitled *Hydrodynamica* in which he explained that an increase of the inviscid flow of a fluid (i.e., the flow of an ideal, zero-viscosity liquid or gas) resulted in a decrease of static pressure exerted by the fluid. Bernoulli's famous equation is $P + \frac{1}{2}\rho v^2$ = a constant, where P = pressure (a force exerted divided by the area exerted upon); ρ (the Greek letter "rho") = the fluid's density; and v = the fluid's velocity.

The constant in Bernoulli's formula is derived from the scientific principle that energy cannot be created or destroyed – only its form can be changed – and a system's total energy does not increase or decrease.

Conservation laws – conservation of energy

Bernoulli's Principle is based on the conservation of energy, which says that in a steady flow the sum of all forms of mechanical energy – a fluid's potential energy plus its kinetic energy – along a streamline (e.g., a tube) is the same at all points. Thus, greater fluid flow rate (a higher speed) results in increased kinetic energy and dynamic pressure and reduced potential energy and static pressure.

An aircraft filled with fuel has a finite amount of energy. Through combustion in the engine, the fuel's heat energy is converted to kinetic energy, either in the form of jet exhaust or at least one rotating propeller (many types of planes have two or more propellers). Spinning helicopter rotor blades also have kinetic energy.

If an aircraft is airborne when it runs out of fuel, it still has potential energy as a function of its height above the ground. As the pilot noses down to keep air flowing over the airfoils (wings, rotor blades) and create lift, the aircraft's potential energy is transformed into kinetic energy.

Combining Bernoulli's Principle with the fact that airfoils provide lift at varying speeds during different phases of flight (takeoff, climb, cruise, descent, landing), the lift produced in a given instant can be calculated using the following equation: $L = \frac{1}{2}\rho v^2 A C_l$, where L = the lift force, $\frac{1}{2}\rho v^2$ was previously explained, A = the airfoil's area (length multiplied by width), and C_l is the coefficient of lift of the airfoil.

Pilots need to remember that the lifting force on their aircraft is proportional to the density (ρ) of air through which they fly (higher altitude = less dense air), the aircraft's speed, and airfoil angle of attack (AOA).

Conservation of mass

In the scientific field of fluid dynamics, it has been established that a fluid's mass cannot be created or destroyed within a flow of interest (e.g., airflow in sub-zero temperature conditions). Conservation of mass is mathematically expressed as the mass continuity equation.

Conservation of momentum

Momentum, an object's mass times its velocity, cannot be created or destroyed. However, it can be changed through an applied force. Because it involves magnitude and direction, momentum is a vector quantity. It is conserved in all three directions (longitudinally, laterally, and in terms of yaw) simultaneously.

Venturi Effect

To understand how a machine with airfoils can take to the air and remain airborne, we need to examine a phenomenon called the Venturi Effect. In the late 18th century, an Italian physicist, Giovanni Battista Venturi, conducted experiments with a pump and an unusual tube. The diameter of one end of the tube was constant and the circumference of the tube's central portion was smaller. Downstream from the bottleneck, the tube's diameter increased. It was as though someone had squeezed the center of the tube, creating a constriction.

Venturi noticed that as fluids moved through the tube, the flow rate increased (accelerated) and the force (static pressure) against the tube's surface decreased as the diameter became smaller. The opposite phenomenon – reduced flow rate (deceleration) and greater static pressure – happened as the tube diameter downstream of the constriction widened. Venturi published his findings in 1797 and the effect that he observed, measured, and wrote about became associated with his name. It has certainly been integral to aviation since the advent of gliding centuries ago.

If a Venturi tube is cut in half longitudinally, the curvature of the tube wall would look similar to that of an airplane wing's upper surface or the top of helicopter rotor blades. A moving airfoil "slices" the air, forcing molecules to travel along one side or the other. Those moving across the curved side have to travel a greater distance to reach the trailing edge than those moving across the relatively flat side. Consequently, the air molecules moving across the curved surface accelerate, as they did in Venturi's tube, and the static pressure drops.

Because pressure flows from high to low, the static pressure differential experienced between an airfoil's two sides imposes an aerodynamic force acting from the high-pressure (flat) surface to the low-pressure (curved) side. When acting upward, the force is called lift.

Newton's First Law of Motion
A stationary object remains at rest and an object in motion continues to move at the same rate (speed) and in the same direction unless acted upon by a force.

Newton's Second Law of Motion
Acceleration results from a force being applied to an object. The heavier the body, the greater the amount of force needed to accelerate it.

Newton's Third Law of Motion
Sir Isaac Newton (1642–1727) was a brilliant English physicist and mathematician who formulated universal laws of motion, including his third, which said that for every action there is an equal and opposite reaction. Consequently, when an airfoil is deflected up, the airstream flowing over the airfoil reacts by moving downward. Also, when exhaust from jet engines is directed backward the resulting reactive force on the engines, engine pylons, wings, and the rest of the airplane is forward.

Aircraft axes (pronounced "axe-eez")

Aircraft motion occurs around three axes – longitudinal, lateral, and yaw – that go through the machine's center of gravity. The longitudinal axis has been explained; an aircraft rolls around it. The lateral axis is horizontal and perpendicular to the longitudinal axis; on basic airplane images it is depicted as a straight line going through one wingtip to the other. The yaw axis is vertical; an aircraft is said to yaw (rotate) around it.

Flight control

When lift = weight and thrust = drag, the aircraft is either stationary on the ground, or aloft in straight-and-level, unaccelerated flight. To make an aircraft accelerate requires an increase in thrust, which the pilot controls from the cockpit by moving one or more throttle controls (on piston aircraft) or power lever(s) on turbine aircraft.

During takeoff, the airplane accelerates along the runway, strip, or body of water and reaches a speed at which it is going fast enough for the wings to generate lift. To make the plane go skyward, the pilot pulls back on the control column or joystick, which causes (via cables in lighter, smaller aircraft, or a hydraulic system in larger, heavier planes) the hinged elevator to tilt up.

The inclined elevator forces air passing over it to deflect up, resulting in a downward reaction force on the airplane's tail. Because the elevator is aft of the aircraft's center of gravity, as the tail drops the nose of the plane rises and the aircraft climbs.

To make the plane descend, the opposite happens.

To turn an airplane, the pilot moves the control wheel or joystick to the left or right (as desired) to change the machine's direction. The aileron on the wing on the plane's side to where the pilot wants to turn rises into the airstream, forcing the flow upward and reducing the lift produced by the outer portion of the wing where the aileron is located. The result is a wing that drops, rolling (banking) the aircraft.

On the opposite side of the airplane, the aileron moves down into the airstream, deflecting the airflow downward and creating more lift, which causes the wing to rise. With one wing down and the opposite wing up, the airplane rolls to the left or right.

For a coordinated banked turn, the pilot needs to move the aircraft's rudder to the side of the turn (left, right), which is accomplished by pushing on the corresponding pedal in front of him or her. As the pilot does so, the airflow passing over the moved rudder is deflected to the left or right, corresponding to the pushed pedal. The reactive force against the vertical stabilizer is opposite (right, left) and because the tail is aft of the plane's center of gravity, the nose yaws around the yaw axis in the opposite direction (left, right).

Additional aviation terms and definitions

Airfoil: A wing or helicopter blade that generates more lift than drag as air flows over its upper and lower surfaces. A propeller is also an airfoil. Airfoils are carefully designed and can be made of non-metallic materials such as composites.

Angle of attack: The angle between the chord line of an airfoil and its direction of motion relative to the air (i.e., the relative wind). AOA is an aerodynamic angle.

Angle of incidence: In the context of fixed-wing airplanes, the angle of incidence is the inclination of the wing or tail surface attached to the fuselage relative to an imaginary line that is parallel to the aircraft's longitudinal axis.

Anhedral angle: The downward angle of an airplane's wings and tailplane from the horizontal is called the anhedral angle, or negative dihedral angle.

Attitude: An aircraft's position relative to its three axes and a reference such as the earth's horizon.

Center of gravity (CG): An aircraft's center of mass, the theoretical point through which the entire weight of the machine is assumed to be concentrated.

Chord: The distance between the leading and trailing edges along the chord line is an airfoil's chord. In the case of a tapered airfoil, as viewed from above, the chord at its tip will be different than at its root. Average chord describes the average distance.

Chord line: An imaginary straight line from the airfoil's leading (front) edge to its trailing (aft) edge.

Constant speed propeller: A controllable-pitch propeller whose angle is automatically changed in flight by a governor in order to maintain a constant number of revolutions per minute (rpm) despite changing aerodynamic loads.

Controllability: A measure of an aircraft's response relative to flight control inputs from the pilot.

Controllable pitch propeller: A propeller that can be varied in terms of its blade angle by the pilot via a control in the cockpit.

Coordinated flight: When the pilot applies flight and power control inputs to prevent slipping or skidding during any aircraft maneuver, the flight is said to be coordinated.

Critical angle of attack: The angle of attack at which an airfoil stalls (loses lift) regardless of the aircraft's airspeed, attitude, or weight.

Dihedral angle: The upward angle of an airplane's wings and tailplane from the horizontal.

163

Dihedral effect: The amount of roll moment produced per degree of sideslip is called dihedral effect, which is crucial in terms of an aircraft's rolling stability about its longitudinal axis.

Directional stability: An aircraft's initial tendency about its yaw (vertical) axis. When an aircraft is disturbed yaw-wise from its equilibrium state due to a gust, for example, and returns to that state (i.e., aligned with the relative wind) because of the aerodynamic effect of the vertical stabilizer, it is said to be directionally stable.

Downwash: Air that is deflected perpendicular to an airfoil's motion.

Drag coefficient: A dimensionless quantity that represents the drag generated by an airfoil of a particular design.

Drag curve: A constructed image of the amount of aircraft drag at different airspeeds.

Dynamic stability: Describes the tendency of an aircraft after it has been disturbed from straight-and-level flight to restore the aircraft to its original condition of flying straight and level by developing corrective forces and moments.

Equilibrium: In the context of aviation, equilibrium is an aircraft's state when all opposing forces acting on it are balanced, resulting in unaccelerated flight at a constant altitude.

Feathering propeller: A controllable-pitch propeller that can be rotated sufficiently by the pilot (via a control lever in the cockpit connected to a governor in the propeller hub) so that the blade angle is parallel to the line of flight, thereby minimizing propeller drag.

Forward slip: A pilot-controlled maneuver where the aircraft's longitudinal axis is inclined to its flightpath.

Glide ratio: The ratio between altitude lost and distance traversed during non-powered flight (e.g., following an engine failure, in a sailplane).

Glidepath: An aircraft path's across the ground while approaching to land.

Gross weight: An aircraft's total weight when it is fully loaded with aircrew, fuel, oil, passengers and/or cargo (if applicable), weapons, etc.

Gyroscopic precession: The attribute of rotating bodies to manifest movement ninety degrees in the direction of rotation from the point where a force is applied to the spinning body.

Heading: The direction in which the aircraft's nose is pointed.

Inertia: A body's opposition to a change of motion.

Internal combustion engine: A mechanical device that produces power from expanding hot gases created by burning a fuel-air mixture within the device.

Lateral stability (rolling): An aircraft's initial tendency relative to its longitudinal axis after being disturbed, its designed quality to return to level flight following a disturbance such as a gust that causes one of the aircraft's wings to drop.

Lift coefficient: A dimensionless quantity that represents the lift generated by an airfoil of a particular design.

Lift/drag ratio: A number that represents an airfoil's efficiency, the ratio of the lift coefficient to the drag coefficient for a specific angle of attack.

Lift-off: The act of rising from the earth as a result of airfoils lifting the aircraft above the ground.

Load factor: The ratio of load supported by an aircraft's lift-generating airfoils (wings, main rotor blades) to the aircraft's actual weight, including the mass of its contents. Load factor is also known as G-loading ("G" means gravity).

Longitudinal stability: An aircraft's initial tendency relative to its lateral axis after being disturbed, its designed quality to return to its trimmed angle of attack after being disrupted due to a wind gust or other factor.

Maneuverability: An aircraft's ability to change directions in three axes along its flightpath and withstand the associated aerodynamic forces.

Mean camber line: An imaginary line between the leading and trailing edges and halfway between the airfoil's upper (curved) and lower (flat) surfaces.

Minimum drag speed (L/DMAX): The point on the total drag curve where total drag is minimized and lift is maximized (i.e., where the lift-to-drag ratio is greatest).

Nacelle: An enclosure made of metal or another durable material that covers an aircraft engine.

Non-symmetrical airfoil (cambered): When one surface of an airfoil has a specific curvature that the opposite side does not, the airfoil is described as non-symmetrical, or cambered. The advantage of a non-symmetrical wing, for example, is that it produces lift at an AOA of zero degrees (as long as airflow is moving past the blade). Moreover, the lift-to-drag ratio and stall characteristics of a cambered airfoil are better than those of a symmetrical airfoil. Its disadvantages are center of the pressure movement chord-wise by as much as one-fifth the chord line distance, which causes undesirable airfoil torsion, and greater production costs.

Normal category: An airplane intended for non-acrobatic operation that seats a maximum of nine passengers and has a certificated takeoff weight of 12,500 pounds or less.

Payload: In the context of aviation, the weight of an aircraft's occupants, cargo, and baggage.

P-factor (precession factor): A propeller-driven aircraft's tendency to yaw to the left when the propeller rotates clockwise (as seen by the pilot) because the descending propeller blade on the right produces more thrust than the ascending blade on the left. If the propeller rotated counter-clockwise, the yaw tendency would be to the right.

Piston engine: Also known as a reciprocating engine, it is a heat engine that uses one or more pistons to convert pressure created by expanding, hot gases resulting from a combusted fuel-air mixture, or steam pressure, into a rotating motion.

Pitch: An airplane's rotation about its lateral axis, or the angle of a propeller blade as measured from the vertical plane of rotation.

Power lever: The cockpit lever connected to a turbine engine's fuel control unit, which changes the amount of fuel entering the combustion chambers.

Powerplant: An engine and its accessories (e.g., starter-generator, tachometer drive) and the attached propeller (usually via a gearbox).

Propeller blade angle: The angle between the chord of an airplane propeller blade and the propeller's plane of rotation.

Propeller lever: The cockpit control that controls propeller speed and angle.

Propeller slipstream: Air accelerated behind a spinning propeller.

Propeller: A relatively long and narrow blade-like device that produces thrust when it rotates rapidly. In aviation, the term typically includes not only the propeller blades but also the hub and other components that make up the propeller system.

Rate of turn: The rate of a turn expressed in degrees per second.

Reciprocating engine: An engine that converts heat energy created by combusted fuel mixed with air into reciprocating piston movement, which in turn is converted into a rotary motion via a crankshaft.

Reduction gear: A gear or set of gears that turns a propeller at a speed slower than that of the engine.

Relative wind: The direction of airflow relative to an airfoil, a stream of air parallel and opposite to an aircraft's flightpath.

Ruddervator: Two control surfaces on an aircraft's tail that form a "V". When moved together via the control wheel or joystick in the cockpit, the surfaces act as elevators. When the pilot presses his or her foot against one rudder pedal or the other, the ruddervator acts like a conventional plane's rudder.

Sideslip: A flight maneuver controlled by the pilot that involves the airplane's longitudinal axis remaining parallel to the original flightpath, but the aircraft no longer flies forward, as in normal flight. Instead, the horizontal lift component causes the plane to move laterally toward the low wing.

Skid: A flight condition during a turn where the airplane's tail follows a path outside of the path of the aircraft's nose.

Slip: A maneuver used by pilots to increase an aircraft's rate of descent or reduce its airspeed, and to compensate for a crosswind during landing. An unintentional slip also occurs when a pilot does not fly the aircraft in a coordinated manner.

Stability: An aircraft's inherent tendency to return to its original flightpath after a force such as a wind gust disrupts its equilibrium. Aeronautical engineers design most aircraft to be aerodynamically stable.

Stall: A rapid decrease in lift caused by an excessive angle of attack and airflow separating from an airfoil's upper surface. An aircraft can stall at any pitch attitude or airspeed.

Standard-rate turn: A rate of turn of three degrees per second.

Subsonic: Speed below the speed of sound, which varies with altitude.

Supersonic: Speed in excess of the speed of sound, which varies with altitude.

Swept wing: A wing planform involving the tips being further back than the wing root.

Symmetrical airfoil: When an airfoil has identical upper and lower surfaces, it is symmetrical and produces no lift at an AOA of zero degrees. The wings of very high performance aircraft tend to be symmetrical.

Taxiway lights: Blue lights installed at taxiway edges.

Taxiway turnoff lights: Green lights installed level with the taxiway.

Throttle: A mechanical device that meters the amount of fuel-air mixture fed to the engine.

Thrust line: An imaginary line through the center of an airplane's propeller hub and perpendicular to the propeller's plane of rotation, or through the center of each jet engine.

Total aerodynamic force (TAF): Two components comprise the total aerodynamic force: lift and drag. The amount of lift and drag produced by an airfoil are primarily determined by its shape and area.

Torque: A propeller-driven airplane's tendency to roll in the opposite direction of the propeller's rotation. Some multi-engine airplanes have propellers that rotate in opposite directions to eliminate the torque effect.

Trailing edge: The aft part of an airfoil where air that was separated as it hit the wing's front edge and was forced over the upper and lower surfaces comes together.

Transonic: At the speed of sound, which varies with altitude.

Trim tab: A small, hinged control surface on a larger control surface (e.g., aileron, rudder, elevator) that can be adjusted in flight to a position that balances the aerodynamic forces. In still air, a trimmed aircraft in flight requires no control inputs from the pilot to remain straight and level.

T-tail: The description for an airplane's tail involving the horizontal stabilizer mounted on the top of the vertical stabilizer.

Turbulence: The unsteady flow of a fluid (e.g., air).

Utility category: An airplane intended for limited-acrobatic operation that seats a maximum of nine passengers and has a certificated takeoff weight of 12,500 pounds or less.

Vector: A force applied in a certain direction. Depicted visually, a vector shows the force's magnitude and direction.

Velocity: The rate of movement (e.g., miles per hour, knots) in a certain direction.

Vertical stability: An aircraft's designed, inherent behavior relative to its vertical axis, its tendency to return to its former heading after being disturbed by a wind gust or other disruptive force. Also called yawing or directional stability.

V-tail: A design involving two slanted tail surfaces that aerodynamically behave similar to a conventional elevator and rudder, i.e., as horizontal and vertical stabilizers.

Wing: An airfoil attached to a fuselage that creates a lifting force when the aircraft has reached a certain speed.

Wing area: A wing's total surface, including its control surfaces, and winglets, if so equipped.

Wing in ground effect (WIG): When an aircraft flies at a very low altitude, one roughly equal to its wing span, it experiences WIG. The effect increases as the airplane descends closer to the surface (runway, land, water) and supports the aircraft on a cushion of air best at an altitude of one half the wing span.

Winglet: A surface installed on a wingtip that is angled to the wing and improves its efficiency by smoothing the airflow across the upper wing near the tip and reducing induced drag. Winglets improve an aircraft's lift-to-drag ratio.

Wing span: The maximum distance between wingtips.

Wingtip vortices: A spinning mass of air generated at a wing's tip created by outward-flowing high pressure air from underneath the wing meeting inward-flowing low air pressure on the wing's upper surface. The intensity of a wing vortex – also referred to as wake turbulence – is dependent on an airplane's weight, speed, and configuration.

Wing twist: A wing design feature that improves the effectiveness of aileron control at high angles of attack during an approach to a stall.

Aviation Information – Practice Test Questions

1. A propeller-driven airplane:

    A. Is part of the rotary class of aircraft (because the propeller spins).
    B. Has a reciprocating engine only.
    C. Is a fixed-wing aircraft.
    D. Has a reverse thrust feature in all types of military and civilian aircraft.

2. Military aircraft are categorized:

    A. As normal, utility, acrobatic, special mission, or transport.
    B. Based on the mission they perform.
    C. In accordance with Department of Defense directives since 1947.
    D. None of the above.

3. A propeller is:

    A. An airfoil.
    B. A secondary source of thrust.
    C. Part of a balanced thrust system involving only 2, 4, or 6 blades.
    D. An extendible thrust-generation device used at high altitudes.

4. The four main forces acting on an aircraft are:

    A. Deflection, exponential thrust, torque, and the total mass vector modified by the earth's Coriolis Effect.
    B.   Lift, weight, thrust, and drag.
    C.   Wind gusts, gravity, pressure differentials, and tangential rotation.
    D.   All of the above.

5. Turbine aircraft:

    A. Have a propeller source of thrust in some cases.
    B. Never have a propeller source of thrust (only jets are turbine aircraft).
    C. Have a turbocharged engine.
    D. Utilize a ducted wind fan that spins an electrical generator.

6. The empennage consists of:

   A. A vertical stabilizer and a hinged rudder.
   B. The back half of the fuselage and the tailplane.
   C. The "T" tail and nacelle.
   D. The ruddervator and associated hydraulic system.

7. Flaps are used:

   A. To decrease Dutch roll.
   B. To eliminate wingtip vortices.
   C. During takeoff only.
   D. None of the above.

8. Hinged wing panels that move upward and destroy lift after landing are called:

   A. Air brakes.
   B. Spoilers.
   C. Winglets.
   D. Vertical stabilizers.

9. Swept back wings:

   A.   Delay the drag associated with air compressibility at approach speeds.
   B.   Delay the drag associated with air compressibility at low subsonic speeds.
   C.   Delay the drag associated with air compressibility at high subsonic speeds.
   D.   All of the above.

10. Profile drag is the sum of:

    A. Skin friction and form drag.
    B. Skin friction and induced drag.
    C. Form drag and supplementary drag.
    D. Parasite drag and vortex drag.

11. Slats are located:

    A. Along the horizontal stabilizer's leading edge.
    B. Along the leading edge of both wings and the horizontal stabilizer.
    C. Along the trailing edge of the right aileron.
    D. Along the leading edge of both wings.

12. The laws of conservation that pertain to aircraft are:

    A. The law of conservation of mass, kinetic energy, and fluid flow.
    B. The law of conservation of mass, torque, and potential energy.
    C. The law of conservation of weight, thrust, and lift.
    D. The law of conservation of mass, energy, and momentum.

13. According to 18th century Swiss scientist Daniel Bernoulli:

    A. Accelerated fluid flow results in a decrease of dynamic pressure.
    B. Accelerated fluid flow results in a decrease of static pressure.
    C. Accelerated fluid flow results in an increase of total system energy.
    D. All of the above.

14. Lift produced by an airfoil is proportional to:

    A. The rate of air compressibility and the coefficients of lift and drag.
    B. The angle of airflow deflection, the relative wind's vertical vector component, and the reduction of induced drag as the aircraft accelerates.
    C. Air density, aircraft speed, wing area, and airfoil shape.
    D. None of the above.

15. The angle of attack is:

    A. The chord line's orientation in relation to the aircraft's longitudinal axis.
    B. The acute angle between the chord line of an airfoil and the relative wind.
    C. The sum of the angle of incidence of the wings and tailplane.
    D. The aircraft's downward inclination when shooting targets on the ground.

16. Parasite drag is produced by:

    A. Extended slats and flaps.
    B. Aircraft parts that do not contribute to producing lift.
    C. Improperly set trim tabs.
    D. A difference in propeller rpm on multi-engine airplanes.

17. Thrust opposes:

    A. Drag.
    B. Rudder deflection.
    C. Gyroscopic precession.
    D. Gravity.

18. Ailerons move:

    A. In opposing directions.
    B. Downward.
    C. Up or down, depending on the rudder pedal pushed by the pilot.
    D. None of the above.

19. The main types of turbine propulsion are:

    A. Axial and centrifugal flow.
    B. Non-afterburning, after-burning, and turbocharged.
    C. Turbofan, turbojet, and turboprop.
    D. Turbocharged, turbofan, and ramjet.

20. An aircraft's three axes are:

    A. Longitudinal, gyroscopic, and lateral.
    B. Directional, pitch, and gyroscopic.
    C. Yaw, longitudinal, and lateral.
    D. Deflectional, lateral, and induced.

21. Increasing an aircraft's bank in a coordinated turn, _____ its _____ and _____:

    A. increases; angle of attack; lift.
    B. increases; weight (due to "G" loading); rate of turn.
    C. decreases; angle of attack; drag.
    D. decreases; weight (due to "G" loading); angle of attack.

22. When the pilot pulls back on the control column or joystick:

A. The elevator moves up.
B. The elevator moves down.
C. The left aileron moves down.
D. None of the above.

23. To move the rudder to the right, the pilot:

A. Turns the control wheel to the right.
B. Pulls back on the right power lever.
C. Moves the right throttle lever forward while pushing the right pedal.
D. Pushes the right pedal.

24. From a physics perspective, an aircraft's total weight force is deemed to act through the _____:

A. Weight and balance reference datum.
B. Center of pressure.
C. Center of gravity.
D. Center of momentum.

25. An air vortex at the wingtip creates:

A. Form drag.
B. Profile drag.
C. Induced drag.
D. Parasite drag.

26. Momentum is:

A. An object's mass times its velocity squared.
B. An object's mass times its velocity.
C. An object's weight plus one-half of its velocity squared.
D. An object's forward velocity times its coefficient of lift.

27. When exhaust from jet engines is directed backward, the resulting reactive force on the airplane is _____ :

   A. Forward.
   B. Forward but deflected downward due to the angle of incidence.
   C. Forward but reduced because of the inclined component of the total drag vector.
   D. Determined only by using the conservation of energy equation.

28. Coordinated flight is defined as:

   A. The pilot applying control inputs that are suitable for the aircraft's density altitude.
   B. The pilot applying flight and power control inputs to prevent slipping or skidding during any aircraft maneuver.
   C. The pilot reducing back pressure on the control column or joystick while turning in the opposite direction of the horizontal component of total drag.
   D. All of the above.

29. Anhedral angle is the _____ angle of an airplane's wings and tailplane from the horizontal:

   A. Upward.
   B. Obtuse.
   C. Downward.
   D. Isoceles.

30. Minimum drag speed corresponds to:

   A. The point on the total drag curve where the thrust-to-drag ratio is least.
   B. The point on the total drag curve where the drag-to-mass ratio is least.
   C. The point on the total drag curve where the lift-to-drag ratio is greatest.
   D. The point on the total drag curve where the lift-to-weight ratio is least.

31. An airfoil stalls when:

   A. The downward component of the wingtip vortices are greater than the lift produced by increasing the angle of attack.
   B. There is a rapid decrease in lift caused by an excessive angle of attack and airflow separating from an airfoil's upper surface.
   C. The pilot has mistakenly extended the flaps while flying above the maneuvering airspeed (V_a) .
   D. The pilot deploys the air brakes.

32. A propeller with a blade angle that can be changed by the pilot is called a _____ propeller.

    A. dynamic
    B. rotational
    C. reverse thrust
    D. controllable

33. The attribute of rotating bodies to manifest movement ninety degrees in the direction of rotation from the point where a force is applied to the spinning body is called:

    A. Rotational precession.
    B. Dynamic precession.
    C. Induced precession.
    D. Gyroscopic precession.

34. An aircraft's initial tendency relative to its longitudinal axis after being disturbed and dropping a wing to return to level flight is known as:

    A. Lateral stability.
    B. Longitudinal stability.
    C. Directional stability.
    D. None of the above.

35. An imaginary line from an airfoil's leading edge to its trailing edge that is halfway between the airfoil's upper and lower surfaces is the:

    A. Mean camber line.
    B. Chord line.
    C. Angle of incidence.
    D. Elevator inclination line.

36. When one surface of an airfoil has a specific curvature that the opposite side does not have, the airfoil is described as:

    A. Non-cambered.
    B. Deflected.
    C. Non-symmetrical.
    D. Laterally torqued.

37. The phenomenon of a propeller-driven aircraft's tendency to yaw to the left when the propeller rotates clockwise (as seen by the pilot) because the descending propeller blade on the right produces more thrust than the ascending blade on the left is known as:

A. Asymmetric thrust.
B. Rotational precession.
C. P-factor (precession factor).
D. Directional instability.

38. Airflow parallel and opposite to an aircraft's flightpath is called the:

A. Relative wind.
B. Longitudinal wind.
C. Dynamic wind.
D. None of the above.

39. The speed of sound varies with:

A. Angle of attack.
B. Angle of inclination.
C. Induced drag.
D. Altitude.

40. A propeller-driven airplane tends to roll in the opposite direction of the propeller's rotation because of:

A. The induced plane of rotation.
B. Tangential drag.
C. Torque.
D. Angular momentum.

Aviation Information – Practice Test Answer Key

1. C		21. B	
2. B		22. A	
3. A		23. D	
4. B		24. C	
5. A		25. C	
6. A		26. B	
7. D		27. A	
8. B		28. B	
9. C		29. C	
10. A		30. C	
11. D		31. B	
12. D		32. D	
13. B		33. D	
14. C		34. A	
15. B		35. A	
16. B		36. C	
17. A		37. C	
18. A		38. A	
19. C		39. D	
20. C		40. C	

Chapter 9: General Science

The AFOQT General Science test measures your knowledge of the life sciences (plant and animal biology, human physiology), the earth and space sciences (geology, meteorology, oceanography, astronomy), and the physical sciences (physics and chemistry). You'll be asked 20 questions with a 10-minute time limit. Don't panic! You only need to know those basics learned through about the 11th grade. Of course, you aren't going to be able to cover eleven years of schooling in one book – but this chapter will refresh your memory on those fundamental principles of science required, ensuring that you do well. This is a long chapter since there are so many different aspects that each have to be covered. Here's a breakdown of this chapter:

LIFE SCIENCES:
1. **General Biology (starts on page 182)**
   - Basics of Life
   - Classification of Organisms
   - Microorganisms
   - Animals
   - Plants
   - Ecology

2. **General Physiology (starts on page 210)**
   - Cells, Tissues, and Organs
   - Reproduction
   - Heredity
   - Systems of the Body (Digestive, Skeletal, etc)

PHYSICAL SCIENCES:
1. **Chemistry (starts on page 244)**
   - Elements, Compounds, and Mixtures
   - States of Matter
   - Periodic Table and Chemical Bonds
   - Acids and Bases

2. **Physics (starts on page 258)**
   - Motion, Thermal Physics, Heat Transfer, and Wave Motion and Magnetism

EARTH AND SPACE SCIENCES:
1. **Geology (starts on page 265)**
   - Earth's Structure, The Hydrologic Cycle, and Tides

2. **Meteorology (starts on page 271)**
   - Atmosphere and Clouds

3. **Astronomy (starts on page 279)**
   - Our Solar System

General Biology

This section covers the basics of biology, from the building blocks of life, to the fundamentals of biological chemistry and the classification of organisms.

BASICS OF LIFE

We began learning the difference between living (**animate**) beings and nonliving (**inanimate**) objects from an early age. Living organisms and inanimate objects are all composed of **atoms** from elements. Those atoms are arranged into groups called **molecules**, which serve as the building blocks of everything in existence (as we know it). Molecular interactions are what determine whether something is classified as animate or inanimate. The following is a list of the most commonly-found elements found in the molecules of animate beings:

1. Oxygen
2. Chlorine
3. Carbon
4. Nitrogen
5. Sodium
6. Calcium
7. Magnesium
8. Phosphorous
9. Iodine
10. Iron
11. Sulfur
12. Hydrogen
13. Potassium

Another way to describe living and nonliving things is through the terms **organic** and **inorganic.**

- **Organic molecules** are from living organisms. Organic molecules contain **carbon-hydrogen bonds**.

- **Inorganic molecules** come from non-living resources. They do not contain carbon-hydrogen bonds.

There are four major classes of organic molecules:
1. **Carbohydrates.**
2. **Lipids.**
3. **Proteins.**
4. **Nucleic acids**.

Carbohydrates consist of only hydrogen, oxygen, and carbon atoms. They are the most abundant single class of organic substances found in nature. Carbohydrate molecules provide many basic necessities such as: fiber, vitamins, and minerals; structural components for organisms, especially plants; and, perhaps most importantly, energy. Our bodies break down carbohydrates to make **glucose**: a sugar used to produce that energy which our bodies need in order to operate. Brain cells are exclusively dependent upon a constant source of glucose molecules.

There are two kinds of carbohydrates: simple and complex. **Simple carbohydrates** can be absorbed directly through the cell, and therefore enter the blood stream very quickly. We consume simple carbohydrates in dairy products, fruits, and other sugary foods.

Complex carbohydrates consist of a chain of simple sugars which, over time, our bodies break down into simple sugars (which are also referred to as stored energy.) **Glycogen** is the storage form of glucose in human and animal cells. Complex carbohydrates come from starches like cereal, bread, beans, potatoes, and starchy vegetables.

Lipids, commonly known as fats, are molecules with two functions:

1. They are stored as an energy reserve.

2. They provide a protective cushion for vital organs.

In addition to those two functions, lipids also combine with other molecules to form essential compounds, such as **phospholipids,** which form the membranes around cells. Lipids also combine with other molecules to create naturally-occurring **steroid** hormones, like the hormones estrogen and testosterone.

Proteins are large molecules which our bodies' cells need in order to function properly. Consisting of **amino acids,** proteins aid in maintaining and creating many aspects of our cells: cellular structure, function, and regulation, to name a few. Proteins also work as neurotransmitters and carriers of oxygen in the blood (hemoglobin).

Without protein, our tissues and organs could not exist. Our muscles bones, skin, and many other parts of the body contain significant amounts of protein. **Enzymes**, hormones, and antibodies are proteins.

Enzymes
When heat is applied, chemical reactions are typically sped up. However, the amount of heat required to speed up reactions could be potentially harmful (even fatal) to living organisms. Instead, our bodies use molecules called enzymes to bring reactants closer together, causing them to form a new compound. Thus, the whole reaction rate is increased without heat. Even better – the enzymes are not consumed during the reaction process, and can therefore be used reused. This makes them an important biochemical part of both photosynthesis and respiration.

Nucleic acids are large molecules made up of smaller molecules called **nucleotides. DNA** (deoxyribonucleic acid) transports and transmits genetic information. As you can tell from the name, DNA is a nucleic acid. Since nucleotides make up nucleic acids, they are considered the basis of reproduction and progression.

Practice Drill: Basics of Life

Let's test your knowledge over what you've learned so far!

1. Life depends upon:
    a) The bond energy in molecules.
    b) The energy of protons.
    c) The energy of electrons.
    d) The energy of neutrons.

2. Which of the following elements is **NOT** found in carbohydrates?
    a) Carbon.
    b) Hydrogen.
    c) Oxygen.
    d) Sulfur.

3. Which of the following is a carbohydrate molecule?
    a) Amino acid.
    b) Glycogen.
    c) Sugar.
    d) Lipid.

4. Lipids are commonly known as:
    a) Fat.
    b) Sugar.
    c) Enzymes.
    d) Protein.

5. Proteins are composed of:
    a) Nucleic acids.
    b) Amino acids.
    c) Hormones.
    d) Lipids.

Practice Drill: Basics of Life – Answers

1. a)
2. d)
3. c)
4. a)
5. b)

CELLULAR RESPIRATION

As you can imagine, there are a great deal of processes which require energy: breathing, blood circulation, body temperature control, muscle usage, digestion, brain and nerve functioning are all only a few examples. You can refer to all of the body's physical and chemical processes which convert or use energy as **metabolism**.

All living things in the world, including plants, require energy in order to maintain their metabolisms. Initially, that energy is consumed through food. That energy is processed in plants and animals through **photosynthesis** (for plants) and **respiration** (for animals). **Cellular respiration** produces the actual energy molecules known as **ATP** (Adenosine Tri-Phosphate) molecules.

Plants use ATP during **photosynthesis** for producing glucose, which is then broken down during cellular respiration. This cycle continuously repeats itself throughout the life of the plant.

Photosynthesis: Plants, as well as some Protists and Monerans, can use light energy to bind together small molecules from the environment. These newly-bound molecules are then used as fuel to make more energy. This process is called photosynthesis, and one of its byproducts is none other than oxygen. Most organisms, including plants, require oxygen to fuel the biochemical reactions of metabolism.

You can see in the following equation that plants use the energy taken from light to turn carbon dioxide and water – the small molecules from their environment – into glucose and oxygen.

The photosynthesis equation:

$$CO_2 + H_2O \xrightarrow{\text{Light}} C_6H_{12}O_6 + O_2$$

Carbon Dioxide $\quad$ Water $\qquad$ Glucose (sugar) $\qquad$ Oxygen

Chlorophyll
In order for photosynthesis to occur, however, plants require a specific molecule to capture sunlight. This molecule is called **chlorophyll**. When chlorophyll absorbs sunlight, one of its electrons is stimulated into a higher energy state. This higher-energy electron then passes that energy onto other electrons in other molecules, creating a chain that eventually results in glucose. Chlorophyll absorbs red and blue light, but not green; green light is reflected off of plants, which is why plants appear green to us. It's important to note that chlorophyll is absolutely necessary to the photosynthesis process in plants – if it photosynthesizes, it will have chlorophyll.

The really fascinating aspect of photosynthesis is that raw sunlight energy is a very nonliving thing; however, it is still absorbed by plants to form the chemical bonds between simple inanimate compounds. This produces organic sugar, which is the chemical basis for the formation of all living compounds. Isn't it amazing? Something nonliving is essential to the creation of all living things!

Respiration

Respiration is the metabolic opposite of photosynthesis. There are two types of respiration: **aerobic** (which uses oxygen) and **anaerobic** (which occurs without the use of oxygen).

You may be confused at thinking of the word "respiration" in this way, since many people use respiration to refer to the process of breathing. However, in biology, breathing is thought of as **inspiration** (inhaling) and **expiration** (exhalation); whereas **respiration** is the metabolic, chemical reaction supporting these processes. Both plants and animals produce carbon dioxide through respiration.

Aerobic respiration is the reaction which uses enzymes to combine oxygen with organic matter (food). This yields carbon dioxide, water, and energy.

The respiration equation looks like this:

$$\overset{\textbf{Enzymes}}{C_6H_{12}O_6 + 6O_2 \longrightarrow 7\,6CO_2 + 6H_2O + Energy.}$$

If you look back the equation for photosynthesis, you will see that respiration is almost the same equation, only it goes in the opposite direction. (Photosynthesis uses carbon dioxide and water, with the help of energy, to create oxygen and glucose. Respiration uses oxygen and glucose, with the help of enzymes, to create carbon dioxide, water, and energy.)

Anaerobic respiration is respiration that occurs WITHOUT the use of oxygen. It produces less energy than aerobic respiration produces, yielding only two molecules of ATP per glucose molecule Aerobic respiration produces 38 ATP per glucose molecule.

So, plants convert energy into matter and release oxygen gas – animals then absorb this oxygen gas in order to run their own metabolic reaction and, in the process, release carbon dioxide. That carbon dioxide is then absorbed by plants in the photosynthetic conversion of energy into matter. Everything comes full circle! This is called a **metabolic cycle.**

Practice Drill: Cellular Respiration

1. Which of the following is **NOT** true of enzymes?
   a) Enzymes are lipid molecules.
   b) Enzymes are not consumed in a biochemical reaction.
   c) Enzymes are important in photosynthesis and respiration.
   d) Enzymes speed up reactions and make them more efficient.

2. Plants appear green because chlorophyll:
   a) Absorbs green light.
   b) Reflects red light.
   c) Absorbs blue light.
   d) Reflects green light.

3. Photosynthesis is the opposite of:
   a) Enzymatic hydrolysis.
   b) Protein synthesis.
   c) Respiration.
   d) Reproduction.

4. The compound that absorbs light energy during photosynthesis is:
   a) Chloroform.
   b) Chlorofluorocarbon.
   c) Chlorinated biphenyls.
   d) Chlorophyll.

5. What is the name of the sugar molecule produced during photosynthesis?
   a) Chlorophyll
   b) Glycogen
   c) Glucose
   d) Fructose

Practice Drill: Cellular Respiration – Answers

1. a)
2. d)
3. c)
4. d)
5. c)

CLASSIFICATION OF ORGANISMS

All of Earth's organisms have characteristics which distinguish them from one another. Scientists have developed systems to organize and classify all of Earth's organisms based on those characteristics.

Kingdoms

Through the process of evolution, organisms on Earth have developed into many diverse forms, which have complex relationships. Scientists have organized life into five large groups called **kingdoms**. Each kingdom contains those organisms that share significant characteristics distinguishing them from organisms in other kingdoms. These five kingdoms are named as follows:

1. **Animalia**
2. **Plantae**
3. **Fungi**
4. **Protista**
5. **Monera**

Kingdom Animalia

This kingdom contains multicellular organisms multicellular, or those known as complex organisms. These organisms are generically called **heterotrophs**, which means that they must eat preexisting organic matter (either plants or other animals) in order to sustain themselves.

Those heterotrophs which eat only plants are called **herbivores** (from "herbo," meaning "herb" or "plant"); those that kill and eat other animals for food are called **carnivores** (from "carno," meaning "flesh" or "meat"); and still other animals eat both plants *and* other animals – they are called **omnivores** (from "omnis," which means "all").

Those organisms in the Animal Kingdom have nervous tissue which has developed into nervous systems and brains; they are also able to move from place to place using muscular systems. The Animal Kingdom is divided into two groups: **vertebrates** (with backbones) and **invertebrates** (without backbones).

Kingdom Plantae

As you can guess from its name, the Plant Kingdom contains all plant-based life. Plants are multicellular organisms that use chlorophyll, which is held in specialized cellular structures called **chloroplasts,** to capture sunlight energy. Remember: photosynthesis! They then convert that sunlight energy into organic matter: their food. Because of this, most plants are referred to as **autotrophs** (self-feeders). There are a few organisms included in the Plant Kingdom which are not multicellular – certain types of algae which, while not multicellular, have cells with a nucleus. These algae also contain chlorophyll.

Except for algae, most plants are divided into one of two groups: **vascular plants** (most crops, trees, and flowering plants) and **nonvascular plants** (mosses). Vascular plants have specialized tissue that allows them to transport water and nutrients from their roots, to their leaves, and back again – even when the plant is several hundred feet tall. Nonvascular plants cannot do this, and therefore remain very small in size. Vascular plants are able to grow in both wet and dry environments; whereas nonvascular plants, since they are unable to transport water, are usually found only in wet, marshy areas.

Kingdom Fungi

The Fungi Kingdom contains organisms that share some similarities with plants, but also have other characteristics that make them more animal-like. For example, they resemble animals in that they lack chlorophyll – so they can't perform photosynthesis. This means that they don't produce their own food and are therefore heterotrophs. However, they resemble plants in that they reproduce by spores; they also resemble plants in appearance. The bodies of fungi are made of filaments called **hyphae**, which in turn create the tissue **mycelium.** The most well-known examples of organisms in this Kingdom are mushrooms, yeasts, and molds. Fungi are very common and benefit other organisms, including humans.

Kingdom Protista

This kingdom includes single-celled organisms that contain a nucleus as part of their structure. They are considered a simple cell, but still contain multiple structures and accomplish many functions. This Kingdom includes organisms such as paramecium, amoeba, and slime molds. They often move around using hair-like structures called *cilia* or *flagellums*.

Kingdom Monera

This kingdom contains only bacteria. All of these organisms are single-celled and do not have a nucleus. They have only one chromosome, which is used to transfer genetic information. Sometimes they can also transmit genetic information using small structures called **plasmids.** Like organisms in the Protista Kingdom, they use flagella to move. Bacteria usually reproduce asexually.

There are more forms of bacteria than any other organism on Earth. Some bacteria are beneficial to us, like the ones found in yogurt; others can cause us to get sick such as the bacteria *E. coli.*

KINGDOM	DESCRIPTION	EXAMPLES
Animalia	Multi-celled; parasites; prey; consumers; can be herbivorous, carnivorous, or omnivorous.	Sponges, worms, insects, fish, mammals, reptiles, birds, humans.
Plantae	Multi-celled; autotrophs; mostly producers.	Ferns, angiosperms, gymnosperms, mosses.
Fungi	Can be single or multi-celled; decomposers; parasites; absorb food; asexual; consumers.	Mushrooms, mildew, molds, yeast.
Protista	Single or multi-celled; absorb food; both producers and consumers.	Plankton, algae, amoeba, protozoans.
Monera	Single-celled or a colony of single-cells; decomposers and parasites; move in water; are both producers and consumers.	Bacteria, blue-green algae.

Levels of Classification

Kingdom groupings are not very specific. They contain organisms defined by broad characteristics, and which may not seem similar at all. For example, worms belong in Kingdom Animalia – but then, so do birds. These two organisms are very different, despite sharing the necessary traits to make it into the animal kingdom. Therefore, to further distinguish different organisms, we have multiple levels of classification, which gradually become more specific until we finally reach the actual organism.

We generally start out by grouping organisms into the appropriate kingdom. Within each kingdom, we have other subdivisions: **Phylum, Class, Order, Family, Genus, and Species**. (In some cases, "Species" can be further narrowed down into "Sub-Species.")

As we move down the chain, characteristics become more specific, and the number of organisms in each group decreases. For an example, let's try to classify a grizzly bear. The chart would go as follows:

Kingdom - Insect, fish, bird, pig, dog, bear

Phylum - Fish, bird, pig, dog, bear

Class - Pig, dog, bear

Order - Dog, bear

Family - Panda, brown, grizzly

Genus -
Brown, grizzly

Species -
Grizzly

Here is an easy way to remember the order of terms used in this classification scheme:

Kings Play Cards On Friday, Generally Speaking.
Kingdom, Phylum, Class, Order, Family, Genus, Species

Binomial Nomenclature

Organisms can be positively identified by two Latin words. Therefore, the organism naming system is referred to as a binomial nomenclature ("binomial" referring to the number two, and "nomenclature" referring to a title or name). Previously-used words help illustrate where the organism fits into the whole scheme, but it is only the last two, the genus and species, that specifically name an organism. Both are written in italics. The genus is always capitalized, but the species name is written lowercase.

Grizzly bears fall underneath the genus *Ursus*, species *arctos*, and sub-species *horribilis*. Therefore, the scientific name of the grizzly bear would be *Ursus arctos horribilis*. *Canis familiaris* is the scientific name for a common dog, *Felis domesticus* is a common cat, and humans are *Homo sapiens*.

Practice Drill: Classification of Organisms

1. Which feature distinguishes those organisms in Kingdom Monera from those in other kingdoms? Organisms in Kingdom Monera:
   a) Contain specialized organelles.
   b) Contain a nucleus.
   c) Contain chloroplasts.
   d) Lack a nucleus.

2. Which of the following has the classification levels in the correct order, from most general to most specific?
   a) Kingdom, Phylum, Class, Order, Family, Genus, Species.
   b) Order, Family, Genus, Species, Class, Phylum, Kingdom.
   c) Species, Genus, Family, Order, Class, Phylum, Kingdom.
   d) Kingdom, Phylum, Class, Species, Genus, Family, Order.

3. The _____ contains organisms with both plant-and-animal-like characteristics?
   a) Animal Kingdom.
   b) Plant Kingdom.
   c) Fungi Kingdom.
   d) Monera Kingdom.

4. Which of the following statements is true about the binomial nomenclature system of classification?
   a) The genus and species names describe a specific organism.
   b) The category of kingdom is very specific.
   c) The category of species is very broad.
   d) Three names are needed to correctly specify a particular organism.

5. Which of the following kingdom's members are multicellular AND autotrophic?
   a) Fungi.
   b) Animalia.
   c) Protista.
   d) Plantae.

6. Which of the following kingdom's members have tissue called hyphae?
   a) Fungi.
   b) Animalia.
   c) Protista.
   d) Plantae.

Practice Drill: Classification of Organisms – Answers

1. **d)**
2. **a)**
3. **c)**
4. **a)**
5. **d)**
6. **a)**

MICROORGANISMS

Microorganisms (microbes) are extremely small and cannot be seen with the naked eye. They can be detected using either a microscope or through various chemical tests. These organisms are everywhere, even in such extreme environments as very hot areas, very cold areas, dry areas, and deep in the ocean under tremendous pressure. Some of these organisms cause diseases in animals, plants, and humans. However, most are helpful to us and the Earth's ecosystems. In fact, we are totally dependent upon microbes for our quality of life. There are three types of microorganisms: **bacteria, protists, and fungi.**

Bacteria

Bacteria are microorganisms that do not have a true nucleus; their genetic material simply floats around in the cell. They are very small, simple, one-celled organisms. Bacteria are normally found in three variations: **bacilli** (rod-shaped), **cocci** (sphere-shaped), and **spirilla** (spiral-shaped). Bacteria are widespread in all environments and are important participants within all ecosystems. They are **decomposers**, because they break down dead organic matter into basic molecules.

Bacteria are also an important part of the food-chain, because they are eaten by other organisms. Still, bacteria remain the most numerous organisms on Earth. This is due to the fact that they are small, can live practically anywhere, and have great metabolic flexibility. But most importantly, bacteria have the ability to rapidly reproduce. In the right environment, any bacteria can reproduce every 20 or 30 minutes, each one doubling after each reproduction.

Benefits of Bacteria: Some bacteria are found in our intestinal tracts, where they help to digest our food and make vitamins.

To demonstrate the significance of bacteria, let's look at the cycle of nitrogen, which is used by organisms to make proteins. The cycle starts with dead plants being decomposed by bacteria. The nitrogen from the plant tissue is released into the atmosphere, where nitrifying bacteria convert that nitrogen into ammonia-type compounds. Other bacteria act upon these compounds to form nitrates for plants to absorb. When these new plants die, we are brought back again to the decomposing bacteria releasing the plant's nitrogen into the atmosphere.

Bacterial Diseases: Microorganisms, including bacteria, enter our bodies in a variety of ways: through the air we breathe, ingestion by mouth, or through the skin via a cut or injury. We can eliminate much of this threat by disinfecting utensils and thoroughly washing our hands. This destroys bacteria and other microorganisms which may cause disease.

Protists

Protists are very diversified and include organisms that range greatly in size – from single cells to considerably complex structures, some longer than 100 meters. Protists have a wide variety of reproductive and nutritional strategies, and their genetic material is enclosed within a nucleus. Even though protists are more simplistic than other organisms with cellular nuclei, they are not as primitive as bacteria. Some are autotrophic and contain chlorophyll; others are heterotrophic and consume other organisms to survive. Because protists obtain food in both of these ways, it is generally believed that early protists were both animal- and plant-like. Protists are important to food chains and ecosystems, although some protists do cause disease.

Fungi

Fungi are heterotrophic and can be either single-celled or multi-celled. They play an important decomposition role in an ecosystem, because they consume dead organic matter. This returns nutrients to the soil for eventual uptake by plants.

There are three types of fungi which obtain food: saprophytic, parasitic, and mycorrhizal-associated.

Saprophytic fungi consume dead organic matter; **parasitic** fungi attack living plants and animals; and **mycorrhizal-associated** fungi form close relationships (**symbiosis**) with trees, shrubs, and other plants, where each partner in the relationship mutually benefits. An organism called **lichen** is an example of a symbiotic union between a fungus and algae.

Fungi produce **spores** (reproductive structures) that are highly resistant to extreme temperatures and moisture levels. This gives them the ability to survive for a long time, even in aggressive environments. When their environments become more favorable, the spores **germinate** (sprout) and grow. Spores are able to travel to new areas, which spreads the organism. Fungi absorb food through **hyphae**. A large mass of joined, branched hyphae is called the **mycelium**, which constitutes the main body of the multicellular fungi. However, the mycelium is not usually seen, because it is hidden throughout the food source which is being consumed. The largest organism in the world is believed to be a soil fungus whose mycelium tissue extends for many acres!

What we do usually see of a fungus is the fungal fruiting body. A mushroom is a fruiting body filled with spores. The main body of the mushroom (the **mycelium**) is under the soil surface.

Practice Drill: Microorganisms

1. Fungi are decomposers, which is important for_____.
   a) Making nutrients available for recycling back into the soil.
   b) Producing oxygen by photosynthesizing.
   c) Producing oxygen by respiration.
   d) Living in mostly aquatic environments.

2. Which is the most numerous organism on Earth?
   a) Paramecium from the Protist Kingdom.
   b) Yeast from the Fungi Kingdom.
   c) Euglena from the Protist Kingdom.
   d) Bacteria from the Moneran Kingdom.

3. Which kingdom contains organisms that are able to convert atmospheric nitrogen to nitrate?
   a) Animalia.
   b) Plantae.
   c) Monera.
   d) Protista.

4. Why are spores produced?
   a) They are part of resistance.
   b) To reproduce.
   c) To photosynthesize.
   d) They are part of the support system.

5. Members of the Kingdom Monera are found in our digestive tracts and perform which of the following functions?
   a) Produce carbohydrates.
   b) Produce vitamins.
   c) Produce lipids.
   d) Produce proteins.

Practice Drill: Microorganisms – Answers

1. a)
2. d)
3. c)
4. b)
5. b)

ANIMALS

Animals are multi-celled and unable to produce their own food internally, just like plants. As mentioned previously, the Animal Kingdom is divided into two large groupings: the **invertebrates** and **vertebrates.**

Invertebrates are multicellular, have no back bone or cell walls, reproduce sexually, and are heterotrophic. They make up approximately 97% of the animal population.

Vertebrates, on the other hand, have well-developed internal skeletons, highly developed brains, an advanced nervous system, and an outer covering of protective cellular skin. They make up the remaining 3% of the animals.

What Is an Animal?

All animals, from sponges to human beings, share some fundamental characteristics. One such characteristic is cellular division. At the beginning of reproduction, an egg is fertilized and then undergoes several cell divisions (cleavages); this process quickly produces a cluster of cells. Cell division continues through many distinct stages before finally resulting in an embryo. The full, multi-celled organism then develops tissues and organ systems, eventually developing into its adult form.

All multicellular animals must come up with solutions to several basic problems:

- **Surface-area-to-volume issues**: Nutrients, air, and water must be able to enter an animal's body in order to sustain life; therefore, the surface area of an animal's body must be large enough to allow a sufficient amount of these elements to be consumed by the organism. In single-celled organisms, the cell size is limited to the amount of nutrients able to pass through the cell membrane to support the cell. In multi-celled organisms, specialized tissues and organ systems with very large surface areas bring in the necessary elements and then carry them to the cells. Those specialized tissues are found in the respiratory system, urinary system, excretory system, and the digestive system. These tissues and organs, along with the circulatory system, are able to support a large-sized body.

- **Body support and protection**: All animals have some form of support and protection in the form of their internal or external skeletal systems. These skeletal systems provide support for the animal's body and protect the internal organs from damage.

- **Mobility**: Animals are heterotrophs and must acquire food; this need, along with the need to mate and reproduce, requires the animal to move. Although plants move, they are considered stationary because they are rooted. Animals, on the other hand, move from place to place; this is called **locomotion.** Locomotion requires a muscular system. Muscles are found only in animals; they are not present in plants, fungi, or single-celled microorganisms.

- **Sensory integration**: Animals have many specialized sensory organs: eyes, ears, noses, etc. These organs make animals aware of the environment and give them the ability to respond to environmental stimuli. The integration and coordination of sense organs with other bodily functions requires an organized collection of specialized nervous tissue, known as a **central nervous system** (CNS).

A Few Animal Phyla

Phylum Porifera: Sponges.
Collections of individual cells with no tissues or organs, and no nervous system or skeleton.

Phylum Coelenterata: Jellyfish, sea anemones, and coral.
Bodies symmetrical in a circular fashion with rudimentary organs and systems, but no skeleton.

Phylum Echinodermata: Sea stars and sea urchins.
Bodies have circular symmetry with five body parts arranged around a central axis. They have calcium spines or plates just under the skin.

Phylum Mollusca: Snails, clams, and octopi.
These have a well-developed circulatory system, nervous system, and digestive system; octopuses have particularly well-developed brains.

Phylum Arthropoda: Crustaceans, spiders, and insects.
This phylum has more species than the other phyla. They have exoskeletons, and most undergo **metamorphosis** (a physical transformation that is a part of the growth process). They often have specialized body parts (antennae, pinchers, etc.), and they are well adapted to many environments.

Phylum Chordata: Amphibians, reptiles, fish, birds, and mammals (including humans).
All share four characteristics: a notochord that develops into the vertebral column in vertebrates, a nerve cord that runs along the spinal column, gill slits at some point in our development, and a tail or at least a vestigial tail (humans have the tailbone or coccyx).

Practice Drill: Animals

1. Multicellular animals have developed respiratory and excretory systems to overcome which of the following issues?
   a) Weight versus mass.
   b) Surface-area-to-volume.
   c) Height to weight.
   d) Mass to volume.

2. The two categories of animals are:
   a) Single-celled and multi-celled.
   b) Autotrophic and heterotrophic.
   c) Those that live in water and those that live on land.
   d) Vertebrate and invertebrate.

3. Jellyfish and coral are related to:
   a) Octopi.
   b) Sea anemones.
   c) Sea urchins.
   d) Sponges.

4. The Phylum Arthropoda contains which of the following animals?
   a) Spiders.
   b) Sea stars.
   c) Sponges.
   d) Seals.

5. Humans are classified under which of the following Phyla?
   a) Echinodermata.
   b) Chordata.
   c) Mollusca.
   d) Platyhelminthes.

Practice Drill: Animals – Answers

1. **b)**
2. **d)**
3. **b)**
4. **a)**
5. **b)**

PLANTS

Organisms within Kingdom Plantae are very diverse, but they usually share certain characteristics which make them recognizable as plants. Chlorophyll ensures that some, if not all, of a plants body will have a green color, and their root systems render plants incapable of locomotion. Remember photosynthesis? Plants are autotrophs; they create their own food through photosynthesis, which turns carbon dioxide and water into sugars and oxygen gas. This process takes place using chlorophyll in structures called **chloroplasts**. Plants also have hard cell walls made of the carbohydrate **cellulose**.

Diverse Environments and Plants
Plants are found in nearly every place on Earth. Since plants need light to photosynthesize, their ability to survive in different environments depends upon their access to sources of light. Water is also an important part of a plant's growth and development, partly because the water contained within a plant cells (by the cell wall) provide a plant with structure and support.

Land plants evolved from algae into two large groups: **bryophytes** (nonvascular plants) and **tracheophytes** (vascular plants).

Tracheophytes
These plants have tubes (vessels) which provide both support and a means of transporting water and nutrients throughout their bodies. This support enables them to grow much larger than bryophytes.

The tracheophyte group is further broken down into two types: **seedless** and **seeded** vascular plants.

Seedless vascular plants require moist environments, because they need water to reproduce. Millions of years ago, seedless plants dominated the Earth; you can see many of them still today, such as club mosses, horsetails, and ferns.

Seeded vascular plants have become dominant today because they have developed a reproductive system that includes pollen and seeds. In response to harsh and dangerous conditions, plants have developed **pollen** as a structure to protect sperm cells until they can safely reach the female part of a flower. Another structure which protects plants against the environment is a seed. **Seeds** contain and protect an immature plant in a state of dormancy until conditions are favorable. They then germinate and form a new plant.

Since plants cannot transport themselves (remember: no locomotion), they depend on dispersal systems to establish themselves in new areas. Many systems help distribute seeds, including wind, water, and animals.

Seeded vascular plants are divided into two groups: **gymnosperms** and **angiosperms**.

Gymnosperms are seeded vascular plants that do not flower. They include plants such as pines, spruce, and cypresses. Gymnosperms are adapted to cold dry areas. They have very thin, small leaves covered with a waterproof layer that keeps them from drying out; additionally, a biological antifreeze in their sap keeps them from freezing. Gymnosperms retain green leaves year-round and produce seeds in cones.

Angiosperms are seeded vascular plants that *do* form flowers. These plants have thrived. They dominate the Earth and are highly diverse, largely because they have developed flowers, fruits, and broad leaves.

> **Broad leaves** capture more sunlight, and therefore produce more food than the narrow, thin leaves of the gymnosperms are able to produce.

> **Flowers** are the place in plants where sperm and egg cells are produced – they contain both the male and female sexual parts. A flower is designed to attract animals, which is why their structures are so colorful and fragrant. Animals assist in the pollination process by carrying pollen and other seeds to diverse locations; the animal often receives a "reward" from the plant in the form of nectar or pollen. Bees, for example, receive nectar and pollen for food from flowering plants.

> **Fruits** contain the fully developed seed of flowering seed plants. Animals are attracted to the plant, eat the fruit, and then disperse the seeds.

Bryophytes

Quite different from tracheophytes, bryophytes lack roots, leaves, and stems. Instead, structures called **rhizoids** (root-like hairs) absorb water and nutrients. Since they do not have a tubular system with which to move water throughout their bodies, bryophytes rely on diffusion to distribute water and nutrients. This process is slow, and not efficient enough to support large bodies, so bryophytes cannot grow very large. The largest types of bryophytes are liverworts and mosses.

Practice Drill: Plants

1. Which of the following characteristics is NOT a characteristic of plants?
   a) They are able to engage in locomotion by moving from place to place.
   b) They use chlorophyll contained in chloroplasts.
   c) They produce sugars and oxygen.
   d) They use carbon dioxide and water in photosynthesis.

2. Which of the following is a bryophyte?
   a) Horsetail.
   b) Fern.
   c) Liverwort.
   d) Spruce tree.

3. Which plant group currently dominates the Earth in terms of quantity over other plant groups?
   a) Gymnosperms.
   b) Bryophytes.
   c) Seedless vascular plants.
   d) Angiosperms.

4. "Tracheophytes" is another name for:
   a) Nonvascular plants.
   b) Angiosperm plants.
   c) Gymnosperm plants.
   d) Vascular plants.

5. Which of the following strategies does an angiosperm plant NOT use to attract animals?
   a) It produces pollen.
   b) It produces nectar.
   c) It produces chloroplasts.
   d) It produces fruit.

6. Rhizoids are similar to _____ in vascular plants?
   a) Leaves
   b) Chloroplasts
   c) Roots
   d) Stems

Practice Drill: Plants – Answers

1. a)
2. c)
3. d)
4. d)
5. c)
6. c)

ECOLOGY

Biosphere and Biome

Life is possible due to the presence of air (**atmosphere**), water (**hydrosphere**), and soil (**lithosphere**). These factors interact with each other and the life on Earth to create an environment called a **biosphere**. The biosphere contains all of Earth's living organisms. Smaller living systems called **biomes** exist in large areas, both on land and in water; they are defined by the physical characteristics of the environment which they encompass, and by the organisms living within it.

Ecosystem

An ecosystem is a community of living and non-living things that work together. Ecosystems have no particular size; from large lakes and deserts, to small trees or puddles. Everything in the natural world – water, water temperature, plants, animals, air, light, soil, etc. – all form ecosystems.

The physical environment of an ecosystem includes soils, weather, climate, the topography (or shape) of the land, and many other factors. If there isn't enough light or water within an ecosystem, or if the soil doesn't have the right nutrients, plants will die. If plants die, the animals which depend on them will die. If the animals depending upon the plants die, any other animals depending upon those animals will also die. Regardless of the type of ecosystem they are in, all organisms – even microscopic ones – are affected by each other and their physical surroundings.

There are two components of an ecosystem. The **biotic** (biological) component includes the living organisms; nonliving factors – such as water, minerals, and sunlight – are collectively known as the **abiotic** (non-biological) component. While all ecosystems have different organisms and/or abiotic factors, they all have two primary features:

1. **Energy flows in one direction**. Beginning in the form of chemical bonds from photosynthetic organisms, like green plants or algae, energy flows first to the animals that eat the plants, then to other animals.

2. **Inorganic materials are recycled.** When taken up from the environment through living organisms, inorganic minerals are returned to the environment – mainly via decomposers such as bacteria and fungi. Other organisms called **detritivores** (such as pill bugs, sow bugs, millipedes, and earthworms), help break down large pieces of organic matter into smaller pieces that are handled then by the decomposers.

But since that's a lot of information to take in at once, here's a simple and complete definition of an ecosystem: a combination of biotic and abiotic components, through which energy flows and inorganic material is recycled.

An Organism's Niche

The area in which an organism lives – and therefore acquires the many things needed to sustain their lives – is called a **habitat.** An organism's role within its community, how it affects its habitat and how it is affected by its habitat, are the factors that define the organism's **niche.** A niche is like an organism's "location" and "occupation" within a community.

For example, birds and squirrels both live in a tree habitat; however, they eat different foods, have different living arrangements, and have different food-gathering abilities. Therefore, the do not occupy the same niche.

THE ECOLOGICALORDER OF LIFE

Biosphere - All ecosystems on the planet make up the biosphere.

Ecosystem – Large community of numerous communities, and the physical non-living environment.

Community - A group of populations in a given area.

Population - A group of organisms of the same species in a given area.

Organism - A living thing.

Organ Systems - A group of organs that perform certain functions to form an organism.

Organs - A group of tissues that perform a certain function to form organ systems.

Tissues - A group of cells that perform certain functions to form an organ.

Cells - The building blocks of life which form tissues.

Organelles - Small parts of cells that have specific functions.

One of the most important relationships among organisms exists between predators and their prey. You may have heard of this relationship described through **food chains** and **food webs**.

Food Chains represent the flow of energy obtained from the chemical breakdown of food molecules. When one animal (the predator) consumes another (the prey), the chemical bonds making up the tissues of the prey's body are broken down by the predator's digestive system. This digestive process releases energy and smaller chemical molecules that the predator's body uses to make more tissue. Prior to being the consumed, the prey obtains energy from foods for its own life processes.

Here's a basic example of a food chain:

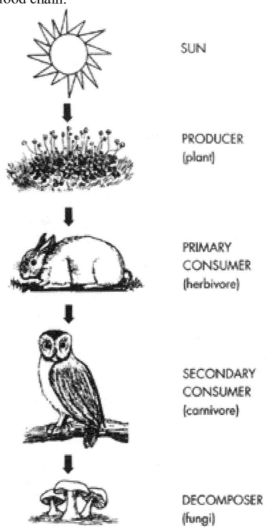

SUN

PRODUCER
(plant)

PRIMARY
CONSUMER
(herbivore)

SECONDARY
CONSUMER
(carnivore)

DECOMPOSER
(fungi)

Food chains are a part of **food webs**, which offer a more complex view of energy transfer. They include more organisms, taking into account more than one predator-prey relationship. Each step along a food chain, or within a food web, is called a **trophic** (or feeding) level. Organisms at that first trophic level are known as **primary producers**, and are always photosynthetic organisms, whether on land or in water.

At the second trophic level, herbivores (referred to as **primary consumers**) eat plants to produce the energy needed for their metabolism. Much of the energy that transfers from the first trophic level to the second level is not turned into tissue. Instead, it is used for the digestive process, locomotion, and is lost as heat. As you move from one trophic level to another, it is estimated that only 10% of the available energy gets turned into body tissue at the next level up.

---

[1] Graphic from: http://www.king.portlandschools.org

The following is an example of a food web:

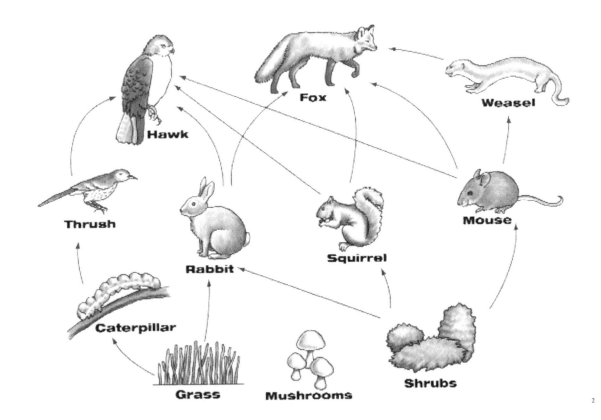

Practice Drill: Ecology

1. Ecology is the study of organisms interacting with:
    a) The physical environment only.
    b) The internal environment only.
    c) The physical environment and each other.
    d) Each other and the internal environment.

2. In terms of energy, an ecosystem is defined as:
    a) Moving energy back and forth between organisms.
    b) Moving energy in one direction from plants to animals.
    c) Not utilizing energy.
    d) Moving energy in one direction from animals to plants.

3. Decomposers are important because they:
    a) Recycle nutrients.
    b) Produce sugars.
    c) Produce oxygen.
    d) Engage in asexual reproduction.

4. Which of the following best describes the concept of an organism's niche?
    a) It is the organism's function, or "occupation", within an ecosystem.
    b) It is the organism's location, or "address", within an ecosystem.
    c) It is both an organism's function and location in an ecosystem.
    d) It is the binomial classification of an organism in an ecosystem.

5. Pillbugs are also known as:
    a) Decomposers.
    b) Detritivores.
    c) Producers.
    d) Autotrophs.

6. The steps in a food chain or food web are called _____ and represent the _____ of an organism.
    a) biome levels; energy level
    b) trophic levels; energy level
    c) trophic levels; feeding level
    d) energy levels; feeding level

7. Another term for herbivores is:
    a) Plants.
    b) Secondary consumers.
    c) Primary consumers
    d) Third trophic-level organisms.

8. Several interacting food chains form a:
  a) Food pyramid.
  b) Food web.
  c) Food column.
  d) Food triangle.

9. Herbivores are at the second trophic level, so they are:
  a) Primary producers.
  b) Primary consumers.
  c) Secondary consumers.
  d) Secondary producers.

Practice Drill: Ecology – Answers

1. c)
2. b)
3. a)
4. c)
5. b)
6. c)
7. c)
8. b)
9. b)

General Physiology

The normal functioning of living organisms, and the activities by which life is maintained, are both studied in physiology. This study includes such things as cell activity, tissues, and organs; as well as processes such as muscle movement, nervous systems, nutrition, digestion, respiration, circulation, and reproduction.

One characteristic of living things is the performance of chemical reactions collectively called metabolism. Cells, the basic units of life, perform many metabolic reactions. In multi-celled organisms, cells group together and form tissues that enable the organisms' functions. Tissues group together and form organs, which in turn work together in an organ system.

CELLS, TISSUES, AND ORGANS

All organisms are composed of microscopic cells, although the type and number of cells may vary. A cell is the minimum amount of organized living matter that is complex enough to carry out the functions of life. This section will briefly review both animal and plant cells, noting their basic similarities and differences.

Cell Structure
Around the cell is the **cell membrane**, which separates the living cell from the rest of the environment and regulates the comings and goings of molecules within the cell. Because the cell membrane allows some molecules to pass through while blocking others, it is considered **semipermeable.** Each cell's membrane communicates and interacts with the membranes of other cells. In additional to a cell membrane, *plants* also have a **cell wall** which is necessary for structural support and protection. Animal cells do not contain a cell wall.

Organelle
Cells are filled with a gelatin-like substance called **protoplasm** which contains various structures called **organelles**; called so because they act like small versions of organs. The diagram on the next page illustrates the basic organelles of both a plant and an animal cell. Pay attention to the differences and similarities between the two.

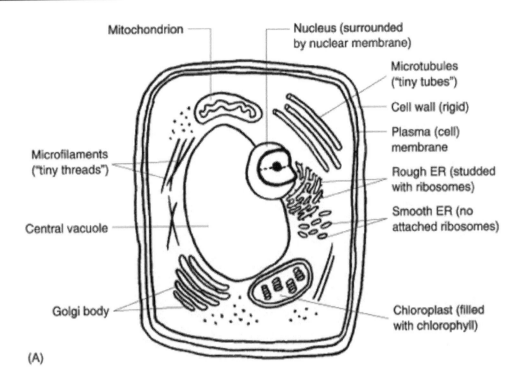

Mitochondrion

Nucleus (surrounded by nuclear membrane)

Microtubules ("tiny tubes")

Cell wall (rigid)

Plasma (cell) membrane

Microfilaments ("tiny threads")

Rough ER (studded with ribosomes)

Smooth ER (no attached ribosomes)

Central vacuole

Golgi body

Chloroplast (filled with chlorophyll)

(A)

ANIMAL CELL (B)

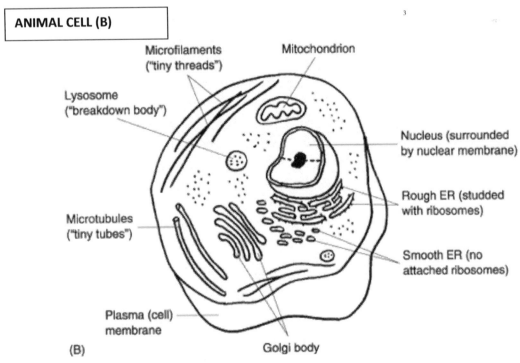

Microfilaments ("tiny threads")

Mitochondrion

Lysosome ("breakdown body")

Nucleus (surrounded by nuclear membrane)

Rough ER (studded with ribosomes)

Microtubules ("tiny tubes")

Smooth ER (no attached ribosomes)

Plasma (cell) membrane

Golgi body

(B)

---

[3] Graphics from: http://www.education.com

Mitochondria are spherical or rod-shaped organelles which carry out the reactions of aerobic respiration. They are the power generators of both plant and animal cells, because they convert oxygen and nutrients into ATP, the chemical energy that powers the cell's metabolic activities.

Ribosomes are extremely tiny spheres that make proteins. These proteins are used either as enzymes or as support for other cell functions.

The **Golgi Apparatus** is essential to the production of polysaccharides (carbohydrates), and made up of a layered stack of flattened sacs.

The **Endoplasmic Reticulum** is important in the synthesis and packaging of proteins. It is a complex system of internal membranes, and is called either rough (when ribosomes are attached), or smooth (no ribosomes attached).

Chloroplasts are only found in plants. They contain the chlorophyll molecule necessary for photosynthesis.

The **Nucleus** controls all of the cell's functions, and contains the all-important genetic information, or DNA, of a cell.

Cellular Differentiation

Single-celled organisms have only one cell to carry out all of their required biochemical and structural functions. On the other hand, multi-celled organisms – except for very primitive ones (i.e. sponges) – have various groups of cells called **tissues** that each perform specific functions (**differentiation**).

There are four main types of tissues: **epithelial**, **connective**, **muscular**, and **nervous**.

Epithelial tissue is made up groups of flattened cells which are grouped tightly together to form a solid surface. Those cells are arranged in one or many layer(s) to form an external or internal covering of the body or organs. Epithelial tissue protects the body from injury and allows for the exchange of gases in the lungs and bronchial tubes. There's even a form of epithelial tissue that produces eggs and sperm, an organism's sex cells.

Connective tissue is made of cells which are surrounded by non-cellular material. For example, bones contain some cells, but they are also surrounded by a considerable amount of non-cellular, extracellular material.

Muscular tissue has the ability to contract. There are three types:
1. **Cardiac** tissue, found in the heart.
2. **Smooth** tissue, located in the walls of hollow internal structures such as blood vessels, the stomach, intestines, and urinary bladder.
3. **Skeletal** (or striated) tissue, found in the muscles.

Nervous tissue consists of cells called **neurons.** Neurons specialize in making many connections with and transmitting electrical impulses to each other. The brain, spinal cord, and peripheral nerves are all made of nervous tissue.

Organs and Organ Systems

As living organisms go through their life cycle, they grow and/or develop. Single-celled organisms grow and develop very rapidly; whereas complex, multi-celled organisms take much longer to progress. All organisms go through changes as they age. These changes involve the development of more complex functions, which in turn require groups of tissues to form larger units called **organs.**

Examples of Organs

1. **The Heart**: Made of cardiac muscle and conjunctive tissue (conjunctive tissue makes up the valves), the heart pumps blood first to the lungs in order to pick up oxygen, then through the rest of the body to deliver the oxygen, and finally back to the lungs to start again.

2. **Roots**: A tree's are covered by an epidermis which is in turn made up of a protective tissue. They are also *composed* of tissue, which allows them to grow. The root organ also contains **conductive tissue** to absorb and transport water and nutrients to the rest of the plant.

Generally, in complex organisms like plants and animals, many organs are grouped together into **systems.** For example, many combinations of tissues make up the many organs which create the digestive system in animals. The organs in the digestive system consist of the mouth, the esophagus, the stomach, small and large intestines, the liver, the pancreas, and the gall bladder.

Practice Drill: Cells, Tissues, and Organs

1. Which statement is true about Earth's organisms?
    a) All organisms are based on the cell as the basic unit of life.
    b) Protists are an exception to the cell theory and are not based on cells.
    c) Only single-celled organisms are based on cells.
    d) All organisms are based on tissues as the basic unit of life.

2. What organelle produces the cell's energy source?
    a) Chloroplast.
    b) Nucleus.
    c) Mitochondrion.
    d) Endoplasmic reticulum.

3. The formation of tissue depends upon:
    a) Cell differentiation.
    b) Cell membranes.
    c) Cell death.
    d) Cell organelles.

4. Cardiac muscle is an example of what tissue?
    a) Smooth muscle.
    b) Nervous.
    c) Contractile.
    d) Connective.

5. Which organelle has two forms: rough and smooth?
    a) Mitochondrion.
    b) Golgi apparatus.
    c) Nucleus.
    d) Endoplasmic reticulum.

6. Which organelle is important in the production of polysaccharides (carbohydrates)?
    a) Mitochondrion.
    b) Golgi apparatus.
    c) Nucleus
    d) Endoplasmic reticulum.

Practice Drill: Cells, Tissues, and Organs – Answers

1. a)
2. c)
3. a)
4. c)
5. d)
6. b)

REPRODUCTION

Individual organisms have limited life spans; however, life continues due to reproduction. There are two types of reproduction. One requires the exchange of genetic material between two organisms (**sexual reproduction**), and the other does not (**asexual reproduction**).

Asexual Reproduction

All kingdoms have organisms that engage in asexual reproduction. Asexual reproduction very quickly produces large numbers of genetically identical (or **cloned**) offspring. Some organisms that engage in asexual reproduction can also engage in sexual reproduction at least part of the time.

	Asexual Reproduction	**Sexual Reproduction**
Number of Organisms Involved:	One.	Two.
Cell Division:	Mitosis.	Meiosis.
Variation in Offspring:	No.	Yes.
Advantages:	Quick. No need to search for mate.	Variation.
Disadvantages:	No variation.	Requires two organisms.

In single-celled organisms such as bacteria and protists, asexual reproduction occurs through a process known as **binary fission** (or **bipartition**). The cell first duplicates parts of itself before splitting into two separate, but identical, cells. Some organisms reproduce asexually using the process of **budding**, wherein an offshoot of their body grows into a complete organism.

Many multi-cellular invertebrates can also reproduce asexually by a process called **fragmentation**, where a portion of the organism's body is separated and then grows into a whole organism. This is similar to budding, except that the original body repairs itself as well, leaving behind two complete organisms.

Plants can reproduce asexually by budding or fragmentation, when they form tubers, rhizomes, bulbs, and other extensions of their bodies. Plants also have a major sexual phase of their life cycle, which is part of a process called **alternation of generations.**

Alternation of Generations

Although asexual reproduction allows plants to reproduce quickly, most plants engage in sexual reproduction, at least part of the time. Sexually reproducing plants cycle between two distinctly different body types. The first is called the **sporophyte**, and the second is called the **gametophyte.**

An adult sporophyte (the part of the plant we see) produces spores. The spores are transported to new areas by animals, wind, water, etc. If the conditions are suitable, those spores will sprout into a **gametophyte** form of the plant, which is not usually seen. This gametophyte produces the eggs and sperm that will join to form a new sporophyte. This change from sporophyte to gametophyte represents an alternation of generations. The gametophyte generation is small and dependent upon the sporophyte generation. An oak tree, for example, is really the sporophyte generation of the plant; the gametophyte generation is contained within its flowers.

Sexual Reproduction

Sexual reproduction is when genetic material from one parent is combined with the genetic material from another, producing offspring that are not identical to either parent. Each parent produces a specialized cell called a **gamete** that contains half of his or her genetic information.

Male animals produce the smaller, more mobile gamete known as a **sperm cell**. Females produce the larger, more sedentary gamete known as an **egg cell**. When these two gametes come into contact, they fuse and combine their genetic information in a process known as **fertilization**. This can happen either externally or internally.

An example of **external fertilization** would be **spawning**, where eggs and sperm are both released into water and must find each other. **Spawning** is dependent upon each gender's reproductive cycle matching the other. For some fish and amphibians, the male and female embrace to motivate the release of the gametes; however, internal fertilization does not take place.

Internal fertilization is dependent upon **copulation**: the process wherein a male deposits sperm cells directly into the reproductive tract of a female. Because a medium like water cannot be used to transport gametes on land, internal fertilization is critical to land-based organisms.

Practice Drill: Reproduction

1. The formation of tubers is an example of what kind of asexual reproduction?
   a) Budding.
   b) Binary fission.
   c) Bipartition.
   d) Root zone development.

2. Which of the following best describes alternation of generation?
   a) The sporophyte produces eggs and sperm that join and lead to the development of a gametophyte.
   b) The gametophyte produces eggs and sperm that join and lead to the development of a sporophyte.
   c) The gametophyte produces eggs and the sporophyte produces sperm that join to form a new plant.
   d) The sporophyte produces eggs and the gametophyte produces sperm that join to form a new plant.

3. In sexually reproducing organisms, gametes come from which parent?
   a) Only the male.
   b) Only the female.
   c) Both the male and female.
   d) Neither.

4. What is the main difference between asexual and sexual reproduction?
   a) Asexual reproduction is only for aquatic organisms.
   b) Asexual reproduction is practiced only by plants.
   c) Humans are the only organisms that utilize sexual reproduction.
   d) Asexual reproduction does not require a mate.

5. Which of the following is **NOT** a form of asexual reproduction?
   a) Fertilization.
   b) Cloning.
   c) Budding.
   d) Fragmentation.

Practice Drill: Reproduction – Answers

1. **a)**
2. **b)**
3. **c)**
4. **d)**
5. **a)**

HEREDITY

A duck's webbed feet, a tree whose leaves change color in the fall, and humans having backbones are all characteristics inherited from parent organisms. These inheritable characteristics are transmitted through **genes** and **chromosomes**. In sexual reproduction, each parent contributes half of his or her genes to the offspring.

Genes

Genes influence both what we look like on the outside and how we work on the inside. They contain the information that our bodies need to make the proteins in our bodies. Genes are made of DNA: a double helix (spiral) molecule that consists of two long, twisted strands of nucleic acids. Each of these strands are made of sugar and phosphate molecules, and are connected by pairs of chemicals called **nitrogenous bases** (just bases, for short). There are four types of bases:

1. **Adenine (A)**
2. **Thymine (T)**
3. **Guanine (G)**
4. **Cytosine (C)**

These bases link in a very specific way: **A** always pairs with **T**, and **C** always pairs with **G**.

A gene is a piece of DNA that codes for a specific protein. Each gene contains the information necessary to produce a single trait in an organism, and each gene is different from any other. For example, one gene will code for the protein insulin, and another will code for hair. For any trait, we inherit one gene from our father and one from our mother. Human beings have 20,000 to 25,000 genes, yet those genes only account for about 3% of our DNA.

Alternate forms of the same gene are called **alleles**. When the alleles are identical, the individual is **homozygous** for that trait. When the alleles are different, the individual is **heterozygous** for that trait.

For example, a child may have red hair because she inherited two identical red color genes from each parent; that would make her homozygous for red hair. However, a second child may have brown hair because he inherited different hair color genes from each parent; this would make him heterozygous for brown hair. When genes exist in a heterozygous pairing, usually one is expressed over the other. The gene which is expressed is **dominant**. The unexpressed gene is called **recessive**.

If you took the DNA from all the cells in your body and lined it up, end to end, it would form a (very thin!) strand 6000 million miles long! DNA molecules, and their important genetic material, are tightly packed around proteins called **histones** to make structures called **chromosomes**. Human beings have 23 pairs of chromosomes in every cell, for 46 chromosomes in total. The sex chromosomes determine whether you are a boy (XY) or a girl (XX). The other chromosomes are called autosomes.

Patterns of Inheritance

Biologists refer to the genetic makeup of an organism as its **genotype**. However, the collection of physical characteristics that result from the action of genes is called an organism's **phenotype.** You can remember this differentiation by looking at the beginning of each word: *geno*type is *gen*etic, and *pheno*type is *phy*sical. Patterns of inheritance can produce surprising results, because the genotype determines the phenotype.

Practice Drill: Heredity

1. On paired chromosomes, two identical alleles are called:
    a) Heterozygous.
    b) Homozygous.
    c) Tetrad.
    d) Binomial.

2. The physical characteristics of an organism are known as its:
    a) Chromosomes.
    b) Genotype.
    c) DNA.
    d) Phenotype.

3. Which of the following is **NOT** a nucleotide found in DNA?
    a) Uracil.
    b) Guanine.
    c) Cytosine.
    d) Thymine.

4. The genotype describes an organism's:
    a) Appearance.
    b) Genetic code.
    c) Type of DNA.
    d) Eye color only.

5. The shape of the DNA molecule is a:
    a) Single spiral.
    b) Double spiral.
    c) Straight chain.
    d) Bent chain.

Practice Drill: Heredity – Answers

1. b)
2. d)
3. a)
4. b)
5. b)

THE RESPIRATORY SYSTEM

The human respiratory system is made up of a series of organs responsible for taking in oxygen and expelling carbon dioxide, and can be divided into two parts: **air conduction** and **gas exchange.** (We'll cover those in more detail soon.)

The respiratory system's primary organs are the lungs, which take in oxygen and expel carbon dioxide when we breathe. Breathing involves **inhalation** (the taking in of air) and **exhalation** (the releasing of air). Blood gathers oxygen from the lungs and transports it to cells throughout the body, where it exchanges the oxygen for carbon dioxide. The carbon dioxide is then transported back to the lungs, where it is exhaled.

Air Conduction
The **diaphragm**, a dome-shaped muscle located at the bottom of the lungs, controls breathing. When a breath is taken, the diaphragm flattens and pulls forward, making more space for the lungs. During exhalation, the diaphragm expands upwards to force air out.

Humans breathe through their noses or mouths, which causes air to enter the **pharynx** (upper part of the throat). The air then passes the **larynx** (the Adam's apple on the inside of the throat). The larynx is also known as the voice box because it changes shape to form sounds. Inhaled air passes into a tube in the center of the chest known as the **trachea**, (the windpipe) which filters the air.

The trachea branches into two **bronchi**, two tubes which carry air into the lungs. Once inside the lungs, each bronchus branches into smaller tubes called **bronchioles**. Bronchioles then lead to sac-like structures called **alveoli**, where the second function of the respiratory system – gas exchange – occurs.

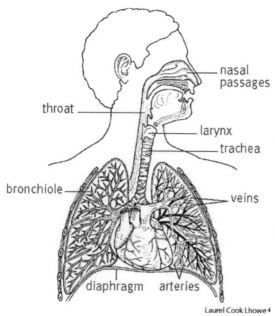

Laurel Cook Lhowe [4]

Gas Exchange

Each lung contains over two million alveoli, which creates a large surface area for gas exchange: approximately 800 square feet!

The alveoli and the surrounding blood vessels have very thin walls, which allows for the diffusion of gases in either direction – specifically oxygen and carbon dioxide. Air entering the lungs from the atmosphere is high in oxygen and low in carbon dioxide. This means that the alveoli have a high concentration of oxygen and a low concentration of carbon dioxide.

The opposite is true for the blood within the alveoli's blood vessels. Blood entering the lungs is *low* in oxygen and *high* in carbon dioxide because of cellular respiration (metabolism).

Because the alveoli have a high concentration of oxygen and a low concentration of carbon dioxide, while their blood vessels have the opposite condition, the two gases flow in opposite directions (gas exchange).

Plants exchange gas as well. Single-celled plants, like their animal counterparts, simply exchange gases through the cell membranes. Multicellular plants use pores on the leaf surface, called **stomata**, to exchange gases with the atmosphere.

Practice Drill: The Respiratory System

1. The conduction of air through the respiratory system follows which of the following paths?
   a) Pharynx, larynx, alveoli, trachea, bronchus, bronchioles.
   b) Alveoli, bronchioles, bronchus, trachea, larynx, pharynx.
   c) Pharynx, larynx, trachea, bronchus, bronchioles, alveoli.
   d) Bronchus, bronchioles, alveoli, pharynx, larynx, trachea.

2. Each alveolus in the lungs is covered by tiny blood vessels to perform which of these functions?
   a) Excretion of fluids.
   b) Gas exchange.
   c) Blood production.
   d) Air intake.

3. The pores on a plant leaf that allow for gas exchange are called:
   a) Alveoli.
   b) Cell pores.
   c) Membrane gaps.
   d) Stomata.

4. Which of the following occurs during gas exchange in a cell?
   a) Oxygen is flowing from a low concentration inside the cell to a high concentration outside the cell.
   b) Oxygen is flowing from a high concentration in the red blood cells to a low concentration inside the body cell.
   c) Carbon dioxide is moving from the red blood cells into the body cells, while oxygen is moving from the body cells into the red blood cells.
   d) Carbon dioxide is flowing from a low concentration outside the cells to a high concentration inside the cells.

5. The lungs are very efficient at gas exchange because they have a:
   a) High mass.
   b) Low volume.
   c) High surface-area-to-volume ratio.
   d) Low surface-area-to-volume ratio.

Practice Drill: The Respiratory System – Answers

1. c)
2. b)
3. d)
4. b)
5. c)

THE SKELETAL SYSTEM

Skeletal systems provide structure, support, form, protection, and movement. Of course, muscles do the actual *moving* of an organism, but bones – a major component of the skeletal system – create the framework through which muscles and organs connect. The bone marrow in animal skeletal systems performs **hematopoiesis** (the manufacturing of both red blood cells and white blood cells).

Skeletal systems come in many different forms - those inside of the body are called **endoskeletons**, while those skeletal structures formed outside of the body are known as **exoskeletons**. Crabs and insects have hard shells made of **chitin** to protect their entire bodies. Some organisms, such as starfish, have skeletons made up of tubes filled with fluids running through their bodies. These fluid skeletal systems are called **hydrostatic**.

Joints are where two bones come together. **Connective tissues** at the joint prevent the bones from damaging each other. Joints can be freely movable (elbow or knee), slightly movable (vertebrae in the back), or immovable (skull).

Plants also have a need for support, shape, and protection. While nonvascular do not have a great need for support (remember, they don't grow very tall), vascular plants require a great deal of support. Remember cell walls (a semi-permeable, rigid structure that surrounds each cell outside the cell membrane)? The support and structure of plant cells are primarily derived from the cell wall. Additional support and structure is provided by the tubes used to move water and nutrients through the plant.

Practice Drill: The Skeletal System

1. Which of the following is NOT a function of the skeletal system in animals?
   a) Transport fluids.
   b) Produce oil.
   c) Placement of internal organs.
   d) Production of blood cells.

2. Which of the following is true of bones?
   a) They contain nerves.
   b) Some are unbreakable.
   c) They are present in vertebrates.
   d) They directly touch each other at a joint.

3. Which of the following animals does **NOT** have an exoskeleton?
   a) Insects.
   b) Crabs.
   c) Lobsters.
   d) Earthworms.

4. What type of tissue is found at joints and protects bones from rubbing against each other and becoming damaged?
   a) Contractile.
   b) Connective.
   c) Conductive.
   d) Catabolic.

5. Fluid skeletal systems are _____.
   a) Hydrostatic.
   b) Hydrolic.
   c) Hydrophobic.
   d) Hydroskeleton.

Practice Drill: The Skeletal System – Answers

1. **b)**
2. **c)**
3. **d)**
4. **b)**
5. **a)**

THE DIGESTIVE SYSTEM

Digestion involves mixing food with digestive juices, moving it through the digestive tract, and breaking down large molecules of food into smaller molecules. The digestive system is made up of the **digestive trac**t: a series of hollow organs joined in a long, twisting tube that leads from the mouth to the anus. Several other organs that help the body break down and absorb food are a part of the digestive system as well.

The organs that make up the digestive tract are the **mouth, esophagus, stomach, small intestine, large intestine (colon), rectum,** and **anus**. These organs are covered with a lining called the **mucosa**. In the mouth, stomach, and small intestine, the mucosa contains tiny glands which produce juices to help break down food.

Two "solid" digestive organs, the **liver** and the **pancreas**, produce digestive juices that travel to the intestine through small tubes called **ducts**. The **gallbladder** stores the liver's digestive juices until they are needed in the intestine. The circulatory and nervous systems are also important to the digestive system.

Digestive pathway

The large, hollow organs of the digestive tract contain a layer of muscle that enables their walls to move. This movement propels food and liquid through the system and assists in mixing the contents within each organ. The movement of food molecules from one organ to the next, through *muscle action*, is called **peristalsis**.

The first major muscle movement occurs when food or liquid is swallowed. Although you are able to start swallowing by choice, once the swallow begins, it becomes involuntary (controlled by nerves).

Swallowed food is pushed into the esophagus, which connects the throat with the stomach. At the junction of the esophagus and stomach, there is a ring-like muscle (**lower esophageal sphincter**) that controls the passage between the two organs. As food approaches the closed sphincter, it relaxes and allows the food to pass through to the stomach.

The stomach has three mechanical tasks:

1. It stores the swallowed food and liquid.

2. It mixes the stored food and liquid with digestive juices produced by the stomach.

3. It empties its contents slowly into the small intestine.

Once in the stomach, the food is churned and bathed in a very strong acid (**gastric acid**). When food in the stomach is partly digested and mixed with stomach acids, it is called **chyme**. Several factors affect how long food molecules remain in the stomach, including the type of food, the degree of muscle action of the emptying stomach, and the breakdown of food occurring in the small intestine. Carbohydrates spend the least amount of time in the stomach, followed by proteins; fats remain in the stomach for the longest amount of time.

From the stomach food molecules enter the first part of the small intestine called the **duodenum**. They then enter the **jejunum**, and then the **ileum** (the final part of the small intestine). In the small intestine, **bile** (produced in the liver and stored in the gall bladder), pancreatic enzymes, and other digestive enzymes produced in the small intestine help break down the food even further. Many accessory organs such as the liver, pancreas, and gall bladder contribute enzymes and buffering fluids to the mix inside of the small intestine; this also aids in the chemical break down of food molecules.

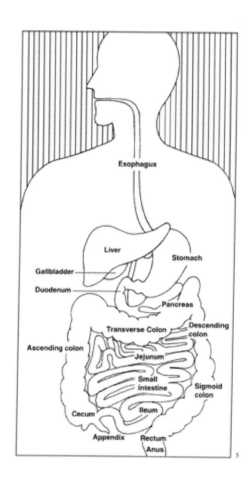

Food then passes into the large intestine, also known as the colon. The main function of the colon is to absorb water, which reduces the undigested matter into a solid waste called feces. Microbes in the large intestine help in the final digestion process. The first part of the large intestine is called the cecum (the appendix is connected to the cecum). Food then travels upward in the ascending colon. The food travels across the abdomen in the transverse colon, goes back down the other side of the body in the descending colon, and then through the sigmoid colon. Solid waste is then stored in the rectum until it is excreted.

---

[5] Graphic from: http://digestive.niddk.nih.gov

Practice Drill: The Digestive System

1. Food begins the digestive process in the:
    a) Esophagus.
    b) Stomach.
    c) Intestines.
    d) Mouth.

2. Chyme is:
    a) Water and completely broken down food molecules.
    b) Acids and completely broken down food molecules.
    c) Acids and partially broken down some food molecules.
    d) Water and partially broken down some food molecules.

3. Where is bile stored?
    a) In the pancreas.
    b) In the gallbladder.
    c) In the liver.
    d) In the small intestines.

4. Which of the following is NOT an accessory organ of the digestive system?
    a) Liver.
    b) Pancreas.
    c) Gall bladder.
    d) Urinary bladder.

5. The chief function of the colon is to:
    a) Absorb water from undigested waste.
    b) Produce sugars.
    c) Absorb protein from undigested waste.
    d) Produce carbohydrates.

Practice Drill: The Digestive System – Answers

1. **d)**
2. **c)**
3. **b)**
4. **d)**
5. **a)**

THE MUSCULAR SYSTEM

Muscles are often viewed as the "machines" of the body. They help move food from one organ to another, and carry out physical movement. There are three types of muscles in our body: cardiac, smooth, and skeletal. The nervous system controls all three types of muscle tissue, both consciously (controlled) and unconsciously (automatic).

Skeletal (or **striated**) muscle tissue is consciously controlled. The muscle is attached to bones, and when it contracts, the bones move. Skeletal tissue also forms visible muscles, as well as much of the body mass.

Smooth muscle is under automatic control and is generally found in the internal organs, especially in the intestinal tract and in the walls of blood vessels.

Cardiac muscle is found only in the heart. This type of muscle tissue is so automated that it will continue to contract even without stimulation from the nervous system. Isolated heart cells in a dish will continue to contract on their own until oxygen or nutrient sources are used up.

Muscle contraction begins when a nerve impulse causes the release of a chemical called a **neurotransmitter**. Muscle contraction is explained as the interaction between two necessary muscle proteins: thick bands of **myosin** and thin bands of **actin**. The thick myosin filaments have small knob-like projections that grab onto the thin actin filaments. As these knobs move slightly, they pull the actin filaments, which slide alongside the myosin filaments. This has the effect of shortening the muscle and thus causing a contraction.

Connective tissues known as **tendons** form a link between muscles and bones (whereas **ligaments** form a link between two bones). The contraction of a muscle causes an exertion of force upon the tendon, which then pulls its attached bone. This movement is synchronized by the central nervous system and results in movement.

Uni-cellular organisms, such as protists and sperm cells, have the ability to move as well. This kind of movement can be accomplished in three different ways. In the case of amoebas, which are one-celled formless blobs of protoplasm, movement is accomplished by extending a portion of the cell itself and then flowing into that portion. Other organisms use **cilia,** which are tiny hair-like projections from the cell membrane, or **flagellum**, which is a tail-like projection that whips around or spins to move.

Practice Drill: The Muscular System

1. What are the three types of muscle cells?
   a) Cardiac, synaptic, and skeletal.
   b) Cardiac, autonomic, and smooth.
   c) Skeletal, cardiac, and smooth.
   d) Smooth, cardiac, and spinal.

2. Which of the following is true about skeletal muscles?
   a) They all contract unconsciously.
   b) All muscle movement is consciously controlled.
   c) They connect directly to one another.
   d) They are also known as striated muscles.

3. What two protein molecules are needed for muscles to contract?
   a) Pepsin and insulin.
   b) Myosin and pepsin.
   c) Hemoglobin and insulin.
   d) Myosin and actin.

4. Flagellum and cilia:
   a) Work with an organism's muscles for movement.
   b) Are parts of all cells and are required for movement.
   c) Are used by organisms without muscular systems.
   d) None of the above.

5. Peristalsis is a process performed by which type of muscle tissue?
   a) Catabolic.
   b) Cardiac.
   c) Smooth.
   d) Skeletal.

Practice Drill: The Muscular System – Answers

1. c)
2. d)
3. d)
4. c)
5. c)

THE CARDIOVASCULAR SYSTEM (CIRCULATORY SYSTEM)

The cells in living organisms need to receive nutrients and have their waste products removed. Single-celled organisms are able to pass these substances to and from their environment directly through the cell membrane. However, in multi-celled organisms, these substances are transported by way of the circulatory system.

The cardiovascular system has three main parts: the heart (which is the pump in the system), the blood vessels providing a route for fluids in the system, and the blood which transports nutrients and oxygen and contains waste products.

Heart

The human heart has four chambers – right atrium, right ventricle, left atrium, and left ventricle – which separate fresh blood from the blood that is full of cellular waste.

When leaving the heart, blood travels through **arteries**. To remember this, imagine that the "a" in "arteries" stands for "away". *A*rteries carry blood *a*way from the heart. On its way to the heart, blood travels through **veins.**

The **superior vena cava** is the vein which brings blood from the body into the top right chamber of the heart. This top right chamber is called the **right atrium**. The right atrium is separated from the chamber below it by a valve, and separated from the chamber next to it by a wall of muscle tissue. The heart relaxes after each beat, which allows blood to flow from the right atrium, through the valve, and into the chamber below called the **right ventricle.**

The right ventricle sends blood through the **pulmonary arteries** to the lungs. Blood picks up oxygen in the lungs and then is moved through the **pulmonary veins** back to the upper part of the heart. But this time, it enters on the left side into the **left atrium.** Use that first-letter rule again to remember this: blood from the *l*ungs enters the *l*eft atrium.

The left atrium – like the right – is separated from the left ventricle below it by a valve. When this valve opens during the relaxed phase of the heart, blood flows into the left ventricle. This chamber has the largest and strongest muscular wall so that it can force blood into the **aorta**, which is the body's largest artery, pulling blood away from the heart to the rest of the body.

The Heart:

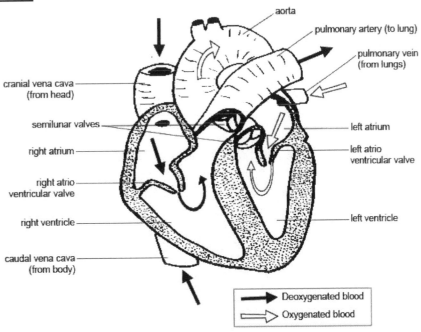

Arteries branch off from the aorta and travel to all parts of the body, continuing to branch and get smaller until they become **arterioles**. Arterioles lead to very small beds of tiny blood vessels called **capillaries**. Capillary beds are the site where the exchange of nutrients, gases, and wastes occurs. Blood that now contains wastes leaves the capillary beds, and enters small vessels called **venules**. These travel back through the body to the heart, becoming larger veins on the way, ending with the **large vena cava vein** that empties into the heart.

This begins the cycle all over again!

Things the Circulatory System Carries:
- Oxygen from the lungs to the body's cells.
- Carbon dioxide from the body's cells to the lungs.
- Nutrients from the digestive system to the cells.
- Waste products, other than carbon dioxide, to the liver and kidneys.
- Hormones and other messenger chemicals, from the glands and organs of their production to the body's cells.

Blood
Blood helps regulate our internal environment and keeps us in a generally constant state known as **homeostasis**. Blood transports and mixes elements up, making it possible for all the organs to contribute to maintaining homeostasis.

---

[6] Graphic from: http://www.en.wikibooks.org

Blood is not a liquid; it is a **suspension** (fluids containing particles suspended inside them). Blood has two components: **plasma**, the liquid part, and the solid **blood cells** suspended throughout. There are three major types of cells: **red blood cells**, **white blood cells**, and cellular fragments called **platelets.**

Plasma is mostly water, in which some substances such as proteins, hormones, and nutrients (glucose sugar, vitamins, amino acids, and fats) are dissolved. Gases (carbon dioxide and oxygen), salts (of calcium, chloride, and potassium), and wastes other than carbon dioxide are also dissolved in blood.

Red blood cells contain a protein molecule called **hemoglobin**, which holds an atom of iron. The hemoglobin molecule binds with oxygen and carbon dioxide, thus providing the mechanism by which the red blood cells can carry these gases around the body.

White blood cells come in many specialized forms and are used in the immune system to fight off invading organisms and keep us from getting diseases.

Platelets release substances at the site of a wound that start the blood-clotting reaction.

Plants

In plants, the transport system is based on the special properties of water.

The cells that make up the vascular tissue of plants form a continuous system of tubes running from the roots, through the stems, and to the leaves. Water and nutrients flow to the leaves through a vascular tissue called **xylem**, where they are used in the process of photosynthesis. Following that process, the products of photosynthesis then flow through a vascular tissue called **phloem** back down to the roots.

Practice Drill: The Cardiovascular System

1. Which of the following is NOT one of the chambers in the four-chambered vertebrate heart?
   a) Right atrium.
   b) Right ventricle.
   c) Left alveolar.
   d) Left ventricle.

2. Which of the following is true about blood flow in the four-chambered vertebrate heart circulatory system?
   a) Blood in the pulmonary vein is oxygenated.
   b) Blood in the pulmonary artery is oxygenated.
   c) Blood in the aorta is not oxygenated.
   d) Blood in the vena cava is oxygenated.

3. Which of the following are the major components of blood?
   a) Proteins and lipids.
   b) Plasma and cells.
   c) Proteins and platelets.
   d) Dells and lipids.

4. Platelets perform which of the following functions?
   a) Blood clotting.
   b) Carrying oxygen.
   c) Carrying carbon dioxide.
   d) Disease protection.

5. Capillary beds occur between:
   a) Arteries and veins.
   b) Aortas and vena cavas.
   c) Arterioles and venules.
   d) Atria and ventricles.

6. Red blood cells perform which of the following functions?
   a) Blood clotting.
   b) Carrying oxygen and carbon dioxide.
   c) Disease protection.
   d) Wound healing.

7. Xylem and phloem are plant tissues that:
   a) Produce sugar molecules and oxygen.
   b) Transport water and nutrients throughout the plant.
   c) Contain chloroplasts.
   d) Produce seeds.

8. The products of photosynthesis in the leaves flow to the roots through vascular tissue called:
   a) Phloem.
   b) Xylem.
   c) Meristem.
   d) Angiosperm.

Practice Drill: The Cardiovascular System – Answers

1. c)
2. a)
3. b)
4. a)
5. c)
6. b)
7. b)
8. a)

THE RENAL SYSTEM (FILTRATION/EXCRETION SYSTEM)

Single-celled organisms excrete toxic substances; either by diffusion through their cell membranes, or through specialized organelles called **vacuoles.** Likewise, metabolic chemical reactions occurring within the cells of organisms produce potentially harmful wastes which must be excreted. Multicellular organisms require special organ systems – specifically the circulatory and excretory systems, in humans – to eliminate wastes.

Organisms must be able to respond to changes in their external environment while still maintaining a relatively constant internal environment. **Homeostasis** – the physical and chemical processes that work to maintain that internal balance of water, temperature, salt concentration, etc. – is maintained by the cooperation of both the circulatory and renal systems

Remember digestion: Food is broken down, absorbed as very small molecules, and carried to the cells by blood. Cells need these broken-down molecules to perform the life-sustaining biochemical reactions of metabolism, which produce wastes.

For example: Aerobic respiration produces water and **carbon dioxide**; anaerobic respiration produces **lactic acid** and carbon dioxide; dehydration synthesis produces water; protein metabolism produces **nitrogenous wastes**, (i.e. **ammonia**); and other metabolic processes can produce salts, oils, etc.

Toxic wastes are disposed of according to their molecular make-up. For example, blood carries gaseous wastes like carbon dioxide to the lungs for exhalation. Other wastes need to first be filtered out of the blood before excretion. Nitrogenous wastes are the result of excess amino acids broken down during cellular respiration. The toxicity (harmfulness) of those nitrogenous wastes varies from: **Extremely Toxic** (Ammonia); **Less Toxic** (Urea); **Non-Toxic** (Uric Acid). **Non-toxic** wastes can be retained, released, or recycled through other reactions.

The Kidneys

Toxic wastes are carried by blood to the liver, where they are converted into **urea.** The blood then carries the urea to the **kidneys** (bean-shaped, fist-sized organs), where it will be converted from urea into **urine.** Urine is able to mix with water and be excreted from the body; the amount of water that is used in this process is regulated by the kidneys in order to prevent body dehydration. The kidneys are complex filtering systems which maintain the proper levels of various life-supporting substances, including sodium; potassium; chloride; calcium; glucose sugar; and amino acids. These life-supporting substances are absorbed by the kidneys from urine before it I expelled. The kidneys also help maintain blood pressure and the acidity (pH) level of the blood.

Each kidney contains at least a million individual units called **nephrons.** Nephrons perform similar functions as the alveoli do in the lungs; but whereas the alveoli function as areas of gas exchange, the kidney nephrons are structured to function as areas of *fluid* interchange. Each nephron contains a bed of capillaries. Those capillaries which are bringing in blood are surrounded by a **Bowman's capsule**.

Bowman's capsules are important parts of the filtration system. They separate the blood into two components: a cleaned blood product, and a filtrate which is moved through the nephron. As the filtrate travels through the nephron, more impurities are removed; and the filtrate concentrates into **urine**, which is then processed for elimination. The collected urine flows into the **ureters**, which take it to the **urinary bladder**. Urine will collect in the urinary bladder until the pressure causes an urge to expel it from the body through the **urethra**. Each of the hundreds of nephrons in the kidneys is attached to its own Bowman's capsule.

Kidneys are remarkably important structures; processing the body's blood about 20 times, each day! They also regulate the amount of water in the bloodstream. If the brain detects depleted levels of water, it increases the release of the **antidiuretic hormone (ADH)**. ADH causes the kidneys to reabsorb water into the bloodstream, preserving water (and concentrating urine) in the body. The reason why you urinate more frequently when drinking alcohol is because alcohol inhibits the ADH signal from the brain.

The kidneys are truly a feat of natural engineering. In fact, despite the medical community's best efforts, it has so far been impossible to build a fully artificial kidney.

Practice Drill: The Renal System

1. The kidneys filter which of the following from blood?
   a) Undigested food.
   b) Metabolic wastes.
   c) Blood cells.
   d) Platelets.

2. Which of the following is **NOT** a function of the kidneys?
   a) Regulating pH (acidity) of blood.
   b) Regulating blood pressure.
   c) Assisting in the maintenance of homeostasis.
   d) Regulating hormone release.

3. The nephron is where _____ is produced.
   a) Urine.
   b) Ammonia.
   c) Nucleic acid.
   d) Amino acid.

4. Waste concentrated in the Bowman's capsule is called:
   a) Urine.
   b) Salts.
   c) Nucleic acids.
   d) Amino acids.

5. Alcohol consumption increases urination because it:
   a) Increases the amount of water in the body.
   b) Increases the action of antidiuretic hormone.
   c) Decreases the action of antidiuretic hormone.
   d) Stops water reabsorption.

Practice Drill: The Renal System – Answers

1. b)
2. d)
3. a)
4. a)
5. c)

THE NERVOUS SYSTEM

Irritability is a term used to describe an organism's response to changes, or **stimuli**, in its surroundings. All living organisms respond to environmental stimulus, usually by taking some sort of action: movement of a muscle, gland secretion, activating entire systems like digestion, etc.

Plants have cellular receptors that use chemical messengers to detect and respond to aspects of their environment such as light, gravity, and touch. For example, the orientation of a plant toward or away from light, called **phototropism** is mediated by hormones.

In multi-celled animals, a nervous system controls these responses.

The functioning unit of the nervous system is the **neuron**, a cell with structures capable of transmitting electrical impulses. A neuron must be able to first receive information from internal or external sources, before integrating the signal and sending it to another neuron, gland, or muscle. In multi-celled vertebrates, each neuron has four regions.

At one end of the neuron, there are branch-like extensions called **dendrites**, which receive signals from other neurons.

The **cell body** of the neuron is where the cellular functions take place and where signals are integrated.

The **axon** is an extension from the cell body which the nerve impulses travel along. Axons can be several feet in length, carrying signals from one end of the body to the other.

At the very end of the axon is the **synaptic terminal**, an area that contains chemical substances called **neurotransmitters.**

When an electrical nerve signal reaches the synaptic terminal, it causes neurotransmitters to be released. Neurotransmitters then move across the small space between the neuron and the next neuron (or gland or muscle). This small space is called the **synapse.** Once across the synapse, the neurotransmitter is received by the dendrites of another neuron (or the receptors on a gland or muscle) and then turned back into an electrical signal to be passed on.

The nervous system is divided into two main systems, the **central nervous system (CNS)** and the **peripheral nervous system (PNS)**.

CNS
The central nervous system consists of the brain and spinal cord (contained within the vertebral column or backbone). The brain integrates all the signals in the nervous system, and therefore is responsible for controlling every aspect of the body.

PNS

The peripheral nervous system consists of the nerves outside of the brain and spinal cord. The main function of the PNS is to connect the CNS to the limbs, organs, and **senses**. Unlike the CNS, the PNS is not protected by the bone of spine and skull. This leaves the PNS exposed to toxins and mechanical injuries. The peripheral nervous system is divided into the **somatic nervous system** and the **autonomic nervous system**.

> The **somatic nervous system** deals with motor functions. Its nerves connect with skeletal muscle and control movement of all kinds, from fine motor skills to walking and running.

> The **autonomic nervous system** works mostly without our conscious control. It is often responsible for critical life functions such as breathing and heart rate. The autonomic nervous system has two divisions.

>> The **sympathetic division** is responsible for the fight-or-flight response; it prepares the body for high-energy, stressful situations.

>> The **parasympathetic division** is responsible for rest and digestion functions, so it tends to slow down the body.

> Nerves from each of these divisions usually make contact with the same organs, but they often have opposite effects.

The Endocrine System

Another important system in our body is the endocrine, or glandular, system. It controls growth rate, feelings of hunger, body temperature, and more. Many organs run the endocrine system: the **pituitary gland**, the **pancreas**, the **ovaries** (only in females) and **testes** (only in males), the **thyroid** gland, the **parathyroid** gland, the **adrenal** glands, etc.

Of all these, the pituitary gland is the most important endocrine gland in your body. About the size of a pea, the pituitary gland hangs down from the base of your brain and produces the hormone which controls growth.

Fun Fact: Humans grow faster at night because more hormones are released into your blood when you are sleeping.

Practice Drill: The Nervous System

1. _____ is the functional unit of the nervous system.
   a) The nephron
   b) The nucleus
   c) The neuron
   d) The neutrophil

2. Which of the following is a part of the CNS?
   a) Autonomic nerves.
   b) Sympathetic nerves.
   c) Peripheral nerves.
   d) Spinal cord nerves.

3. What is the chemical substance that carries a message from one cell to another?
   a) Axon fluid.
   b) Dendrite fluid.
   c) Neurotransmitter.
   d) Hormone.

4. Dendrites receive information from:
   a) The axon of other neurons.
   b) The dendrites of other neurons.
   c) The cell body of other neurons.
   d) The nucleus of other neurons.

5. _____ release neurotransmitters.
   a) Axons.
   b) Dendrites.
   c) Cell bodies.
   d) The nucleus.

6. Which of the following is NOT true about irritability?
   a) Plants do not experience irritability.
   b) Activates neurons in the brain.
   c) Requires axons in animals.
   d) Neurons act upon muscles.

7. The most important gland in the human body is:
   a) The pancreas.
   b) The pituitary.
   c) The ovaries.
   d) The thyroid.

Practice Drill: The Nervous System – Answers

1. c)
2. d)
3. c)
4. a)
5. a)
6. a)
7. b)

Chemistry

General chemistry examines the structure of matter as well as the reaction between matter and energy. It is the science that deals with the properties and transformations of materials. This section will cover the fundamental terms and processes of general chemistry, which include states of matter, chemical bonds, the periodic table, and principles and applications.

ELEMENTS, COMPOUNDS, AND MIXTURES

Matter

Matter is commonly defined as anything that takes up space and has mass. **Mass** is the quantity of matter something possesses, and usually has a unit of weight associated with it.

Matter can undergo two types of change: chemical and physical.

> A **chemical change** occurs when an original substance is transformed into a new substance with different properties. An example would be the burning of wood, which produces ash and smoke.

> Transformations that do not produce new substances, such as stretching a rubber band or melting ice, are called **physical changes**.

The fundamental properties which we use to measure matter are mass, weight, volume, density and specific gravity.

Extrinsic properties are directly related to the amount of material being measured, such as weight and volume.

Intrinsic properties are those which are independent of the quantity of matter present, such as density and specific gravity.

Atom

An atom is the ultimate particle of matter; it is the smallest particle of an element that still is a part of that element. All atoms of the same element have the same mass. Atomic chemical changes involve the transfer of whole atoms from one substance to another; but atoms are not created or destroyed in ordinary chemical changes.

An atom is made up of several parts. The center is called the **nucleus**, and is made up of two particles: a positively-charged particle, called a **proton,** and a particle that does not have a charge, called a **neutron**. The masses of a proton and neutron are about the same.

The nucleus of the atom is surrounded by negatively-charged particles called **electrons**, which move in orbits around the nucleus. The nucleus is only a small portion of the total amount of space an atom takes up, even though most of an atom's mass is contained in the nucleus.

Molecular Weight

A **mole** is the amount of substance that contains 6.02×10^{23} basic particles. This is referred to as **Avogadro's number** and is based on the number of atoms in C_{12} (Carbon 12). For example, a mole of copper is the amount of copper that contains exactly 6.02×10^{23} atoms, and one mole of water contains 6.02×10^{23} H_2O molecules. The weight of one mole of an element is called its **atomic weight**. The atomic weight of an element with isotopes, which are explained further below/on the next page, is the average of the isotopes' individual atomic weights.

The negatively-charged electrons are very light in mass. An atom is described as neutral if it has an equal number of protons and electrons, or if the number of electrons is the same as the atomic number of the atom. You may have already assumed – correctly! – from that information that the atomic number of an atom equals the number of protons in that atom. The **atomic weight** or **mass** of the atom is the total number of protons and neutrons in the atom's nucleus.

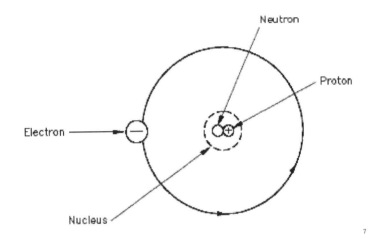

Elements

An element is a substance which cannot be broken down by chemical means; they are composed of atoms that have the same **atomic number** and are defined by the number of protons and neutrons they have. Some elements have more than one form, such as carbon; these alternate forms are called **isotopes.** There are approximately 109 known elements. Eighty-eight of these occur naturally on earth, while the others are **synthesized** (manufactured).

Hydrogen is the most abundant element in the Universe. It is found in 75% of all matter known to exist. **Helium** is the second most abundant element, found in approximately 25% of all known matter. The Earth is composed mostly of iron, oxygen, silicon, and magnesium, though these elements are not evenly distributed. 90% of the human body's mass consists of oxygen, carbon, hydrogen, nitrogen, calcium, and phosphorus. 75% of elements are metals, and eleven are gases in their natural state. We'll cover this more in-depth when we view the periodic table.

Molecules

A molecule is the smallest part of a substance that isn't chemically bonded to another atom. **Chemical formulas** are used to represent the atomic composition of a molecule. For example,

---

[7] Graphic from: http://www.circuitlab.org

one molecule of water contains 2 atoms of Hydrogen and 1 atom of Oxygen; its chemical formula is **2H + O = H₂O**.

Compounds and Mixtures

Substances that contain more than one type of element are called **compounds.** Compounds that are made up of molecules which are all identical are called **pure substances**. A **mixture** consists of two or more substances that are not chemically bonded. Mixtures are generally placed in one of two categories:

Homogeneous Mixture: Components that make up the mixture are uniformly distributed; examples are water and air.

Heterogeneous Mixture: Components of the mixture are not uniform; they sometimes have localized regions with different properties. For example: the different components of soup make it a heterogeneous mixture. Rocks, as well, are not uniform and have localized regions with different properties.

A uniform, or homogenous, mixture of different molecules is called a **solution**. If the solution is a liquid, the material being dissolved is the **solute** and the liquid it is being dissolved in is called the **solvent.** Both solids and gases can dissolve in liquids. A **saturated** has reached a point of maximum concentration; in it, no more solute will dissolve.

Practice Drill: Elements, Compounds, and Mixtures

1. Which statement best describes the density of an atom's nucleus?
    a) The nucleus occupies most of the atom's volume, but contains little of its mass.
    b) The nucleus occupies very little of the atom's volume, and contains little of its mass.
    c) The nucleus occupies most of the atom's volume, and contains most of its mass.
    d) The nucleus occupies very little of the atom's volume, but contains most of its mass.

2. Which of the following is not a physical change?
    a) Melting of aspirin.
    b) Lighting a match.
    c) Putting sugar in tea.
    d) Boiling of antifreeze.

3. A solid melts gradually between 85°C and 95°C to give a milky, oily liquid. When a laser beam shines through the liquid, the path of the beam is clearly visible. The milky liquid is likely to be:
    a) A heterogeneous mixture.
    b) An element.
    c) A compound.
    d) A solution.

4. The identity of an element is determined by:
    a) The number of its protons and neutrons.
    b) The number of its neutrons.
    c) The number of its electrons.
    d) Its atomic mass.

5. True or False? When a match burns, some matter is destroyed.
    a) True.
    b) False.

6. What is the reason for your answer to question 5?
    a) This chemical reaction destroys matter.
    b) Matter is consumed by the flame.
    c) The mass of ash is less than the match it came from.
    d) The atoms are not destroyed, they are only rearranged.
    e) The match weighs less after burning.

7. An unsaturated solution:
   a) Hasn't dissolved as much solute as is theoretically possible.
   b) Has dissolved exactly as much solute as is theoretically possible.
   c) Is unstable because it has dissolved more solute than would be expected.
   d) None of the above.

8. A teaspoon of dry coffee crystals dissolves when mixed in a cup of hot water. This process produces a coffee solution. The original crystals are classified as a:
   a) Solute.
   b) Solvent.
   c) Reactant.
   d) Product.

Practice Drill: Elements, Compounds, and Mixtures – Answers

1. **d)**
2. **b)**
3. **c)**
4. **a)**
5. **b)**
6. **d)**
7. **a)**
8. **a)**

STATES OF MATTER

The physical states of matter are generally grouped into three main categories:

1. **Solids**: Rigid; they maintain their shape and have strong intermolecular forces.

2. **Liquids**: Cannot maintain their own shape, conform to their containers, and contain forces strong enough to keep molecules from dispersing into spaces.

3. **Gases**: Have indefinite shape; disperse rapidly through space due to random movement and are able to occupy any volume. They are held together by weak forces.

Two specific states of matter are **liquid crystals**, which can maintain their shape as well as be made to flow, and **plasmas**, gases in which electrons are stripped from their nuclei.

Gases

There are four physical properties of gases that are related to each other. If any one of these changes, a change will occur in at least one of the remaining three.

1. Volume of the gas.
2. Pressure of the gas.
3. Temperature of the gas.
4. The number of gas molecules.

The laws that relate these properties to each other are:

Boyle's Law: The volume of a given amount of gas at a constant temperature is inversely proportional to pressure. In other words; if the initial volume decreases by half, the pressure will double and vice versa. The representative equation is: $P_1V_1 = P_2V_2$.

Charles's Law: The volume of a given amount of gas at a constant pressure is directly proportional to absolute (Kelvin) temperature. If the temperature of the gas increases, the volume of the gas also increases and vice versa. The representative equation is: $V_1/T_1 = V_2/T_2$.

Avogadro's Law: Equal volumes of all gases under identical conditions of pressure and temperature contain the same number of molecules. The molar volume of all ideal gases at 0° C and a pressure of 1 atm. is 22.4 liters.

The **kinetic theory of gases** assumes that gas molecules are very small compared to the distance between the molecules. Gas molecules are in constant, random motion; they frequently collide with each other and with the walls of whatever container they are in.

Practice Drill: States of Matter

1. Under the same conditions of pressure and temperature, a liquid differs from a gas because the molecules of the liquid:
   a) Have no regular arrangement.
   b) Are in constant motion.
   c) Have stronger forces of attraction between them.
   d) Take the shape of the container they are in.

2. Methane (CH_4) gas diffuses through air because the molecules are:
   a) Moving randomly.
   b) Dissolving quickly.
   c) Traveling slowly.
   d) Expanding steadily.

3. Which of the following would not change if the number of gas molecules changed?
   a) Volume of the gas.
   b) Type of gas.
   c) Pressure of the gas.
   d) Temperature of gas.

4. When the pressure is increased on a can filled with gas, its volume _____.
   a) Stays the same.
   b) Increases.
   c) Decreases.
   d) Turns to liquid.

5. Equal volumes of all gases at the same temperature and pressure contain the same number of molecules. This statement is known as:
   a) Kinetic theory of gases.
   b) Charles's Law.
   c) Boyle's Law.
   d) Avogadro's Law.

Practice Drill: States of Matter – Answers

1. c)
2. a)
3. b)
4. c)
5. d)

PERIODIC TABLE AND CHEMICAL BONDS

The Periodic table

The Periodic Table is a chart which arranges the chemical elements in a useful, logical manner. Elements are listed in order of increasing atomic number, lined up so that elements which exhibit similar properties are arranged in the same row or column as each other.

1a																	0
1 H 1.008	IIa											IIIb	IVa	Va	VIa	VIIa	2 He 4.00
3 Li 6.94	4 Be 9.01		12 Mg 24.31 <- Atomic number <- Chemical symbol <- Atomic weight									5 B 10.81	6 C 12.01	7 N 14.00	8 O 15.99	9 F 18.99	10 Ne 20.18
11 Na 22.99	12 Mg 24.31	IIIb	IVb	Vb	VIb		VIII		Ib	IIb		13 Al 26.98	14 Si 28.09	15 P 30.97	16 S 32.06	17 Cl 35.45	18 Ar 39.95
19 K 39.10	20 Ca 40.08	21 Sc 44.6	22 Ti 47.90	23 V 50.94	24 Cr 51.99	25 Mn 54.94	26 Fe 55.85	27 Co 58.93	28 Ni 58.71	29 Cu 63.54	30 Zn 65.37	31 Ga 69.72	32 Ge 72.59	33 As 74.92	34 Se 78.96	35 Br 79.91	36 Kr 83.80
37 Rb 85.47	38 Sr 87.62	39 Y 88.91	40 Zr 91.22	41 Nb 92.91	42 Mo 95.94	43 Tc 99	44 Ru 101.97	45 Rh 102.91	46 Pd 106.4	47 Ag 107.87	48 Cd 112.40	49 In 114.82	50 Sn 118.69	51 Sb 121.75	52 Te 127.60	53 I 126.90	54 Xe 131.30
55 Cs 132.91	56 Ba 137.34	57-71 see below	72 Hf 178.49	73 Ta 180.95	74 W 183.85	75 Re 186.2	76 Os 190.2	77 Ir 192.2	78 Pt 195.09	79 Au 196.97	80 Hg 200.59	81 Tl 204.37	82 Pb 207.19	83 Bi 208.98	84 Po 210	85 At 210	86 Rn 222
87 Fr 223	88 Ra 226	89-103 see below	104 Rf 261	105 Ha 260	106 Sg 263												

57 La 138.91	58 Ce 140.12	59 Pr 140.91	60 Nd 144.24	61 Pm 147	62 Sm 150.35	63 Eu 151.96	64 Gd 157.24	65 Tb 158.92	66 Dy 162.50	67 Ho 164.93	68 Er 167.26	69 Tm 168.93	70 Yb 173.04	71 Lu 174.97
89 Ac 227	90 Th 232.04	91 Pa 231	92 U 238.03	93 Np 237	94 Pu 242	95 Am 243	96 Cm 247	97 Bk 247	98 Cf 251	99 Es 254	100 Fm 253	101 Md 256	102 No 254	103 Lw 257

[8]

Note the following characteristics:

Each box contains the symbol of the element, its atomic number, and its atomic weight.

The elements appear in increasing order according to their atomic numbers, except for the two separate rows.

The vertical columns are called **groups**. Elements within a group share several common properties and often have the same outer electron arrangement. There are two categories: the main group and the transition elements.

> The number of the main group corresponds to the number of valence electrons. Most of the transition elements contain 2 electrons in their valence shells.

The horizontal rows are called **periods** and correspond to the number of occupied electron shells of the atom.

---

[8] Graphic from: http://volcano.oregonstatevolcano.oregonstate.edu.

The elements set below the main table are the **lanthanoids** (upper row) and **actinoids**. They also usually have two electrons in their outer shells.

Most of the elements on the periodic table are metals. The alkali metals, alkaline earths, basic metals, transition metals, lanthanides, and actinides are all groups of metals.

In general, the elements increase in mass from left to right and from top to bottom.

The main difference between the modern periodic table and the one Mendeleev (the periodic table's creator) came up with is that Mendeleev's original table arranged the elements in order of increasing atomic weight, while the modern table orders the elements by increasing atomic number.

Electronic Structure of Atoms

The electrons of an atom have fixed energy levels. Those in the principle energy levels are said to be in **electron shells**. Shells which correspond to the highest energy levels, called **valance shells**, include the electrons usually involved in chemical bonding. Chemical formulas of simple compounds can often be predicted from valences. The valence electrons increase in number as you go across the periodic table.

The electrons in the outer orbit can combine with other atoms by giving up electrons or taking on electrons. Atoms that give up electrons (**cations**) change from being neutral to having a *positive* charge. Atoms that gain electrons (**ions**) change from being neutral to having a *negative* charge. The **octet rule** is a chemical rule which states that atoms of a low atomic number will share, gain, or lose electrons in order to fill outer electron shells with eight electrons. This is achieved through different types of bonding.

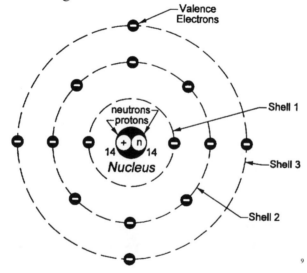

[9] Graphic from: http://www.circuitlab.org

Chemical Bonds

Electromagnetism is involved in all chemical behavior, including the chemical bonds which hold atoms together to form molecules, as well as those holding molecules together to form all substances. **Electronegativity** measures the tendency of an atom to attract a bonding pair of electrons, and is affected by both the atomic number, and the distance between the valence electrons and the charged nucleus. The higher the assigned electronegativity number, the more an element or compound attracts electrons.

There are two main types of bonds formed between atoms: **Ionic** and **Covalent bonds.** Anions and cations, being negatively and positively charged respectively, exist because of the attraction of opposite charges, and usually form **ionic bonds**.

A covalent bond forms when atoms share valence electrons. However, atoms do not always share electrons equally, resulting in a **polar covalent bond**. Electrons shared by two metallic atoms, form a **metallic bond**. Those electrons participating in metallic bonds may be shared between any of the metal atoms in the region.

If the electronegativity values of two atoms are similar, then:
- Metallic bonds form between two metal atoms.
- Covalent bonds form between two non-metal atoms.
- Non-polar covalent bonds form when the electronegativity values are very similar.
- Polar covalent bonds form when the electronegativity values are a little further apart.

If the electronegativity values of two atoms are different, then ionic bonds are formed.

Most metals have less than 4 valence electrons, which allows them to either gain a few electrons or lose a few; they generally tend to lose electrons, which causes them to become more positive. (This means that metals tend to form cations.)

A **hydrogen bond** is not considered a chemical bond. Instead, in a hydrogen bond, the attractive force between hydrogen is attached to an electronegative atom of one molecule and an electronegative atom of a different molecule. Usually the electronegative atom is oxygen, nitrogen, or fluorine, which have partial negative charges. The hydrogen has the partial positive charge. Hydrogen bonds are much weaker than both ionic and covalent bonds.

Practice Drill: Periodic Table and Chemical Bonds

1. When cations and anions join, they form what kind of chemical bond?
   a) Ionic.
   b) Hydrogen.
   c) Metallic.
   d) Covalent.

2. Generally, how do atomic masses vary throughout the periodic table of the elements?
   a) They decrease from left to right and increase from top to bottom.
   b) They increase from left to right and increase bottom to top.
   c) They increase from left to right and increase top to bottom.
   d) They increase from right to left and decrease bottom to top.

3. The force involved in all chemical behavior is:
   a) Electronegativity.
   b) Covalent bonds.
   c) Electromagnetism.
   d) Ionic bonds.

4. Which one of the following is not a form of chemical bonding?
   a) Covalent bonding.
   b) Hydrogen bonding.
   c) Ionic bonding.
   d) Metallic bonding.

5. Two atoms which do not share electrons equally will form what type of bond?
   a) Metallic bonds.
   b) Polar covalent.
   c) Ionic bonds.
   d) They cannot form bonds.

6. Chemical bonding:
   a) Uses electrons that are closest to the nucleus of the atoms bonding.
   b) Always uses electrons from only one of the atoms involved.
   c) Uses all the electrons in all atoms involved.
   d) Uses the valence electrons of all the atoms involved.

Practice Drill: Periodic Table and Chemical Bonds – Answers

1. a)
2. c)
3. c)
4. b)
5. b)
6. d)

ACIDS AND BASES

Acids

Naturally-occurring **acid solutions**, in which the solvent is always water, have several characteristic properties in common. They have a sour taste; speed up the corrosion, or rusting, of metals; conduct electricity; and introduce H^+ cations into aqueous solutions.

These characteristic properties can be changed by the addition of a base.

Bases (Alkalis)

Bases don't occur in as many common materials as do acids. A few examples of bases are: lime, lye, and soap. Basic solutions, as opposed to acidic solutions, have a bitter taste; conduct electricity, when their solvent is water; and introduce OH^- ions into an aqueous solution.

The characteristic properties can be changed by the addition of an acid.

The acidity or basicity of a solution is expressed by **pH values**. A neutral solution is defined by the following: it has equal concentrations of H^+ cations and OH^- ions, and a pH of 7. Neutrality is based on the pH of pure water. The more acidic a solution, the lower the pH is below 7. The more basic the solution, the higher the pH is above 7. The pH scale is based on logarithms of base 10. (If one solution has a pH of 8 and another has a pH of 10, then there is a 10^2 or 100 fold difference between the two.)

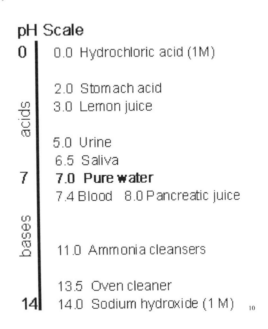

A **buffer** is used to make a solution which exhibits very little change in its pH when small amounts of an acid or base are added to it.

---

[10] Graphic from: http://bioserv.fiu.edu

An acidic buffer solution is simply one which has a pH less than 7. Acidic buffer solutions are commonly made from a weak acid and one of its salts - often a sodium salt. A strong basic solution can be weakened by adding an acidic buffer.

An alkaline buffer solution has a pH greater than 7. Alkaline buffer solutions are commonly made from a weak base and one of its salts. A strong acid can be made weaker by adding an alkaline buffer.

The human body contains many enzymes that only function at a specific pH. Once outside of this range, the enzymes are either unable to catalyze reactions or, in some cases, will break down. Our bodies produce a buffer solution that is a mixture of carbonic acid and bicarbonate, in order to keep the pH of blood at 7.4.

Practice Drill: Acids and Bases

1. One of the characteristic properties of an acid is that they introduce:
   a) Hydrogen ions.
   b) Hydroxyl ions.
   c) Hydride ions.
   d) Oxide ions.

2. A solution with a pH of 12 is:
   a) Very acidic.
   b) Neutral.
   c) Very basic.
   d) You can't have a solution with a pH of 12.

3. Buffers keep the pH of a solution from changing by:
   a) Converting strong acids to weak ones.
   b) Converting weak acids to strong ones.
   c) Converting weak bases to strong ones.
   d) More than one of the above answers is correct.

4. Proper blood pH level for humans is:
   a) 7.0.
   b) 7.2.
   c) 7.6.
   d) 7.4.

5. All of the following are properties of alkalis except:
   a) Bitter taste.
   b) Basic solutions are high conductors of electricity.
   c) Introduce OH⁻ ions into an aqueous solution.
   d) The characteristic properties can be changed by the addition of an acid.

Practice Drill: Acids and Bases – Answers

1. a)
2. c)
3. a)
4. d)
5. b)

Physics

Physics is the science of matter and energy, and of interactions between the two, grouped in traditional fields such as acoustics, optics, mechanics, thermodynamics, and electromagnetism.

MOTION

Speed is a scalar quantity and is defined as distance divided by time. (Ex: miles per hour.) **Velocity** is a vector quantity that describes speed and the direction of travel. **Magnitude of Acceleration** is defined as the change in velocity divided by the time interval. A **scalar quantity** is described only by its magnitude, whereas a **vector quantity** is described by magnitude and direction.

Acceleration is change in velocity divided by time; an object accelerates not only when it speeds up, but also when slowing down or turning. The **acceleration due to gravity** of a falling object near the Earth is a constant $9.8 m/s^2$; therefore an object's magnitude increases as it falls and decreases as it rises.

Newton's Three Laws of Motion

1. An object at rest will remain at rest unless acted on by an unbalanced force. An object in motion continues in motion with the same speed and in the same direction unless acted upon by an unbalanced force. This law is often called "**the law of inertia**".

2. Acceleration is produced when a force acts on a mass. The greater the mass (of the object being accelerated) the greater the amount of force needed (to accelerate the object). Think of it like this: it takes a greater amount of force to push a boulder, than it does to push a feather.

3. Every action requires an equal and opposite reaction. This means that for every force, there is a reacting force both equal in size and opposite in direction. (I.e. whenever an object pushes another object, it gets pushed back in the opposite direction with equal force.)

An object's **density** is its mass divided by its volume. **Frictional forces** arise when one object tries move over or around another; the frictional forces act in the opposite direction to oppose such a motion. **Pressure** is the force per unit area which acts upon a surface.

There are **Three Important Conservation Laws** which are embodied within Newton's Laws. They offer a different and sometimes more powerful way to consider motion:

1. **Conservation of Momentum**: Embodied in Newton's first law (Law of Inertia), this reiterates that the momentum of a system is constant if no external forces act upon the system.

2. **Conservation of Energy**: Energy is neither created nor destroyed; it can be converted from one form to another (i.e. potential energy converted to kinetic energy), but the total amount of energy within the domain remains fixed.

3. **Conservation of Angular Momentum**: If the system is subjected to no external force, then the total angular momentum of a system has constant magnitude and direction. This is the common physics behind figure-skating and planetary orbits.

Energy and Forces

The energy stored within an object is called its **potential energy** – it has the potential to do work. But where does that energy come from? When gravity pulls down on an object (**gravitational energy**) the object receives potential energy. **Kinetic energy**, the energy of motion, is the energy possessed because of an object's motion.

The sum of an object's kinetic and potential energies is called the total **mechanical energy** (or, **internal energy**).

Frictional forces convert kinetic energy and gravitational potential energy into **thermal energy**. **Power** is the energy converted from one form to another, divided by the time needed to make the conversion. A **simple machine** is a device that alters the magnitude or direction of an applied force. Example: an inclined plane or lever.

Objects that move in a curved path have acceleration towards the center of that path. That acceleration is called a **centripetal acceleration**. **Centripetal force** is the inward force causing that object to move in the curved path. If the centripetal force is the action, the (opposite) reaction is an outwardly-directed **centrifugal force**.

THERMAL PHYSICS

Temperature and Heat

Heat and temperature are two different things. **Heat** is a measure of the work required to change the speeds in a collection of atoms or molecules. **Temperature** is a measure of the average kinetic energy of the atoms or molecules of a substance.

A **calorie** is the amount of heat required to raise the temperature of 1 gram of water by 1 degree Celsius. The **specific heat** of a substance is the ratio of the amount of heat added to a substance, divided by the mass and the temperature change of the substance.

The change of a substance from solid to liquid, or liquid to gas, etc., is called a **phase change**.

> **Heat of Fusion:** The amount of heat required to change a unit mass of a substance from solid to liquid at the *melting point*.

> **Heat of Vaporization:** The amount of heat needed to change a unit mass of a substance from liquid to vapor at the *boiling point*.

HEAT TRANSFER

Temperature Scales

There are three common temperature scales: **Celsius**, **Fahrenheit**, and **Kelvin**. Because it is based upon what we believe to be **absolute zero** (the lowest theoretical temperature possible before life ceases), the Kelvin scale is also known as the **absolute scale**.

Temperature Scale	Point at Which Water Freezes
Celsius	0° C
Fahrenheit	32° F
Kelvin	273K

The Two Mechanisms of Heat Transfer

Conduction: Heat transfer via conduction can occur in a substance of any phase (solid, liquid, or gas), but is mostly seen in solids.

Convection: Convection heat transfer occurs only in fluids (liquids and gases).

Both types of heat transfer are caused by molecular movement in the substance of interest.

WAVE MOTION (SOUND) AND MAGNETISM

Waves

Waves can be placed in one of two categories: **longitudinal** or **transverse**.

In a **transverse wave**, the motion of the medium is perpendicular to the motion of the wave; for example, waves on water. In a **longitudinal wave**, the motion of the medium is parallel to the motion of the wave. Sound waves are transverse waves.

A wave's **wavelength** is the distance between successive high points (**crests**) and low points (**troughs**). The **speed of a wave** is the rate at which it moves. **Frequency** – measured in **Hertz** (Hz) – is the number of repetitions, or cycles, occurring per second. The **amplitude** is the intensity (or strength) of the wave.

Sound

When vibrations disturb the air, they create sound waves. The **speed of a sound wave** is approximately 331m/s at 0° C. Human ears are capable of hearing frequencies between 20 to 16,000 Hz. The **decibel** (dB) scale is used to measure the loudness (amount of energy) of a sound wave. The scale starts at zero, which is the softest audio, and increases tenfold in intensity for every 10dB.

Magnetism is a force which either pulls magnetic materials together or pushes them apart. Iron and nickel are the most common magnetic materials. All magnetic materials are made up of tiny groups of atoms called domains. Each domain is like a mini-magnet with north and south poles. When material is magnetized, millions of domains line up.

Around every magnet there is a region in which its effects are felt, called its **magnetic field**. The magnetic field around a planet or a star is called the **magnetosphere**. Most of the planets in the Solar System, including Earth, have a magnetic field. Planets have magnetic fields because of the liquid iron in their cores. As the planets rotate, so does the iron swirl, generating electric currents which create a magnetic field. The strength of a magnet is measured in **teslas**. The Earth's magnetic field is 0.00005 teslas.

An electric current creates its own magnetic field. **Electromagnetism** (the force created together by magnetism and electricity) is one of the four fundamental forces in the Universe; the other three are gravity and the two basic forces of the atomic nucleus.

A magnet has two poles: a north pole and a south pole. Like (similar) poles (e.g. two north poles) repel each other; unlike poles attract each other. The Earth has a magnetic field that is created by electric currents within its iron core. The magnetic north pole is close to the geographic North Pole. If left to swivel freely, a magnet will turn so that its north pole points to the Earth's magnetic north pole.

Practice Drill: Physics

1. The temperature at which all molecular motion stops is:
   a) $-460\ °C$.
   b) $-273\ K$.
   c) $0\ K$.
   d) $0C$.

2. What is the amount of heat required to raise the temperature of 1 gram of water by 1 degree Celsius?
   a) Specific heat
   b) Heat of fusion
   c) calorie
   d) Heat of vaporization

3. An object that has kinetic energy must be:
   a) Moving.
   b) Falling.
   c) At an elevated position.
   d) At rest.

4. The amount of heat required to melt an ice cube is called:
   a) Conduction.
   b) Specific Heat.
   c) A calorie.
   d) Heat of fusion.

5. A moving object has
   a) Velocity.
   b) Momentum.
   c) Energy.
   d) All of these.

6. Heat transferred between a pot of boiling water and the air above it is an example of:
   a) Conduction.
   b) Convection.
   c) Heat of vaporization.
   d) Phase change.

7. _____ increases, decreases, or changes the direction of a force.
   a) A simple machine.
   b) Energy.
   c) Momentum.
   d) Inertia.

8. _____ is a measure of the average kinetic energy of the atoms or molecules of a substance.
   a) Specific Heat
   b) Temperature
   c) Heat
   d) Force

9. Average speed is:
   a) A measure of how fast something is moving.
   b) The distance covered per unit of time.
   c) Always measured in terms of a unit of distance divided by a unit of time.
   d) All of the above.

10. Which of the following controls can change a car's velocity?
   a) The steering wheel.
   b) The brake pedal.
   c) Both A and B.
   d) None of the above.

11. The distance between two corresponding parts of a wave.
   a) Wavelength.
   b) Crest.
   c) Energy.
   d) Equidistance.

12. The high part of a transverse wave.
   a) Height.
   b) Period.
   c) Crest.
   d) Wavelength.

13. The magnetic field around a planet or a star is called a(an):
   a) Electromagnetic field.
   b) Magnetosphere.
   c) Magnetic field.
   d) Magnetic energy field.

14. The number of waves that pass a given point in one second.
   a) Trough.
   b) Energy.
   c) Crest.
   d) Frequency.

15. Unit of measurement for wave frequency.

    a) Crest.

    b) Decibel.

    c) Hertz (Hz).

    d) Period.

Practice Drill: Physics – Answers

1. c)

2. c)

3. a)

4. d)

5. d)

6. b)

7. a)

8. b)

9. d)

10. c)

11. a)

12. c)

13. b)

14. d)

15. c)

Geology

Geology is a branch of science which deals with the study of the Earth, the materials of which it is made, the structure of those materials, and the processes acting upon them. A very important part of geology is the study of how Earth's materials, structures, processes and organisms have changed over time. It includes such areas as volcanoes, rocks, minerals, gemstones, earthquakes, fossil fuels, and tectonics.

EARTH'S STRUCTURE

When the Earth first formed – about 4.54 billion years ago – it looked like a ball of bubbling-hot liquid rocks; rocks with different chemical elements, compounds, sizes, and weights. After a while, the heavier rocks started to "sink" towards the center of the Earth, while the lighter rocks moved towards the Earth's surface. This separation of rocks took millions of years. The Earth has a circumference of 24, 901 miles, and is made of several – sometimes overlapping – layers. These layers can be classified in two ways: by chemical composition, and by physical properties.

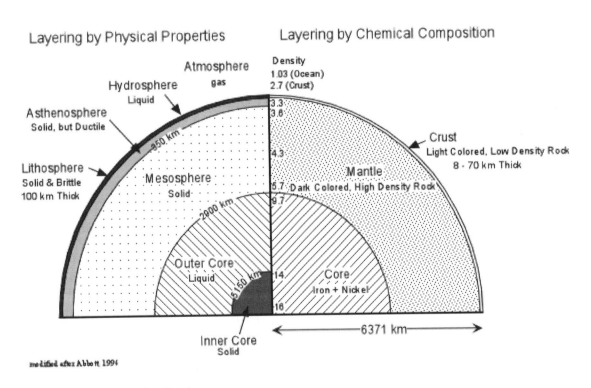

modified after Abbott 1994

There are six levels to the Earth:

> **Inner Core:** Made of *solid* iron and nickel.
> **Outer Core:** *Molten* (hot liquid) iron and nickel, surrounding the inner core.
> **Mantle (mesosphere):** A large solid layer surrounding the **core**.
> **Asthenosphere:** The semi-fluid and flexible upper section of the mantle.

265

Lithosphere: Includes the surface crust and the uppermost portion of the mantle.
Hydrosphere: The liquid water component of the Earth.

Rocks

A **mineral** is a naturally-occurring inorganic solid that has a definite chemical composition and crystal structure. Mineral deposits are formed by many processes: separation by gravity, formation of placer deposits in streams (ex. gold) and lakes, chemical deposition of minerals in sea water, and more.

A **rock** is defined as a natural solid made up of minerals or other natural solids. For example, granite is a rock and quartz is a mineral.

> **Igneous rocks** are formed directly from molten magma, or lava.

> **Sedimentary rocks** are formed from sediments that are compressed or cemented together.

> **Metamorphic rocks** are formed when other types of rock are heated and compressed over long periods of time.

Plate Tectonic Theory

Those independent sections of the Earth's lithosphere which move are called **tectonic plates**. Plate Tectonic Theory states that approximately 320 million years ago, the precursors to today's continents converged into a single land mass. Then, around 180 million years ago, that mass broke apart into seven tectonic plates: the African, North American, South American, Eurasian, Australian, Antarctic, and Pacific plates. Several minor plates also exist, including the Arabian, Nazca, and Philippines plates.

These plates all move around like cars in a demolition derby, at different speeds (from 2 cm to 10 cm per year--about the speed at which your fingernails grow!) and in different directions. A place where two plates meet is called a **plate boundary**. Boundaries have different names depending on how the two plates are moving in relationship to each other. If they are crashing, they are called **convergent** boundaries; pulling apart: **divergent** boundaries; sideswiping: **transform** boundaries.

Earthquakes generally occur where plates slip past each other; where one plate is sub-ducted (pushed under another; or at mid-ocean ridges, where plates are separating. **Volcanoes** occur when magma rapidly rises to the surface.

Mountain ranges are also formed through various processes – the Andes formed along a sub-duction zone, while the Himalayas were formed when two continental plates collided; the modern Rockies were formed by a compression followed by expansion.

Weathering is the deterioration of rock into small pieces, either through chemical or mechanical processes.

> **Chemical weathering** involves the direct effect of atmospheric or biologically-produced *chemicals* on rocks.

> **Mechanical (or physical) weathering** involves the breakdown of rocks through atmospheric *conditions* such as temperature changes, biological processes, moving water, wind, and glaciers.

Erosion is the movement of small bits of rock and soil. **Fossil fuel** deposits are partially decomposed organic debris. **Soil** is a mixture of pulverized rock and organic debris. Soil conditions are regulated by **humus:** a complex mixture of compounds resulting from the decomposition of plant tissue (stems and leaves).

THE HYDROLOGIC CYCLE (WATER CYCLE)

The movement of water on Earth is called the hydrologic cycle, the methods of which can be broken down into three different categories: **evaporation**, **precipitation**, and **run off**. The hydrologic cycle utilizes all three forms of water: vapor, liquid and solid.

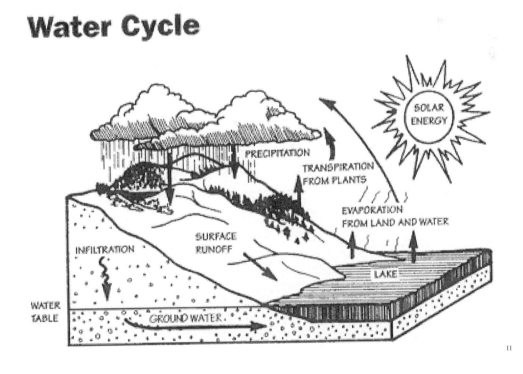

[11] Graphic from: greatswamp.org

Evaporation is the transformation of liquid water to water vapor. Water can also vaporize through plant tissue, especially leaf surfaces. This process is known as **transpiration.**

Water which enters the atmosphere must first condense into a liquid (clouds and rain) or a solid (snow, hail, and sleet) before it can descend. **Precipitation** includes all forms by which atmospheric water falls to the Earth: snow, rain, hail, and sleet.

Runoff is the flow of water back to bodies of water, either by land (rivers and streams take this route) or through underground sources.

Ground water is found in spaces between soil particles underground (located in the zone of saturation).

Infiltration is the process by which ground water accumulates and soaks into the ground. There it either replenishes shallow aquifers, or seeps into deep aquifers. **Aquifers** serve as underground beds of saturated soil or rock which yield significant quantities of water. **Shallow aquifers** flow into and replenish rivers and streams, while **deep aquifers** serve as large underground reservoirs of freshwater. Water may remain in deep aquifers for centuries, gradually moving towards and into the sea, where it then evaporates again into the atmosphere.

TIDES

Most places on Earth have two high tides and two low tides which follow a cycle coinciding with the 24-hour 50-minute lunar day (or, the time it takes Earth to make one complete rotation relative to the moon). Along America's Atlantic Coast, two high and low tides occur daily, with relatively little difference between successive high and low waters. Such tides are called **semi-diurnal**. On the north shore of the Gulf of Mexico, the tide is **diurnal**, moving in and out again only once a day. The Pacific Northwest gets **mixed tides**, two highs and two lows day, characterized by significant gaps between successive tides.

An incoming tidal flow is called a **flood current** or **flood tide**; an outgoing flow is an **ebb current** or **ebb tide**. The time between the two tides, with little to no current, is called **slack water** or **slack tide.**

The moon's phases also greatly affect tides. Whenever the moon aligns with the earth and sun during its full-moon and new-moon phases, we have extremely high and extremely low tides, known as **spring tides**: a term that has nothing to do with the actual spring season.

Between these phases, when the moon is in its first and third quarters, the moon is at right angles to the sun. This position counterbalances the gravitational interaction of the moon and sun, resulting in a period when the range between high and low tides is minimal. These are known as **neap tides**. A **riptide** is a strong, subsurface tidal current that conflicts with another current or currents. They cause a violent underwater disturbance, usually in a direction contrary to that of the surface water.

Practice Drill: Geology

1. Which of the following is NOT a type of plate boundary?
   a) Transform.
   b) Translational.
   c) Divergent.
   d) Convergent.

2. In which scenario below would you be likely to hire a geologist to help better understand the situation?
   a) A spacecraft uses radar to map the surface of a planet in our Solar System.
   b) A volcano is erupting on a Pacific island.
   c) A small community is worried about contamination of their water wells from an industrial waste site.
   d) Geologists might be employed in all of these scenarios.

3. The most voluminous portion of the Earth is known to geologists as:
   a) The lithosphere.
   b) The mantle.
   c) The core.
   d) The crust.

4. The lithosphere is that portion of the Earth where rocks behave as:
   a) Rocks.
   b) Fluids.
   c) Plastic solids.
   d) Brittle solids.

5. Igneous, sedimentary, and metamorphic are:
   a) Three types of plate boundaries.
   b) Three divisions of Earth.
   c) Ways to describe soils.
   d) The three major classes of rocks.

6. Which of the following is **NOT** a subdivision of Earth's interior?
   a) The magnetosphere.
   b) The lithosphere.
   c) The core.
   d) The mantle.

7. What is transpiration?
    a) Transpiration is a process where water vapor enters the atmosphere when animals breathe.
    b) Transpiration is a process where water vapor forms clouds.
    c) Transpiration is a process where water vapor exits a plant through holes in the leaves.
    d) Transpiration is a process where water vapor enters the atmosphere as water and evaporates from the ground.

8. What are the three states of water on Earth?
    a) Groundwater, lakes, and clouds.
    b) Liquid water, frozen water, and water vapor.
    c) Gas, steam, and vapor.
    d) Groundwater, oceans, and ice.

9. What word means the change of state from liquid to a gas?
    a) Evaporation.
    b) Condensation.
    c) Eutrophication.
    d) Precipitation.

10. Spring tides occur:
    a) At new moon and first quarter moon.
    b) At first quarter and third quarter moons.
    c) At new moon and full moon.
    d) At third quarter and full moons.

Practice Drill: Geology – Answers

1. **b)**
2. **d)**
3. **b)**
4. **d)**
5. **d)**
6. **a)**
7. **c)**
8. **b)**
9. **a)**
10. **c)**

Meteorology

Meteorology is the study of the changes in temperature, air pressure, moisture, and wind direction in the troposphere.

ATMOSPHERE

Atmospheric Properties

The thin envelope of air surrounding our planet is a mixture of gases, each with its own physical properties. Two gases make up the bulk of the Earth's atmosphere: nitrogen, which comprises 78% of the atmosphere, and oxygen, which accounts for 21% of the volume of air.

The other 1% is composed of **trace** gases, the most prevalent of which is the inert gaseous element argon. The rest of the trace gases, although present in only minute amounts, are very important to life on earth. Two in particular, carbon dioxide and ozone, can have a large impact on atmospheric processes. Another gas, water vapor, also exists in small amounts and varies in concentration: almost non-existent over desert regions, and about 4% over oceans. Water vapor is important to weather production since it exists in gaseous, liquid, and solid phases; it also absorbs radiant energy from the earth.

Energy Balance

The energy balance of the Earth is achieved by an opposition of energy flow to and from the ground level and all the atmospheric layers. The general temperature gradient from the poles to the equator, as well as the change in seasons, is caused by the spherical nature of the Earth and its tilt.

Pressure Systems

Our global atmospheric circulation is dominated by four major pressure zones: high pressure at the poles; low pressure at 60 degrees latitude; high pressure at 30 degrees; and low pressure at the equator. A detailed explanation of why this is so would get into the weeds of complicated physics. However, it is possible to make a general argument that substantially explains things.

If the Earth didn't spin, but could somehow be heated at the equator (all the way around) while being cooled at the poles, then naturally air would rise at the equator and sink at the poles. Surface pressure would therefore be low at the equator and high at the poles; and surface winds would always and everywhere be from the north in the northern hemisphere and the south in the southern. But the Earth *does* spin. This introduces a force, the **Coriolis force**, on moving air. Now the surface winds are turning, and the north and south winds may be east winds – and these winds will have an equator-ward component in order to continue the transport of heat between equator and pole.

Air pressure is measured with **barometers** and reported in millibars (mb). One type of barometer is **mercurial**, which is very accurate but not portable. A mercurial barometer measures air pressure in inches of mercury, which are then converted to millibars. Another type of barometer is the **aneroid**, which measures air pressure in millibars and is portable.

Atmospheric Structure

The atmosphere is divided into four layers based on temperature: the **troposphere**, **stratosphere**, **mesosphere**, and **thermosphere**.

Troposphere

About 75% of the air in the atmosphere is compressed into the lowest layer, which is called the troposphere. In this layer, wherein clouds form and air masses continuously mix, the change of temperature in relation to height is relatively large. Within the troposphere, air consists of 78% nitrogen; 21% oxygen; and 1% argon, carbon dioxide, and minute amounts of other gases; tropospheric air also contains variable amounts of water vapor and a mixture of minute impurities, such as particles of dust and salt. The thickness of the troposphere varies with the season of the year.

Tropopause

The top of the troposphere is known as the tropopause. It is a transition zone between the troposphere and the stratosphere, and acts as a lid to "hold in" the lower atmosphere. This lid contains occasional breaks and overlaps, which provide paths for high-velocity winds called **jet streams**. The jet streams cause constant turbulence and a mixing of the lower atmosphere. This mixing of air masses causes our weather.

The Greenhouse Effect

Heat from the sun warms the Earth's surface, but most of it is radiated and sent back into space. Water vapor and carbon dioxide in the troposphere trap some of this heat, preventing it from escaping; this keeps the Earth warm. However, if there is too much carbon dioxide in the troposphere, then too much heat will be trapped.

Stratosphere

The layer immediately above the tropopause is the stratosphere. It has a stable temperature in the lower half of the layer and an almost complete lack of clouds. In the upper half of the stratosphere, at about 25 kilometers, the temperature begins to increase with height up to about 50 kilometers at the **stratopause**. In the stratopause, the temperature is about the same as that at the earth's surface; this warmth is caused by the presence of **ozone**, which absorbs part of the ultraviolet radiation from the sun. Without the ozone layer, life on Earth would be difficult, if not impossible.

The Ozone Layer is a thin layer of ozone which absorbs most of the harmful ultraviolet radiation from the sun. The ozone layer is being depleted ("holes" are appearing), growing thinner over Europe, Asia, North American and Antarctica.

Mesosphere

Extending 50 to 80 km above the Earth's surface, the mesosphere is a cold layer in which the temperature generally decreases as altitude increases. The atmosphere is very dense, and is thick enough to slow down meteors plunging into the atmosphere, until they burn up.

Thermosphere

The thermosphere extends from 80 km above the Earth's surface to outer space. The temperature is hot, with temperatures as high as thousands of degrees, because the few molecules present in the thermosphere receive extraordinarily large amounts of energy from the sun.

The Ionosphere

Scientists call the ionosphere an extension of the thermosphere; so technically, the ionosphere is not another atmospheric layer. The ionosphere represents less than 0.1% of the total mass of the Earth's atmosphere. But even though it is such a small part, it is extremely important! The upper atmosphere is ionized by **solar radiation**. This means that the Sun's energy is so strong at this level, that it breaks apart molecules. When the Sun is active, more and more ionization happens! Different regions of the ionosphere make long-distance radio communication possible by reflecting the radio waves back to Earth. It is also home to auroras. Temperatures in the ionosphere increase as altitude increases.

The Atmosphere:

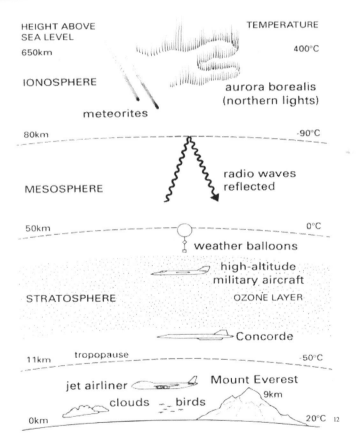

The General Circulation of the Atmosphere

The circulation on a spinning Earth is not really so much different from what we'd expect -- just a little more elaborate. The overall pattern includes two high-pressure systems and two low-

---

[12] Graphic from: http://media.photobucket.com

pressure systems: high-pressure at the poles and at 30 degrees latitude, and low-pressure at the equator and at 60 degrees latitude.

The resulting wind systems are: **easterlies** between 60 degrees and the pole, known appropriately as **polar easterlies**; **westerly** winds from 30 to 60 degrees, commonly called the mid-latitude **westerlies**; and the **tropical easterlies**, known as **trade winds**. The **doldrums** is a region around the equator where heated air is rising. This air falls at the **horse latitudes**. Between the two, trade winds blow in a steady and predictable pattern. Many wind systems arise because the temperature of the oceans gradually changes in response to a change in solar radiation.

CLOUDS

Condensation is the process whereby water vapor is changed into small droplets of water; and may result from a decrease in temperature, a decrease of pressure, or an increase of water vapor in the air. In the atmosphere, condensation normally occurs when warm, moist air rises and cools by expansion. Frontal activity, terrain features, and unequal heating of land and sea surfaces cause the air to be lifted.

For condensation to occur, there must be something present in the atmosphere upon which the water vapor can condense. Virtually billions of minute particles – which result from ordinary dust, combustion products, and sea salt crystals – exist in the atmosphere. Condensation of water vapor upon these particles forms clouds and fog.

Clouds do not always produce precipitation; some clouds are only made of extremely small water droplets that simply float in the atmosphere. Still other forms of precipitation may fall from clouds and then evaporate, all without ever reaching the Earth's surface. This phenomenon is called **virga**.

Cloud Types

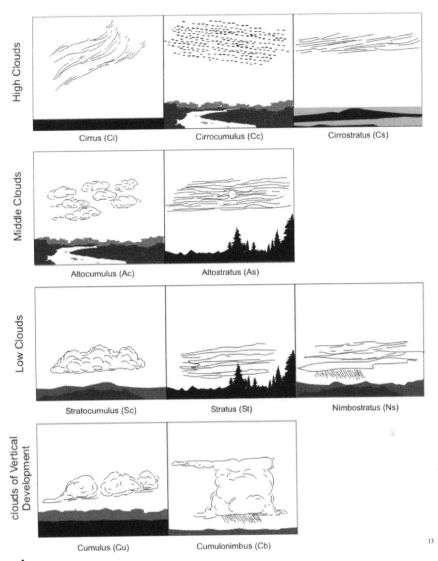

Cirrus (Ci) Cirrocumulus (Cc) Cirrostratus (Cs)

Altocumulus (Ac) Altostratus (As)

Stratocumulus (Sc) Stratus (St) Nimbostratus (Ns)

Cumulus (Cu) Cumulonimbus (Cb) [13]

Cloud Categories

Clouds are classified by both their appearances and the physical processes which produce them. All clouds, by their shape, fall into two general categories: **cumuliform (cumulus)** and **stratiform (stratus)**

> **Cumulus** means heaped or accumulated; and these heaped clouds are formed by rising air currents. Cumulus clouds may produce local showers or severe thunderstorms, as well as extremely strong vertical air currents.

> **Stratus**, or sheet-like, clouds are formed when a layer of air is cooled below its saturation point without pronounced vertical motion. The vertical thickness of stratiform-type clouds may range from several meters, up to a few kilometers. Precipitation from stratiform clouds is generally continuous, with only gradual changes in intensity, and covers a relatively large area.

---

[13] Graphic from: cmos.ca

Cloud Classification
Clouds may be further classified as low, middle, high, and towering.

Low
When the bases of clouds are lower than 2,000 meters above the surface of the Earth, the clouds generally are designated as cumulus or stratus, unless they are producing precipitation. In that case, they are referred to as **cumulonimbus** or **nimbostratus**. (Nimbus means "rain cloud.")

A common cloud called **stratocumulus** has some characteristic of both cumulus and stratus clouds.

Middle
Between 2,000 and 6,000 meters, these clouds generally are identified with the prefix *alto*. **Altocumulus** and **altostratus** clouds are in this category.

High
Above 6,000 meters, high clouds are composed of ice crystals and generally have a delicate appearance. These clouds are designated as **cirrocumulus** and **cirrostratus**. **Cirrus** clouds exist at still greater altitudes, and are fibrous types of clouds composed of ice crystals. They appear as curly wisps.

Towering
Bases of towering clouds may be as low as the typical low clouds, but their tops may extend to, or even above, the tropopause.

Practice Drill: Meteorology

1. What are the two most abundant gases in the Earth's atmosphere?
   a) Nitrogen and oxygen.
   b) Oxygen and carbon monoxide.
   c) Water vapor and argon.
   d) Methane and hydrogen.

2. The layer of the Earth's atmosphere in which weather occurs is the:
   a) Stratosphere.
   b) Mesosphere.
   c) Thermosphere.
   d) Troposphere.

3. What causes the Earth's mesosphere (also known as the ozone layer) to be warmer than layers just above or below it?
   a) Chemical reactions involving ozone produce heat.
   b) Ozone absorbs solar energy.
   c) Heat is transported into the ozone layer by convection from the troposphere.
   d) Energetic particles hit the mesosphere to produce heat and aurorae.

4. The thick, dense region of the atmosphere is known as:
   a) Ionosphere.
   b) Mesosphere.
   c) Stratosphere.
   d) Hydrosphere.

5. The names of all three high-cloud genera contain which of the following words in some form?
   a) Alto.
   b) Cumulus.
   c) Cirrus.
   d) Stratus.

6. A cloud with some of the characteristics of both cumulus and stratus clouds is:
   a) Stratocumulus.
   b) Cirrus.
   c) Altostratus.
   d) Nimbostratus.

Practice Drill: Meteorology – Answers

1. a)
2. d)
3. b)
4. b)
5. c)
6. a)

ASTRONOMY

Astronomy is the scientific study of matter in outer space, especially the positions, dimensions, distribution, motion, composition, energy, and development of celestial bodies and occurrences.

OUR SOLAR SYSTEM

Our solar system is located in the **Milky Way Galaxy**, a collection of 200 billion stars and their solar systems. The Milky Way Galaxy is located in a group of 30+ galaxies we call the **Local Group**. The Local Group is a part of a local **super-cluster** of 100+ galaxies (called the Virgo Super-cluster). This super-cluster is one of millions of super-clusters in the universe.

Our solar system consists of the Sun, planets, **dwarf planets** (or **plutoids**), moons, an asteroid belt, comets, meteors, and other objects. The Sun is the center of our solar system; the planets, over 61 moons, the asteroids, comets, meteoroids, and other rocks and gas all orbit the Sun. The Earth is the third planet from the Sun in our solar system.

The Sun is about 26,000 light-years from the center of the Milky Way Galaxy, which is about 80,000 to 120,000 light-years across. Our solar system is located toward the edge of one of the Milky Way's spiral arms. It takes the Sun and our solar system roughly 200-250 million years to orbit once around the Milky Way. In this orbit, our solar system is traveling at a velocity of about 155 miles/sec (250 km/sec). A **light year** is a unit of length equal to about 6 trillion miles.

Planets

The nine planets that orbit the sun are, in order from closest to the Sun to farthest from the Sun: Mercury, Venus, Earth, Mars, Jupiter (the biggest planet in our solar system), Saturn (with large, orbiting rings), Uranus, Neptune, and Pluto (a dwarf planet or plutoid). A belt of asteroids, minor planets made of rock and metal orbits between Mars and Jupiter. These objects all orbit the sun in roughly circular orbits that lie in the same plane, referred to as the **ecliptic**. Pluto is an exception; this dwarf planet has an elliptical orbit tilted over 17° from the ecliptic.

> The **inner planets**, planets that orbit close to the Sun, are quite different from the **outer planets**, those planets that orbit far from the Sun. The inner planets are Mercury, Venus, Earth, and Mars. They are relatively small, composed mostly of rock, and have few or no moons.

> The **outer planets** include Jupiter, Saturn, Uranus, and Neptune. They are much larger, mostly gaseous, ringed, and have many moons. Pluto is a dwarf planet that has one large moon and two small moons.

Small Bodies

There are other smaller object that orbit the Sun, including **asteroids**, **comets**, **meteoroids,** and dwarf planets.

- Asteroids (also called minor planets) are rocky or metallic objects, most of which orbit the Sun in the asteroid belt between Mars and Jupiter.
- Comets are small, icy bodies that orbit the sun. They have very long dust tails.
- Meteoroids are small bodies that travel through space. They are stony and/or metallic and are smaller than asteroids. In fact, most are very tiny.

Practice Drill: Astronomy

1. What are the components of our solar system?
   a) Planets, the Sun, asteroids, meteors, and comets.
   b) Planets and asteroids.
   c) Meteors and comets.
   d) Planets, asteroids, the Sun.

2. What is the center of our solar system?
   a) The Milky Way.
   b) An asteroid belt.
   c) The Sun.
   d) The moon.

3. What planet is best known for its rings?
   a) Saturn.
   b) Uranus.
   c) Jupiter.
   d) Neptune.

4. The closest star to Earth is:
   a) The moon.
   b) The Milky Way.
   c) Venus.
   d) The Sun.

5. What is the name of a frozen chunk of ice and dust that orbits the sun?
   a) Comet.
   b) Meteorite.
   c) Asteroid.
   d) Meteor.

Practice Drill: Astronomy – Answers

1. **a)**
2. **c)**
3. **a)**
4. **d)**
5. **a)**

Chapter 10: Rotated Blocks

The Rotated blocks section is deceptively simple, which as you can probably tell by now is a recurring theme for the AFOQT exam. In this section, you have 13 minutes to complete 15 questions, so approximately 50 seconds per question.

The objective in the Rotated Blocks section is straight forward enough: you are given an image of a 3D "block" (or some shape or object) and must find the block that matches but is shown from a different angle. You'll be given 5 answer choices.

The trick is that the blocks are extremely similar and the differences can be quite subtle. The general idea of the shape will be there for each answer choice, except one might be a little shorter on one side, or a little thicker, or the hole is placed slightly differently, etc. This is one of those sections that is incredibly difficult to "study for". Frankly, most people either get it or they don't, depending on their innate ability to visualize three dimensional objects. Even if you are not one of the lucky ones who are a natural at this, you can still do well with practice and using a systematic approach. Regardless of which category you might fall into, a good suggestion is to find a small detail of the shape and cull out any answer choices that don't match correctly. It might just be a single protrusion, the location of a hole, etc. What you want to avoid is getting distracted as you look through the answer choices. Review one aspect, then go back and look for another. If you get scatter brained and are trying to remember 5 different aspects at once, you'll never keep straight in your mind which ones were potential matches or not. A final reminder, don't forget how similar the answer choices are. Even once you think you found the answer, look through the choices just one more time to be sure.

Those 50 seconds per question can go by quickly for some people, so do not forget about time management and give yourself enough time at the end to fill in guesses for any remaining questions.

With that, let's get started on some practice on the next page!

1)

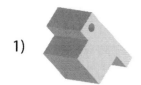

A) 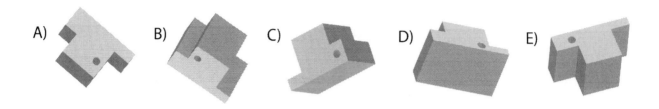 B) C) D) E)

2)

A) 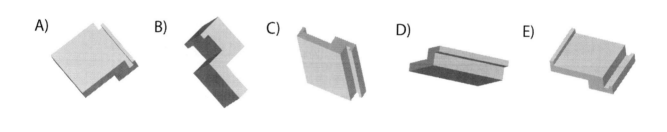 B) C) D) E)

3)

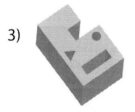

A) 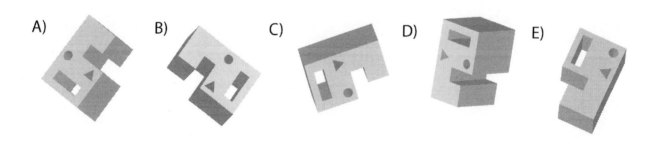 B) C) D) E)

4)

A)   B)   C)   D)   E)

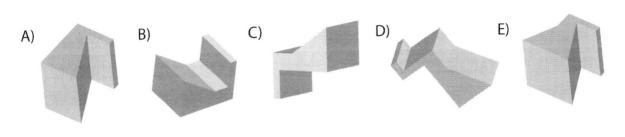

5)

A)   B)   C)   D)   E)

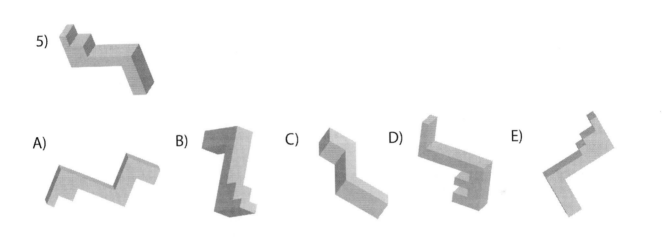

6)

A)   B)   C)   D)   E)

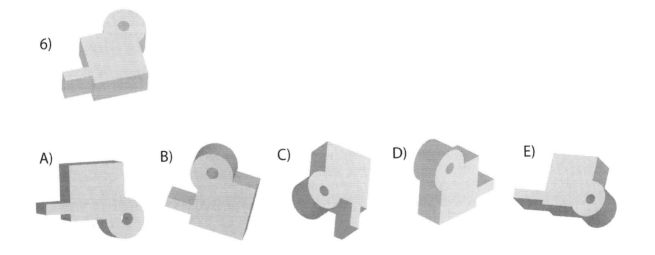

7)

A) B) C) D) E)

8)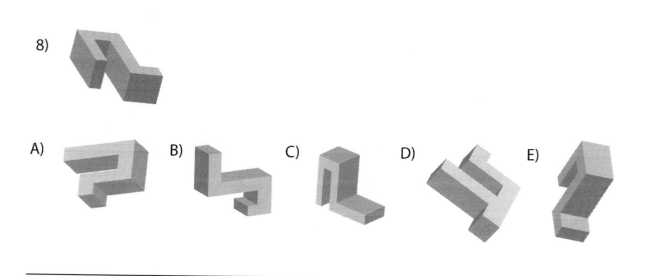

A) B) C) D) E)

9)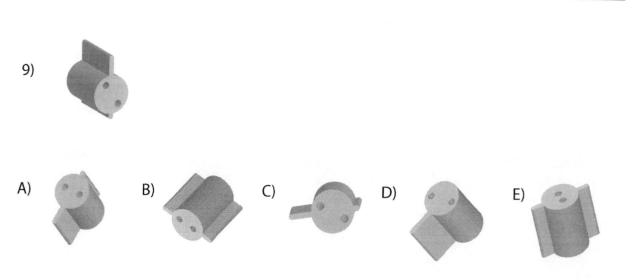

A) B) C) D) E)

10)

A)   B)   C)   D)   E)

11)

A)   B)   C)   D)   E)

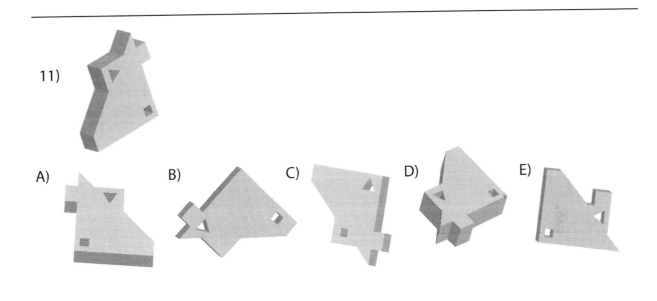

12)

    B)   C)   D)   E)

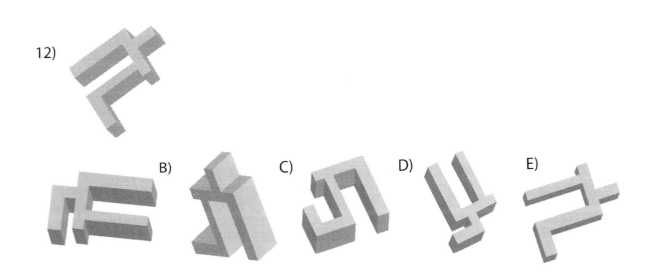

13)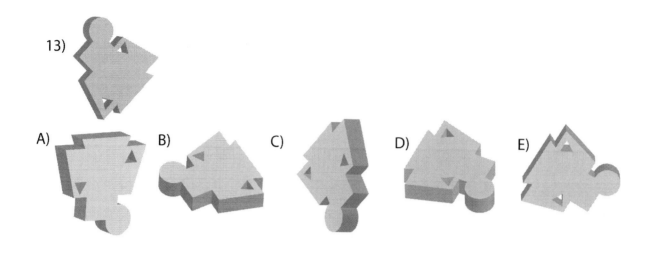

14)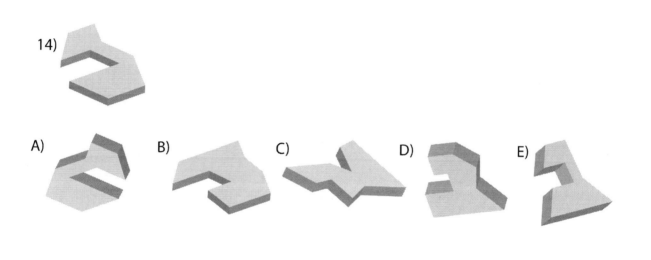

15)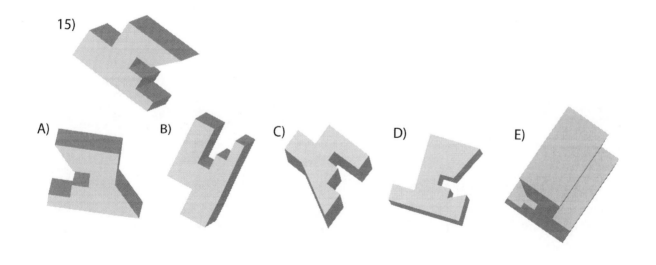

Rotated Blocks – Answer Key

1. C
2. A
3. D
4. C
5. B
6. D
7. A
8. E
9. C
10. C
11. D
12. B
13. D
14. A
15. E

Chapter 11: Hidden Figures

In the hidden figures section, you will have 8 minutes to complete 15 items. The first thing you will notice about this section is the formatting of the questions is totally different than any other section. You will be given 5 shapes with correlating answer choices A, B, C, D, & E. Below those answer choices, you will be presented the questions which is a box with a lot of zig-zagging lines in all directions. Somewhere in those zig-zagged lines is a shape that matches one of the 5 answer choices.

This section is straightforward enough, but a few things to remember that can help you:

- First and foremost, it is imperative to remember that the shape in the hidden figure will always match the same size, position, and orientation as shown in the answer choice selections. Do not over-analyze and think you see a figure that is rotated 90 degrees or slightly bigger or smaller because the AFOQT will never present questions that way on this section.
- Find a defining feature of the answer choices. That one long section or sharply angled protrusion can help you quickly ID the shape in many cases.
- Finally, this works for some and not for others, but if you squint and almost blur out the hidden figure image a little, sometimes the shapes will just kind of "appear" because there is a pattern to them, whereas the other lines in the box are just meant to distract and conceal. Not very scientific, we know, but this has been a life-saver for many people.

Let's get started with some practice on the next page. Do not let the hidden figure section overwhelm you. Even if you are struggling with it, just give it your best shot for a while, but focus your attention on the other sections as they are more important, require more study time, and you will see more results from your study effort elsewhere.

For questions 1-5, use the below shapes as answer choices:

A. B. C. D. E.

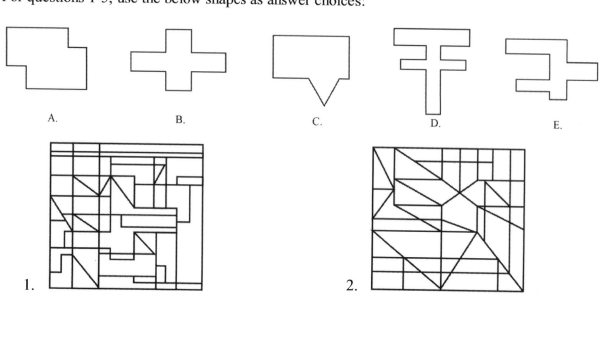

1.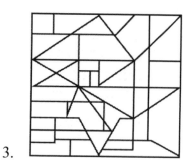

2.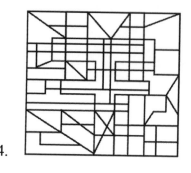

3.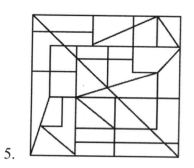

4.

5.

For questions 6-10, use the below shapes as answer choices:

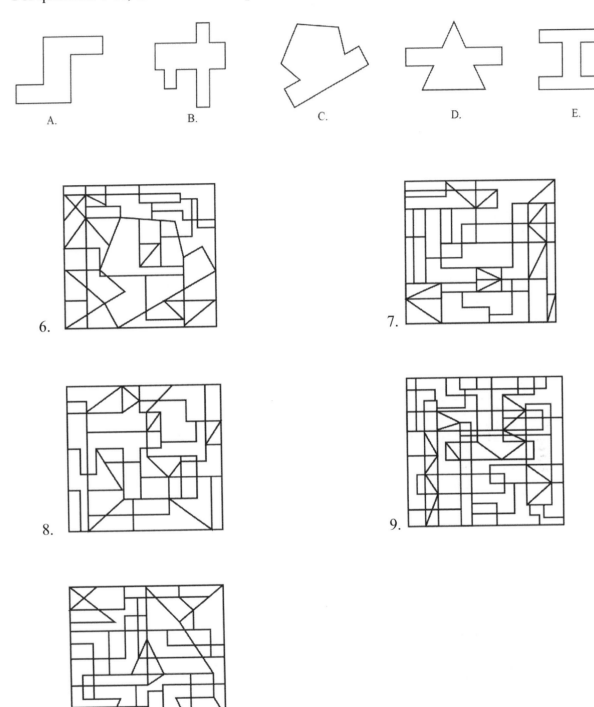

A.

B.

C.

D.

E.

6.

7.

8.

9.

10.

293

For questions 11-15, use the below shapes as answer choices:

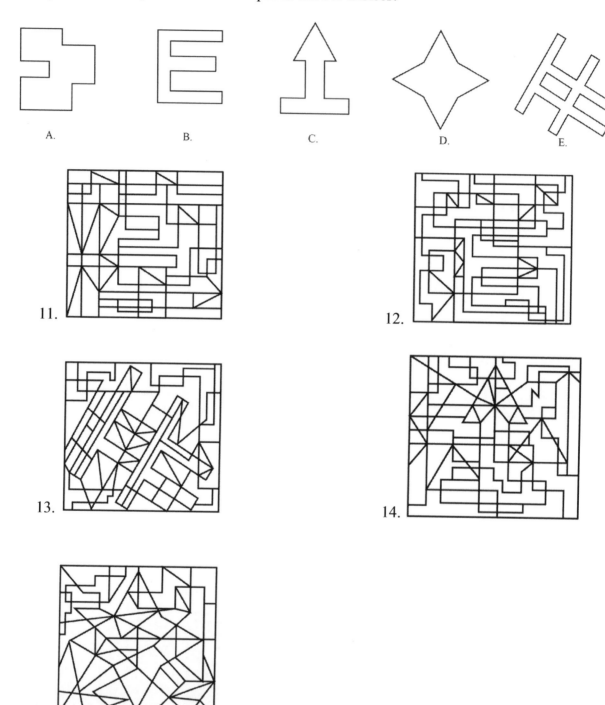

A.

B.

C.

D.

E.

11.

12.

13.

14.

15.

294

Hidden Figures Practice Test – Answers

1. E
2. B
3. C
4. D
5. A
6. C
7. A
8. B
9. E
10. D
11. A
12. B
13. E
14. C
15. D

Made in the USA
Lexington, KY
30 July 2014